# Windows Assembly Language Programming

Daniel H. Rosenthal

12 March 2020

@ 2020 Daniel H. Rosenthal

Table of contents

| | |
|---|---|
| 5 | Introduction |
| 11 | A short Program to create two windows |
| 17 | A usb camera window and saving the image |
| 25 | Hexadecimal view of working message structure |
| 35 | A program for an animation of bending lines |
| 50 | About procedures, and a small Dll example |
| 66 | How to rearrange WindowProc's start so not to look like a procedure |
| 68 | Creating a typing cursor and typing without edit controls |
| 80 | Setting a timer |
| 83 | Creating a menu without pictures and with them |
| 100 | Downloading a page from a website |
| 104 | Allocating memory. Global alloc, Virtual alloc |
| 115 | Loading and saving files, 32 and 64 bit |
| 135 | Sending Emails, an experiment by Assembly language and SMTP |
| 145 | The program as complete code for the emails experiment |
| 165 | About stop starts with animation |
| 172 | Saving to the Clipboard |
| 181 | Something about edit controls |
| 193 | Sound waves and the Riff header |
| 213 | A Random sounds program |
| 228 | Something about using the floating point unit |
| 239 | An error of recursion |
| 244 | Converting a floating point number into text. And creating a new Dll |
| 250 | About 64 bit calling |
| 254 | Mouse Inputs        260  Keyboard Inputs |

## Introduction.

This is about creating computer programs which run with the Windows 7 Operating system, in 100% pure assembly language. Writing programs is sometimes called creating Applications.
I assume that the reader already knows Basic Assembly language to some extent.

This book contains some long stretches of assembly code without any proper explanations, but I don't think there is anything I can do about that, and I have left it that way.
I think examples of assembly language programming can be useful when you teach yourself, and so I felt one could make a book which is mainly made of examples of programming.
This could be very useful to someone who is teaching himself Windows Assembly programming, but there are several different methods of learning the subject.
And this book is only about one of several different ways of learning. Which is to download a free assembler, called 'flat assembler,' and then do practice with it, and follow examples which they give you with it.
This is all amateur, not professional.

This book is not intended to be complete or comprehensive on any subject. I have noticed very few books have examples of assembly programming. I wonder whether writers have avoided doing that for some good reason?
I will not ever claim to show the right way of doing things. The language is pure assembly, since I have deliberately avoided something confusing which is not pure assembly.
The assembler used for programming is always the "flat assembler" which is very easy to find and download on the internet.
It's a good thing that the flat assembler download is not bulky, it comes in a really small 1 megabyte zip file.

This book should contain about six complete examples of code, of short computer programs which can run with the Windows 7 operating system, and nearly always this should work with Windows 10 as well. They are 100% my own writing.
When you have an example of code, then you can sometimes notice that sections of it can be used to do something with a specific purpose. At other times sections of program code are very hard to read, but also may be used as a vague example, of how to do something?

This book assumes that you already know some Basic Assembly Language, since it cannot teach the basic beginning of the language. But it is at a level which could only interest a beginner. An expert would know all of it already.

There are examples of simple loading and saving memory areas as a file, keyboard inputs, creating a menu.  And creating a moving picture with a Dibsection, and saving the still picture  as a bmp file. And creating a sound track, and saving sound as a file. And there is one experiment for sending emails using assembly language, but that doesn't always work.

When you start writing programs which run with Windows, you find it easy to add more and more to them and build them up to be much longer.

I have never tried to use Microsoft's Visual Studio, but I think the flat assembler is a lot better for me. When I looked at descriptions of Visual Studio I thought it would be making things difficult.

A few years ago, though I knew basic Assembly Language from a computer school, I did not know how to apply the basic Assembly language to creating Windows 7 programs. I have taught myself, so I am ignorant in some fields which specialist courses would teach.

I have to assume that the reader is in a similar situation to me since you naturally understand your own viewpoint best.

I am going to try to upload only a few of my programs to a Source Forge web page.  I meant the "sourceforge.net" website, for free software projects. in which I had a project I called "sound effect". If you look for "https://sourceforge.net/directory/" and enter the word 'sound effect', you may be able to find the program..

The "flat assembler" is also called the Fasmw. (Flat assembler Windows version, which includes a text editor for the program text.) The flat assembler is completely free.

As you download it ,  it comes with lots of short examples of computer programming. For me their examples of programming were important, as I used them to teach myself.

 The best way to learn to create Windows programs must be to start with really short examples, to assemble them, to run them, and to experiment by making changes to them.

I decided not to duplicate any of the information that is clearly written on Microsoft's websites , and that means if you use this book you should still need to look up Microsoft's free information about "Windows API" and functions,  with the internet.

The programming here is completely my own.

The free flat assembler package could come mainly from this address:

https://flatassembler.net


And it can also be downloaded from some other place,  in the Source Forge website , .

The Fasmw is very easy and convenient to use. You just click on the word "run" and the Fasmw saves,  assembles, and runs your program immediately, doing all of that together.  Its good that it does all those things in one operation.

The flat assembler zip file was about 1 megabyte long, and even unzipped, only about 2.5 megabytes.

I have also tried masm32. The masm32 package has a lot of short example programs which are written in a different syntax, and translating the syntax to another assembler's syntax is hard work. I think you can Google "masm32" to find it, and recently a free Microsoft package comes from this address:

www.masm32.com/download.htm
I think that from here onward I should not include anything for Masm32, since this is all about programming with the flat assembler. It is a better assembler, in some ways.

A lot of information about "Windows Api" is easy to find on the internet as it is given out by the Microsoft websites. (API stands for Application Programming Interface.) But Microsoft's website has very few examples of pure assembly language programming, because Microsoft's examples are usually written in the C language. I could not read that, I don't know the C language.

To me the C language looks like a mistake, which would create difficulties where there shouldn't be any. I think plain assembly language is much easier to read. I felt I needed to see programming written in plain pure assembly language. And about twenty examples like that do come free, downloaded with the flat assembler. But actually you wish there were many more examples.

I have wanted to know for certain that an example I was trying to learn from, can work to do something specific. If you don't know for certain that an example can work, there is not much point to it. So I only include my own examples which I created if I am absolutely sure that they did work. For me the Microsoft information was not really enough. I did my programming with a
laptop computer which has the Windows 7 operating system, but a few tests have shown that
the programs could nearly always work with other versions of Windows, like Windows XP
and Windows 10.
;--------
The flat assembler for Windows, is very easy and convenient to use. Its only fault is that at the lower end of your programs you have to include an 'import section', and if you write out the import section yourself, it is quite hard work to type that all in.
But you can also try to write a shorter form of the import section which works with the include files. I prefer the shorter form of it which uses the include files. Once the import section has been typed it, you can use copy & paste it easily to use it in your other programs.

The Flat Assembler comes in a zip file which includes many folders with all the include files and special files which you need to start.
Examples are in a folder called "examples". Nearly all of their examples did work quickly. Just click on "run" and the program is saved, assembled, and starts to run instantly.

In general assembly language may be hard to read, but to me C++ is much harder. Reading a program could take hours since one needs to work out the logic and trace where the conditional relative jumps go. Tracing where the computer goes seems harder in Windows programming because the operating system might call the special procedure called WindowProc at times when you might not expect it. You can do an experiment to count up how many times different parts of a program have been running, to find out where the computer is actually running.

Some of the examples in the flat assembler package were in 64 bit mode, and it was interesting. The 64 bit mode should be much better than 32 bit mode, but they have almost ruined it by creating a strange rule which says that the lowest 4 binary bits of the stack pointer have to be zeros, and you need to get used to it.

My second laptop, which was cheap second hand, is not capable of doing the 64 bit mode at all. I mean its Central processing unit can't do 64 bit at all, even though it does do floating point numbers which are often 64 bit size, but they are working in the FPU, not in the main processor.
The floating point coprocessor was useful and even easy to use, but at first in the beginning I had trouble with it, since the floating point coprocessor can crash if you make a mistake of a certain kind.
It's almost as if someone had wanted to sabotage a coprocessor that is otherwise very good.
The mistake which can crash it seems to be that the floating point register at the bottom of the floating point stack should not be "lost" unless it is "empty". So you either make sure it is not going to be "lost", or mark it as being "empty" with the instruction ffree st7, which marks as 'empty'.

Unfortunately 64 bit mode is not going to work for many of the older computers. For a while I converted some of my 32 bit programs so they could work with 64 bit. 64 bit mode has an improved set of extra registers named r8 to r15. And it has some new types of load instructions which work relative to the instructions pointer, and that might be useful, though I have hardly used them (called RIP addressing for Relative to Instructions Pointer).
Microsoft has made some strange rules about the 64 bit stack pointer, the rules say that its lowest 4 binary bits should be zero when you start running functions. This is quite strange and purposeless.

After the flat assembler is downloaded and unzipped, I find the Fasmw.exe and right click on it to make a shortcut to it. I put the shortcut on my desktop. Whenever I want to start programming, I just click on the shortcut to Fasmw.exe. I am mentioning masm32, but this book has nothing on that.
With the different Masm32 system, the file to run is called "Qeditor.exe" and I would make a shortcut to it.
It may automatically create a shortcut to Qeditor, the shortcut is named "masm32 editor".
The Qeditor.exe is slightly harder to use than the Fasmw, for one specific reason. Because with the Qeditor, one must remember to always "save" the program, and then click on "Console Build all", and then, click on "run".

Because the Qeditor.exe strangely does not assemble and run the ASM file which you actually see on its editing screen. Instead, it assembles and runs an earlier copy which you have saved to the hard drive. Whenever I forgot to click on "save", the Qeditor kept assembling an older version of the program, not the one I could see on the screen.

Whereas with the flat assembler, a click on "run" does all of it automatically in an instant. Saving , compiling, and running all at once. Another useful thing about the Fasmw, is that it can load several programs at the same time , and you see tabs with the file names at the bottom of the screen. This is something really useful. Because you often want to compare two programs, or copy & paste sections from one to another.

How does a Windows program start? Looking at a short example program is much better than reading a description about it in words. I assume that you are going to look at the short examples that come with the flat assembler, since looking at them will show you how to start a program better than my words can. It starts with registering then creating a window. It also starts with a module handle which I notice is not necessary.
The same way of starting a program can be used for many totally different programs.
 Just simply copy the start method which you see in their free example programs.

You can copy the first few lines at the start and the end of their examples, without really understanding it and it will work.
I notice Microsoft calls the system of programming and invocations an Application Programming Interface, or API.
Microsoft gives out lots of free information about specific functions and their parameters , and flags.

And to find it I type in the Google Search "Windows API", plus the name of the particular subject I would like information on.
I noticed that frequently Microsoft's is not easy to understand, and I thought that was partly because their information was in a C language rather than in pure assembly language. Personally I could not have managed to learn anything without an example program in plain assembly.

 I also thought it was not right to use too many macros in the program, since a macro might hide the details of how a program works, and that could make it harder to understand. I am writing programs  without using any macros.

Clearly the middle of a program can be written in any way you like. The beginning and the ending has to follow a specific pattern for the Windows operating system. But the middle of it can be your own original work for anything you want.

I think an interesting subject is having a direct access to the pixels in a picture, or an image, using address registers. That must be very important. And the strange thing is that Microsoft calls the picture with direct access to pixels a "Dibsection". That is a strange sounding word for something so necessary. Why use such a word for something so commonly necessary, which everyone should want?

I am including in this book an example of creating a Dibsection. And making an animated picture on the Dibsection using address registers to write the pixels. One should learn to create a Dibsection because you have access to the pixels in a picture. To do drawings, animations, or to adjust pictures for example.

All Fasmw programs have to have at their bottom something called an "Import section" which has to contain double lists of every function which you are using. I don't really understand the import section, but just copy its pattern.

I think that the flat assembler uses this as a space in which to write the addresses of DLL functions, and then the addresses of those DLLs are actually used whenever you write "invoke" with the function name, and so the import section is very important to this assembler.

The Flat assembler normally comes with some include files which already contain in them this "import section". There are at least 8 of them. And by writing the word "include" then the path and file names of those specific 8 include files, you should be able to simplify and shorten the appearance of your import section.

For example the following include file contains in it a part of the import section which you need:

   include 'INCLUDE\API\USER32.INC'

For some reason the import section for sound was not in the include files, so that has to be typed in.

I have not investigated the range of books, so I only know a few.

A book with some information about computer registers and basic Assembly Language is title "IBM PC Assembly Language and programming" By Peter Abel.  It teaches some basic assembly language,  but a lot of it is about DOS which is maybe obsolete?

A good book about Windows Assembly Language is the book title "Programming Windows 95 By Charles Petzold" Microsoft press, 1996.  Copies of it are low in price and really useful,  but I could only recommend this 1996 book, because I have looked at a more recent book which I thought might be in its series and I thought that was not interesting. The older book was good, but I think it uses  a form of C language instead of pure assembly, and you have to do a bit of mental calculation if you convert the bits of C language into Assembly.

There are many things I do not like at all about the Windows operating system, the worst is, that they have intentionally made the Windows programming as different as possible from Operating systems programming.  Surely they did that to try to confuse and prevent creation of new operating systems?

# A Short Program to Create two Windows

This is a very short complete program I wrote which should create 2 normal small windows. Then if you press on the "b" key it should ask you for a file name, and it should load a .bmp Picture file, if there is one, and it should show the picture in the left side window.

```
                                                        ;6 pages long

    format PE               ;****
    entry start                                 ;start: (Below here) is where it starts running
    include 'win32a.inc'


    section '.data' data readable writeable              ;Starts a data section.

     hInstance dd 0
     _title db 'Window' , 0                       ;word appearing in top left corner
     _class db 'Window' , 0


     h_Window1 dd 0
     h_Window2 dd 0
     hDC1 dd 0
     hDC2 dd 0

     wc WNDCLASSEX 0             ; the window class structure with the label "wc"
     msg MSG                     ; the message structure, with the label "msg"

    ;==========    ;(Uses szTextFilter for loading bmp files. It ends in 2 binary zeros)

     szTextFilter db "Bmp picture Files" , 0 , "*.bmp" , 0 , "All Files" , 0 , "*.*" , 0 , 0
     szTextPath rb MAX_PATH
     szText db ".bmp" , 0 , 0                        ;".bmp" needs the full stop
     ofn OPENFILENAME                                ; the get open file name structure

     hBitmap1 dd 0
     memDC dd 0
     actual dd 0

     top_left_X dd 0                            ;these X and Y are for BitBlt
     top_left_Y dd 70
```

```
    X_size dd 1300
    Y_size dd 1300
                                        ; warning: the word "writable" can trigger Avast false positives

section '.code' code readable executable            ;start the code section

  start:                                            ;start: where it starts running
    invoke  GetModuleHandle , 0                     ;
    mov [hInstance] , eax                           ;
    ;===========================
    mov dword [wc.cbSize] , sizeof.WNDCLASSEX       ;size = 48 bytes
    mov  [wc.hInstance] , eax                       ;hInstance is maybe not necessary
    invoke  LoadCursor , 0 , IDC_ARROW
    mov  [wc.hCursor] , eax
    mov [wc.style] , 0
    mov [wc.lpfnWndProc] , WindowProc      ;gives Operating System the address of WindowProc

    mov [wc.hbrBackground] , COLOR_WINDOW+1   ;background +3=black +1=white
    mov [wc.lpszMenuName] , _class
    mov [wc.lpszClassName] , _class
    ;------------
    invoke  RegisterClassEx , wc                    ;register the window class
    ;====================                           ;Then Creates the first window

    invoke  CreateWindowEx , 0 , _class , \         ; \ slash for continued on next line
    _title , WS_OVERLAPPEDWINDOW , \
    1 , 1 , 400 , 400 , 0 , 0 , 0 , 0

    mov [h_Window1] , eax
    invoke GetDC , [h_Window1]                      ;Get device context of the window
    mov [hDC1] , eax

    ;==================
       invoke ShowWindow , [h_Window1] , SW_SHOWNORMAL

    invoke  CreateWindowEx , 0 , _class , \         ;Creates the second window
    _title , WS_OVERLAPPEDWINDOW , \                ;
    410 , 1 , 300 , 300 , 0 , 0 , 0 , 0
```

```
        mov [h_Window2] , eax
        invoke GetDC , [h_Window2]              ;Get device context of the second window
        mov [hDC2] , eax
    ;==================
        invoke ShowWindow , [h_Window2] , SW_SHOWNORMAL

    invoke FreeConsole
    call text1

    msg_loop:                                   ;A message loop.

        invoke  GetMessage , msg , 0 , 0 , 0
        cmp    eax , 1
        jb     ending
        jne    msg_loop

        invoke  TranslateMessage , msg

        invoke  DispatchMessage , msg
        cmp [msg.message] , WM_CHAR             ;Detect any alphabet key press
        jnz no1
        cmp [msg.wParam] , "b"                  ;Pressing the "b" key to load picture file
        jnz no2

        call load_picture_file
    no2:
        call show_bitmap                        ;pressing any key to rerun BitBlt.

    no1:  call text1                            ;shows a line of text in each window
        jmp msg_loop

      text: db " First  window  Press 'b' key    " ,0     ;One text line
      text2: db "Second window     ",0

text1:
    invoke TextOut , [hDC1] , 10 , 20 , text , 30        ;Text to first window
    invoke TextOut , [hDC2] , 10 , 20 , text2 , 15       ;Text to second window
    ret
;==============================
```

```
show_bitmap:                                    ;Show a bitmap picture (if one loaded)

   mov edi , [hBitmap1]

   invoke CreateCompatibleDC , [hDC1]
   mov [memDC] , eax
   invoke SelectObject , [memDC] , edi          ;edi held the handle of a bitmap

   invoke BitBlt , [hDC1] , [top_left_X] , [top_left_Y] , \    ;\ a slash means continued
        [X_size] , [Y_size] , [memDC] , 10 , 10 , SRCCOPY
          ;-------------------------------
   invoke DeleteDC , [memDC]
   ret


   ;=============================
;maybe hInstance not necessary when load from file?

load_picture_file:
        invoke DeleteObject , [hBitmap1]
        call ofn_structure                      ;Get the Openfilename structure ready

        invoke GetOpenFileName , ofn            ;This gets a complete file name into szTextPath

        invoke LoadImage , 0 , szTextPath , 0 , 600 , 600 , LR_LOADFROMFILE

        cmp eax , 0
        jz returns

        mov [hBitmap1] , eax
        call show_bitmap
   returns:
        ret

;---------------------------- To Fill in the ofn data structure
   ofn_structure:

   invoke RtlZeroMemory , ofn , sizeof.OPENFILENAME
   invoke RtlZeroMemory , szTextPath , MAX_PATH
```

```
    mov [ofn.lStructSize] ,  sizeof.OPENFILENAME
    mov eax  ,  [h_Window1]
    mov [ofn.hwndOwner] ,   eax
    mov [ofn.lpstrFilter] ,   szTextFilter
    mov [ofn.lpstrFile] ,   szTextPath            ;szTextPath gets filled with path & file name

    mov [ofn.nMaxFile] ,   MAX_PATH
    mov eax ,   OFN_EXPLORER OR OFN_PATHMUSTEXIST OR  \       ; \ slash for Continued
    OFN_HIDEREADONLY OR OFN_OVERWRITEPROMPT
    mov [ofn.Flags] ,   eax
    mov [ofn.lpstrDefExt] ,   szText
    ret


    ;=========================================
proc WindowProc hwnd , wmsg , wparam , lparam

    cmp     [wmsg] , WM_CHAR
    je      .esca
    cmp     [wmsg] , WM_DESTROY
    je      .wmdestroy

  .def:

  invoke  DefWindowProc , [hwnd] , [wmsg] , [wparam] , [lparam]      ;Does default processing

    ret

  .esca:
        mov eax , [wparam]
        cmp eax , 27                     ;Detects escape key, it's character 27
        jz .wmdestroy
        jmp .def                         ;jump to .def was essential

  .wmdestroy:

    invoke  PostQuitMessage , 0           ;
    xor    eax , eax
    ret
endp
```

;==============================

ending:                                                                                                          ;
                                                                        ;;End the running program.
            invoke DeleteObject , [hBitmap1]
            invoke ReleaseDC , [h_Window1] , [hDC1]
            invoke ReleaseDC , [h_Window2] , [hDC2]
            invoke FreeConsole
            invoke DestroyWindow , [h_Window1]
            invoke DestroyWindow , [h_Window2]
            invoke ExitProcess , 0


;==============================

section '.idata' import data readable writeable          ;Start of the import section

  library kernel32 , 'KERNEL32.DLL' , \
         user32 , 'USER32.DLL' , \
         gdi32 , 'GDI32.DLL' , \
         comctl32 , 'COMCTL32.DLL' , \
         winmm , 'WINMM.DLL' , \
         avicap ,  'AVICAP32.DLL' , \                    ;use avicap for webcam pictures
         comdlg32 , 'COMDLG32.DLL'

     include 'INCLUDE\API\ADVAPI32.INC'                  ;Include files come with the assembler
     include 'INCLUDE\API\COMCTL32.INC'
     include 'INCLUDE\API\COMDLG32.INC'
     include 'INCLUDE\API\GDI32.INC'
     include 'INCLUDE\API\KERNEL32.INC'
     include 'INCLUDE\API\SHELL32.INC'
     include 'INCLUDE\API\USER32.INC'
     include 'INCLUDE\API\WSOCK32.INC'

This is the end of the short program which creates two windows. About 6 pages.
;=================================================

## A USB Camera Window and Saving Pictures

A program for working a web camera came together with my flat assembler. The program worked, and it made it easy to record a video from the camera. I made a few changes to the program, adding a try again loop to it which seems to improve it.

Now a camera window is created on its own. A dialog box often asks you to chose a camera.
With the menu function, the program simply saves the camera picture as a BMP picture file, and it can also save a video recording until you press the escape key to stop recording.
A file called "avicap32.dll" is necessary to make this work, and I don't understand how that works.
I found it in this folder:   "windows/System32/avicap32.dll" I wonder if it is a permanent part of Windows?

A normal window can so easily be added to this program, so it will have two windows.
 In the case when you create two windows, invoke BitBlt can use their device contexts to copy the camera picture from one to the other. The same invoke BitBlt can also be used to copy the camera picture to a Dibsection, if you have made one.

```
            ;About 7 pages. A Camera window alone

   format PE            ;*******************
   entry start
   include 'win32a.inc'


section '.data' data readable writeable           ;Start of a data section

  hInstance dd 0

; _title db 'Window' ,0
 _class db 'Window',0
    nDevice   dd   0            ; Device Number can range from 0 to 9 ?
 nFPS    dd 20          ; Speed. Is this milliseconds per frame? 1000 was jerky, 20 better

   hWebcam       dd 0
   _camtitle       db 'FASM_WEBCAM',0

 video_name db "A Video saved.avi",0          ;The video recording was Ok.

 _filename  db 'A Camera image.BMP',0       ; This determines the picture's Filename
```

```
;--------------------------
 h_menu1 dd 0
 h_menu2 dd 0
 h_menu3 dd 0

 h_DC dd 0
 start_sign dd 0                            ;my signal to start the camera
 window_address dd 0


 T1 db " Exit",0
 W1 db "End program",0                      ;500


 T2 db " Camera ",0
 W2 db "Stop Camera ",0                     ;501
 W3 db "Restart Camera",0                   ;502
 W4 db "SAVE PICTURE",0                     ;510
 W5 db "Save Video until escape key",0      ;511
 wc WNDCLASSEX 0
 msg MSG
                    ;; note: the word "writable" can trigger avast false positives

 section '.code' code readable executable                  ;Start the code section

                                        ;This is called to create a camera window.
create_capture_window:
     mov eax, [hWebcam]

     cmp eax, 0              ;Flag WS_OVERLAPPEDWINDOW caused right corner buttons
     jnz srt
   invoke  capCreateCaptureWindowA , _class, WS_OVERLAPPEDWINDOW or  WS_VISIBLE ,\
                                 100, 40, 600, 600, 0, [h_menu1]
     mov    [hWebcam], eax
     invoke GetDC, [hWebcam]       ;Get the device context of camera picture [h_DC]
     mov [h_DC], eax

invoke SetWindowLongA, [hWebcam], GWL_WNDPROC, WindowProc

     mov [window_address], eax        ;(this is to let menu and messages work.)
    srt:
```

```
        ret
    ;;*With the device context, BitBlt can copy pictures to another window or to a dibsection.
    ;=========================
     start_camera:

        cmp [hWebcam], 0
        jz skips

        mov ecx,10              ;Try Again Counter.

    try_again1:
        push ecx
        invoke SendMessage, [hWebcam], WM_CAP_DRIVER_CONNECT, [nDevice], 0
        pop ecx
        cmp eax,1               ; the try again improved this
        jz is_ok
        dec ecx
        jnz try_again1

     is_ok:

      invoke  SendMessage, [hWebcam], WM_CAP_SET_SCALE, TRUE, 0
      invoke  SendMessage, [hWebcam], WM_CAP_SET_PREVIEWRATE, [nFPS], 0    ;nFps is in data
      invoke  SendMessage, [hWebcam], WM_CAP_SET_PREVIEW, TRUE, 0
     skips:
        ret

  ;=========================
stop_camera:
        invoke SendMessage, [hWebcam], WM_CAP_DRIVER_DISCONNECT, _camtitle, 0

;;;  invoke  SendMessage, [hWebcam], WM_CAP_DRIVER_DISCONNECT, [nDevice], 0
        ret
    ;=========================
     save_picture_as_file:           ;* worked easily, saved the screen as "camera image.BMP"

      invoke  SendMessage, [hWebcam], WM_CAP_FILE_SAVEDIB, 0, _filename
        ret
    ;=========================
```

```
    save_video:                          ;* it worked right away!  escape key stops recording

    invoke  SendMessage, [hWebcam], WM_CAP_FILE_SET_CAPTURE_FILE, 0, video_name
    invoke  SendMessage, [hWebcam], WM_CAP_SEQUENCE, 0, 0
    ret

;===========================
    start:                    ;the program  starts running this spot, and calls above

    invoke  GetModuleHandle, 0      ;it can work without this module handle
    mov [hInstance], eax
      ;===========================
    mov dword [wc.cbSize], 48              ;size of this structure is 48 bytes
    mov    [wc.hInstance], eax             ;hInstance was not necessary
    invoke  LoadCursor, 0, IDC_ARROW
    mov    [wc.hCursor], eax
    mov [wc.style], 0
    mov [wc.lpfnWndProc], WindowProc
    mov [wc.hbrBackground], COLOR_WINDOW+1    ;background +3=black +1=white
    mov [wc.lpszMenuName], _class
    mov [wc.lpszClassName], _class
      ;------------
    invoke  RegisterClassEx, wc  ;
  ;------------------------------------
    invoke CreateMenu
    mov [h_menu1], eax

    invoke CreateMenu
    mov [h_menu2], eax
    invoke CreateMenu
    mov [h_menu3], eax
;---------------------------------------------
    invoke AppendMenuA, [h_menu1], MF_POPUP, [h_menu2], T1       ;exit
    invoke AppendMenuA,[h_menu2],0,500, W1                        ;End program

    invoke AppendMenuA, [h_menu1], MF_POPUP, [h_menu3], T2

    invoke AppendMenuA, [h_menu3], 0, 501, W2
    invoke AppendMenuA, [h_menu3], 0, 502, W3
```

```
    ;------------------------------------
    invoke AppendMenuA, [h_menu3], 0, 510, W4            ;save picture
    ;----------------
    invoke AppendMenuA, [h_menu3], 0, 511, W5            ;save as Video
;---------------------------------------------
            ;;As well, creating a normal window can be added here, to make 2 windows.

    call create_capture_window                ;Call to create the camera window.

    invoke ShowWindow, [hWebcam], SW_SHOWNORMAL
     ;====================
    call start_camera
    invoke FreeConsole

  msg_loop:

       invoke  GetMessage, msg, 0, 0, 0
       cmp    eax,1
       jb     ending
       jne    msg_loop


       invoke  TranslateMessage, msg

       invoke  DispatchMessage, msg

       cmp [start_sign], 1
       jnz no1
       mov [start_sign], 0         ;erase it to 0
       call start_camera
       jmp no1

   no1:
       jmp msg_loop


    ;===========================
proc WindowProc hwnd, wmsg, wparam, lparam

    cmp    [wmsg], WM_COMMAND
    je     .command
```

```
        cmp     [wmsg], WM_CHAR
        je      .character
        cmp     [wmsg], WM_DESTROY
        je      .wmdestroy

 .def:
        mov edx, [hWebcam]          ;CallWindowProc Allows camera window to do messages
        cmp edx, [hwnd]             ;But run DefWindowProc is also necessary here.
        jnz .def2
        invoke CallWindowProc, [window_address], [hwnd], [wmsg], [wparam], [lparam]
        ret

  .def2:
        invoke  DefWindowProc, [hwnd], [wmsg], [wparam], [lparam]
        ret

 .command:
        mov eax, [wparam]
        cmp eax, 500                          ;menu click on exit
        jz .wmdestroy
        cmp eax, 501
        jnz .com1
        call stop_camera
        ret
.com1:
        cmp eax, 502
        jnz .com2
        mov [start_sign], 1                   ;a signal to start the camera.
        ;;; call start_camera         ;starting camera worked better from message loop?
        ret
.com2:
        cmp eax, 510
        jnz .com3
        call save_picture_as_file    ;working simply. previous picture was overwritten
        ret
.com3:
        cmp eax, 511
        jnz .def
```

```
        call save_video          ;saved a video recording until escape key stops it.
        ret

    .character:
        mov eax,[wparam]
        cmp eax, 27               ;Here escape is as a character 27
        jz .wmdestroy
        jmp .def                  ;*essential .def

    .wmdestroy:
        invoke  PostQuitMessage, 0
        xor    eax, eax
        ret
    endp
;===========================

ending:
        invoke  SendMessage, [hWebcam], WM_CAP_DRIVER_DISCONNECT, _camtitle, 0

        invoke ReleaseDC, [hWebcam], [h_DC]
        invoke FreeConsole
        invoke DestroyWindow, [hWebcam]
        invoke ExitProcess, 0                     ;Ends the running

;=========== camera constants? Some necessary. 1024 = 400h

    WM_USER = 1024
    WM_CAP_FILE_SET_CAPTURE_FILE = 1024 + 20
    WM_CAP_SEQUENCE              = 1024 + 62
;-------
    WM_CAP_START                 = 1024
    WM_CAP_COPY                  = 1024 + 30
    WM_CAP_GET_FRAME             = 1024 + 60
    WM_CAP_DLG_VIDEOFORMAT       = 1024 + 41
    WM_CAP_DLG_VIDEOSOURCE       = 1024 + 42
    WM_CAP_DLG_VIDEODISPLAY      = 1024 + 43
    WM_CAP_GET_VIDEOFORMAT       = 1024 + 44
    WM_CAP_SET_VIDEOFORMAT       = 1024 + 45
    WM_CAP_DLG_VIDEOCOMPRESSION  = 1024 + 46
```

```
    WM_CAP_ABORT              = 445h   ;did not do anything
    WM_CAP_STOP               = 444h   ;did not do anything

    WM_CAP_DRIVER_CONNECT            = 1024 + 10
    WM_CAP_DRIVER_DISCONNECT         = 1024 + 11
    WM_CAP_FILE_SAVEDIB              = 1024 + 25
    WM_CAP_SET_PREVIEW               = 1024 + 50
    WM_CAP_SET_PREVIEWRATE           = 1024 + 52
    WM_CAP_SET_SCALE                 = 1024 + 53
;==============================
section '.idata' import data readable writeable

 library kernel32,'KERNEL32.DLL',\
       user32,'USER32.DLL',\
       gdi32,'GDI32.DLL',\
       comctl32,'COMCTL32.DLL',\
       winmm,'WINMM.DLL',\
       avicap, 'AVICAP32.DLL',\           ;Avicap32 used for camera
       comdlg32,'COMDLG32.DLL'

   include 'INCLUDE\API\ADVAPI32.INC'
   include 'INCLUDE\API\COMCTL32.INC'
   include 'INCLUDE\API\COMDLG32.INC'
   include 'INCLUDE\API\GDI32.INC'
   include 'INCLUDE\API\KERNEL32.INC'
   include 'INCLUDE\API\SHELL32.INC'
   include 'INCLUDE\API\USER32.INC'
   include 'INCLUDE\API\WSOCK32.INC'

    import  avicap,\
        capCreateCaptureWindowA, 'capCreateCaptureWindowA'          ;necessary.

;;necessary for the web cam  I find avicap32.dll in "windows/System32/avicap32.dll"

;This is the end of the camera window program . About 7 pages.
;==================================================
```

# Hexadecimal View of working message structure

This program creates a viewing of the memory as hexadecimal numbers.
It can be adjusted to show different areas of memory in hexadecimal, and now it shows the MSG message structure while it's running. And you see in it the keyboard inputs, the mouse coordinates, and all the other fields of the message structure.
The program creates 2 windows, a normal window on the left with a hexadecimal display, and on the right, an edit control window,.
You can type into the edit control, but that doesn't do anything.

The hexadecimal view shows everything in MSG except that it avoids the annoying message coming from the edit control cursor blinking. By testing for message 118h and skipping that.
Below the hexadecimal view of MSG, there is another hexadecimal view which you can address to show anything else such as a test of floating point numbers maybe.

The writing of the program demonstrates how one can give a functioning menu to an edit control.
This program is about 9 pages long.

```
format PE                  ;*******************
entry start
include 'win32a.inc'

section '.data' data readable writeable              ;start a data section

 hInstance dd 0
 text_set rb 300                    ;small memory area for text coming from edit window
 ;--------
 _title db "Window  MSG structure in Hex" , 0
 _title2 db "Edit control window " , 0

  _class db 'normal' , 0
  _edit db 'EDIT' , 0       ;This word is seen by the operating system, and that creates edit control

  pointing1 dd 0
   ;------
   h_menu1 dd 0
   h_menu2 dd 0
   h_menu3 dd 0
```

```
h_DC dd 0
h_Window dd 0
h_Edit_Window dd 0
window_address dd 0
h_Font dd 0

T1 db " Exit" , 0
W1 db "End program" , 0                                    ;ID=500
W2 db "Text Go from window into memory (Get) " , 0         ; ID=501

T2 db " Top" , 0
W3 db " Text go from memory into window (Set) " , 0        ;ID=502


fontname db "Verdana" , 0

X0 dd 0
X1 dd 0
Y1 dd 0100
letter_colour dd 0
letter1 dq 0                          ; letter1 is A field for writing 2 hex digits

wc WNDCLASSEX 0
msg MSG
rb 100                                ;rb puts zeroes to see it without clutter
sixteen dd 16                         ;a test number for floating point
blank rb 100h                         ;could show a floating point operation?

                    ; Note: The word "writable" can trigger a false positive.

section '.code' code readable executable      ; This line starts the Code section


start:

    invoke  GetModuleHandle , 0       ; Module handle is not really necessary?
    mov [hInstance] , eax
    ;===========================
    mov dword [wc.cbSize] , sizeof.WNDCLASSEX    ;the size is always = 48 bytes.
```

```
        mov   [wc.hInstance] , eax              ;Is [hInstance] sometimes necessary?
        invoke  LoadCursor , 0 , IDC_ARROW
        mov   [wc.hCursor] , eax
        mov [wc.style] ,  CS_DBLCLKS            ;only makes detecting double clicks possible
        mov [wc.lpfnWndProc] , WindowProc       ;Give the address of WindowProc
        mov [wc.hbrBackground] , COLOR_WINDOW+3  ;background +3=black +1=white
        mov [wc.lpszClassName] , _class
        ;----------
        invoke  RegisterClassEx , wc

     ;-------------------------------------
       invoke CreateMenu
       mov [h_menu1] , eax

       invoke CreateMenu
       mov [h_menu2] , eax
       invoke CreateMenu
       mov [h_menu3] , eax
 ;-------------------------------------------
        invoke AppendMenuA , [h_menu1] , MF_POPUP , [h_menu2] , T1       ;exit
        invoke AppendMenuA , [h_menu2] , 0 , 500 , W1                    ; ends the program
   ;--------
        invoke AppendMenuA , [h_menu1] , MF_POPUP , [h_menu3] , T2
        invoke AppendMenuA , [h_menu3] , 0 , 501 , W2
        invoke AppendMenuA , [h_menu3] , 0 , 502 , W3
      ;-----------------------------------------------

        invoke  CreateWindowEx , 0 , _class , \           ;Create a normal window
        _title , WS_OVERLAPPEDWINDOW or WS_VISIBLE , \
        1 , 1 , 610 , 700 , 0 , [h_menu1] , 0 , 0

        mov [h_Window] , eax
     ;--------------------------------- ;Create an Edit control type of window.
invoke  CreateWindowEx , 0 , _edit , \
  _title2 , ES_MULTILINE or ES_AUTOHSCROLL or ES_AUTOVSCROLL or \    ; \ continued
   WS_OVERLAPPEDWINDOW or WS_VISIBLE , \                             ; \ continued
   615 , 1 , 400 , 400 , 0 , [h_menu1] , 0 , 0

       mov [h_Edit_Window] , eax
```

```
                                    ;Then SetWindowLongA allows edit window to use WindowProc

    invoke SetWindowLongA , [h_Edit_Window] , GWL_WNDPROC , WindowProc
    mov [window_address] , eax


    invoke ShowWindow , [h_Window] , SW_SHOWNORMAL

;======================  Allocated memory
    invoke GlobalAlloc , 0 , 1000000h                ;not actually used in this program?
    mov [pointing1] , eax
     ;--------------
    invoke GetDC , [h_Window]     ;Get Device Context  that is necessary for TextOut and for BitBlt
    mov [h_DC] , eax
;==================== Enlarge font size a little After GetDC.

    invoke CreateFont , 18 , 9 , 0 , 0 , 40 , 0 , 0 , 0 , 0 , \       ;First two numbers are font size.
                0 , 0 , 0 , 0 ,  fontname                     ;(address of fontname)

    mov [h_Font] , eax                          ;Save handle of font
    invoke SelectObject , [h_DC] , eax     ;So the font size will be affecting text in the window
    invoke SetBkColor , [h_DC] , 0101010h          ; set background colour here
;=====================
 msg_loop:                                                ;The message loop

    invoke  GetMessage , msg , 0 , 0 , 0

    cmp    eax , 1
    jb     endinga
    jne    msg_loop

    invoke  TranslateMessage , msg

    invoke  DispatchMessage , msg

    call hexasquare1              ; To view in hexadecimal numbers
    call hexasquare2

    jmp msg_loop
```

```
hexasquare1:                                ;* See the MSG data structure.

    cmp [msg.message] , 118h                ;Avoid when edit window sends a cursor blinking message
        jnz he1
        ret                                 ;ahead only when not a cursor blink
  he1:

            mov [X0] , 20                   ;X0= horizontal position
            mov [Y1] , 100                  ;Y1= vertical position
            mov ebx , msg                   ;Display the message structure , in hexadecimal
            mov ch , 4
            jmp hexadecimal_view            ;(adjusted for little-endian).

    hexasquare2:                            ;The address in ebx can be changed

            mov ebx , blank
            fild [sixteen]                  ;load an integer by pushing it to st0
            fst qword [ebx]                 ;store it as a floating point number
            fmul st0 , st0                  ;square of sixteen
            fistp qword [ebx+10h]           ;save result as integer and pop


            mov [X0] , 20
            mov [Y1] , 300                  ;Y1 lower down on screen

            mov ch , 4
            jmp hexadecimal_view

;==============================

    write_two_digits:

        push ecx                            ;save ecx here or else a crash
        push ebx
        mov ebx , letter1
        mov [ebx] , ax                      ; The 2 hex letters in ax  to be  shown
        mov byte [ebx+2] , 20h                          ; And a space

        invoke SetTextColor , [h_DC] , [letter_colour]
```

```
        invoke TextOut , [h_DC] , [X1] , [Y1] , letter1 , 3        ;Writes 2 digits and a space
        pop ebx
        pop ecx
        ret

hexadecimal_view:
row_loop:
        mov eax , [X0]                          ;Start every line at the left side
        mov [X1] , eax
        mov cl , 16                             ;number of double characters per row
byte_loop:
        mov al , [ebx]                          ;Read a Byte to be Translated
        mov edx , 0ffaa55h                      ;color for number 0 , is blue
        cmp al , 0
        jz tohex1
        mov edx , 055ffffh                      ;a color for hex numbers below ascii
        cmp al , 20h
        jb tohex2                               ;Note; deleting these 2 jumps made blue and white color
        cmp al , 80h
        jb tohex1
tohex2:
        mov edx , 0ffffffh                      ;a color for lower case letters
tohex1:
        mov [letter_colour] , edx

        call two_hex          ; It returns with 2 ascii hexadecimal digits ,  in AH and AL

        call write_two_digits

        add [X1] , 26 ;
        dec cl
        test cl , 3
        jnz tohex3
        add [X1] , 4
tohex3:
        inc ebx
        test cl , 0ffh
        jnz byte_loop
```

```
        add [Y1] , 30
        jb endhex
        cmp [Y1] , 600
        jnb endhex
        dec ch
        jnz row_loop
endhex:
        ret

two_hex:                        ;call two_hex  with a binary value in al 0-255
        push ecx
        mov ah , al
        call into_ascii
        mov ch , al                     ;save lower digit in ch
        mov al , ah
        ror al , 4

        call into_ascii
        mov ah , ch             ;recover lower digit in ch
        pop ecx
        ret             ;return with AL=upper hex digit and AH=lower hex digit

into_ascii:
        and al , 0fh            ;to convert byte in AL into hexadecimal ASCII Text
        mov cl , "0"            ;= 30h number 0 as text
        cmp al , 10
        jnb as1
        add al , cl
        ret
as1:
        sub al , 10
        mov cl , "A"                    ;= 41h
        add al , cl
        ret

;==========================
```

```
proc WindowProc  hwnd , wmsg , wparam , lparam                    ; WindowProc

    cmp    [wmsg] , WM_COMMAND
    jz     .command
    cmp    [wmsg] , WM_CHAR
    je     .character
    cmp    [wmsg] , WM_DESTROY
    je     .wmdestroy

.def:
.defwndproc:
   mov edx , [h_Edit_Window]      ;Go One or the other depending on which window handle.
   cmp edx , [hwnd]               ;For edit control windows , (also needed SetWindowLongA)
    jnz .def2
    invoke CallWindowProc , [window_address] , [hwnd] , [wmsg] , [wparam] , [lparam]
    ret

 .def2:                           ;For normal windows, default message processing

    invoke  DefWindowProc , [hwnd] , [wmsg] , [wparam] , [lparam]
    ret


 .command:
    mov eax , [wparam]
    cmp eax , 500
    jz .wmdestroy
    cmp eax , 501                 ;GetWindowTextA  has a length parameter at its end
    jnz .nott2
    invoke GetWindowTextA , [h_Edit_Window] ,  text_set , 200
    ret

.nott2: cmp eax , 502             ;No length parameter. From memory to window
    jnz .def
    invoke SetWindowTextA , [h_Edit_Window] ,  text_set
    ret


 .character:
    mov eax , [wparam]
    cmp eax , 27                                      ; The escape key is 27
```

```
        jz .wmdestroy
        jmp .def

 .wmdestroy:
        invoke  PostQuitMessage , 0
        xor    eax , eax
        ret
 endp
;==================
endinga:
             invoke GlobalFree , [pointing1]
             invoke DeleteObject , [h_Font]              ;Delete object essential
             invoke ReleaseDC , [h_Window] , [h_DC]
             invoke FreeConsole
             invoke DestroyWindow , [h_Edit_Window]
             invoke DestroyWindow , [h_Window]
             invoke ExitProcess , 0


   ;==================
section '.idata' import data readable writeable           ;Start the import section

 library kernel32 , 'KERNEL32.DLL' , \
        user32 , 'USER32.DLL' , \
        gdi32 , 'GDI32.DLL' , \
        comctl32 , 'COMCTL32.DLL' , \
        winmm , 'WINMM.DLL' , \
        comdlg32 , 'COMDLG32.DLL'

    include 'INCLUDE\API\ADVAPI32.INC'
    include 'INCLUDE\API\COMCTL32.INC'
    include 'INCLUDE\API\COMDLG32.INC'
    include 'INCLUDE\API\GDI32.INC'
    include 'INCLUDE\API\KERNEL32.INC'
    include 'INCLUDE\API\SHELL32.INC'
    include 'INCLUDE\API\USER32.INC'
    include 'INCLUDE\API\WSOCK32.INC'
```

I think this is the 32 bit message structure, it is defined in an include file, USER32.INC

### 32 bit msg structure.

The case sensitive names are for the Fasmw

| Offset hex | Offset | Length in bytes | Name (case sensitive) | |
|---|---|---|---|---|
| 0 | 0 | 4 | hwnd | A handle to the window |
| 4 | 4 | 4 | message | Identifies what kind of message |
| 8 | 8 | 4 | wParam | Message information |
| 0Ch | 12 | 4 | lParam | Extra message information |
| 10h | 16 | 4 | time | The time a message was posted |
| 14h | 20 | 4+4 | pt | Point structure is X,Y |

### The 64 bit message structure.

### 64 bit msg structure.

The case sensitive names are for the Fasmw

| Offset hex | Offset | Length in bytes | Name (case sensitive) | |
|---|---|---|---|---|
| 0 | 0 | 8 | hwnd | A handle to the window |
| 8 | 8 | 4 | message | Identifies what kind of message |
| 10h | 16 | 8 | wParam | Message information |
| 18h | 24 | 8 | lParam | Extra message information |
| 20h | 32 | 4 | time | The time when message was posted |
| 24h | 36 | 4+4 | pt | Point structure is X,Y |

This is a drawing of the function BitBlt

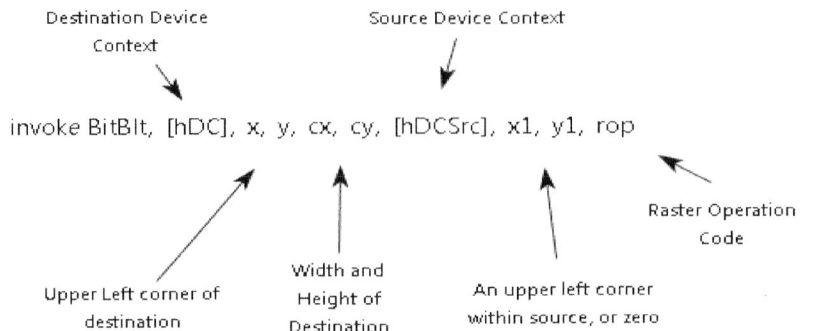

# A program for an animation of bending lines

The following is a complete program to animate a pattern of lines which bend and curl in different directions. The animated drawing is drawn onto a Dibsection and this is copied to the front window using invoke BitBlt.

The principle created a steady animation and the method can work for many different kinds of drawings.

The program can also save the picture as a .bmp image file. This also demonstrates how you can ask for a file name and then save a picture, with in this case a bmp file header.

```
                        ;about 15 pages
    format PE           ;****************** Start of the program, to make an .exe file.
    entry start                             ;On starting it will go to the label "start:"
    include 'win32a.inc'   ;

    section '.data' data readable writeable            ;Starting the data section

    hInstance dd 0

    _title db 'turning' , 0                 ;word appearing in top left corner
    _class db 'window' , 0

    pointing1 dd 0
    ;------
    h_menu_1 dd 0
    h_menu_2 dd 0
    h_menu_3 dd 0

    hDC dd 0
    h_Window dd 0
    hDC_Bmp dd 0
    hBitmap dd 0


    B2 db "Box border" , 0
    B1 db "Message Box text" , 0

    T1 db " Exit" , 0
    W1 db "End program" , 0                 ;500
    T2 db " Menu   " , 0                    ;501
```

```
W2 db " Save screen as a .BMP File " , 0   ;
W3 db " Make message Box   " , 0                              ;502
  ;------------
actual dd 0
hcf dd 0
background dd 0                                               ;switch black/white background?

  szTextFilter db "Bmp picture File" , 0 , "*.bmp" , 0 , "All Files" , 0 , "*.*" , 0 , 0
      szTextPath rb MAX_PATH
      szText db "bmp" , 0
;---------------

wc WNDCLASSEX
msg MSG
ofn OPENFILENAME
                           ;Here the word "writable" is used but can cause a false positive.
  ;--------
section '.code' code readable writable executable             ;Start the code section

  start:                                                      ;start running here

      invoke  GetModuleHandle , 0
      mov [hInstance] , eax
      ;=========================
      mov dword [wc.cbSize] , 30h
      mov     [wc.hInstance] , eax
      invoke  LoadCursor , 0 , IDC_ARROW
      mov     [wc.hCursor] , eax
      mov [wc.style] , CS_DBLCLKS                ;to make detecting double clicks possible
      mov [wc.lpfnWndProc] , WindowProc          ;Give the OS the address of WindowProc
      mov [wc.cbClsExtra] , 0
      mov [wc.cbWndExtra] , 0
      mov [wc.hbrBackground] , COLOR_WINDOW+1    ;background +3=black +1=white
      mov [wc.lpszMenuName] , _class                  ;_title
      mov [wc.lpszClassName] , _class
      ;------------
      invoke  RegisterClassEx , wc  ;

      ;==============
```

```
    invoke CreateMenu                                      ; Collect several menu handles
    mov [h_menu_1] , eax

    invoke CreateMenu
    mov [h_menu_2] , eax
    invoke CreateMenu
    mov [h_menu_3] , eax

;------------------------------------

    invoke AppendMenuA , [h_menu_1] , MF_POPUP , [h_menu_2] , T1     ;exit
    invoke AppendMenuA , [h_menu_2] , 0 , 500 , W1                   ;End the program
;--------
    invoke AppendMenuA , [h_menu_1] , MF_POPUP , [h_menu_3] , T2
    invoke AppendMenuA , [h_menu_3] , 0 , 501 , W2
                                                                     ;save as a bmp file
    invoke AppendMenuA , [h_menu_3] , 0 , 502 , W3

;--------------------- To create the window

    invoke  CreateWindowEx , 0 , _class , \                  ; \ continued on next lines
    _title , WS_OVERLAPPEDWINDOW , \
    1 , 1 , 710 , 700 , 0 , [h_menu_1] , 0 , 0

    mov [h_Window] , eax

    invoke ShowWindow , [h_Window] , SW_SHOWNORMAL
     ;=======================
                                                           ;To allocate memory
    invoke GlobalAlloc , 0 , 1000000h            ; But the memory is not necessary in this
    mov [pointing1] , eax
       ;-----
    call start_dibsection           ;Call to create a Dibsection memory for animations.
                                    ;timer ID , milliseconds , zero for call windowproc
 invoke SetTimer , [h_Window] , 300 , 16 , 0


;====================

    msg_loop:
```

```
    invoke  GetMessage , msg , 0 , 0 , 0
    cmp     eax , 1
    jb      endinga
    jne     msg_loop

    invoke  TranslateMessage , msg

    invoke  DispatchMessage , msg

    cmp word [msg.message] , WM_CHAR
    jnz no1
    cmp [msg.wParam] , 20h
    jnz no1
    inc [background]

 no1:
    cmp [msg.message] , WM_TIMER            ; Detects when there is a timer message
    jnz msg_loop
    mov [msg.message] , 0
    cmp [msg.wParam] , 300    ; compare to user defined timer ID ( not really necessary )
    jnz msg_loop
    test [background] , 1
    jz black
invoke BitBlt , [hDC_Bmp] , 0 , 0 , 700 , 700 , [hDC_Bmp] , 0 , 0 , WHITENESS        ;Erases
    jmp white
black:
invoke BitBlt , [hDC_Bmp] , 0 , 0 , 700 , 700 , [hDC_Bmp] , 0 , 0 , BLACKNESS     ; Erasing
  white:
    call draws_line1

invoke BitBlt , [hDC] , 0 , 0 , 700 , 700 , [hDC_Bmp] , 0 , 0 , SRCCOPY         ; Copy the image

    jmp   msg_loop

                  ; (The lower BitBlt copies the Dibsection image to the visible window.)
      ;=====================
```

```
draws_line1:                                    ;Draw the animation
    fld1
    fst [accumulateX]
    fstp [accumulateY]                          ;start off X , Y as 1
    mov ecx , 290                               ;290 1st stem
    fld [angle1]
    fstp [angle]
    mov [colour] , 0ffffffh                     ;set a white colour
    call line_loop                              ;draw a bending line
    ;--
    call red_circle
     ;---
    call branch

    mov ecx , 300
    add [colour] , 0ffh                         ;change the color
    call line_loop
    call red_circle
    call branch

    mov ecx , 300
    add [colour] , 0ffh
    call line_loop
    call red_circle
    ;--
    fld1
    fst [accumulateX]
    fstp [accumulateY]                          ;start off X , Y as 1
    ;--                                         ;now readying for the next frame
    fld1                                        ;load a constant number 1
    fidiv [divisor]         ;divide it , a smaller divisor makes faster turning
    fadd [angle1]
    fstp [angle1]                               ;increase the angle
    ret

branch:
    fld1
    fidiv [divisor]                             ;saves for branches , divisor is integer.
```

```
            fadd [branchangle]
            fadd st0 , st0
            fstp [angle]
            fld [branchX]
            fstp [accumulateX]
            fld [branchY]
            fstp [accumulateY]
            ret

line_loop:  fld [angle]
            fsin
            fadd [accumulateX]              ;sine of the angle times radius = X
            fst [accumulateX]
            fistp [X]
            fld [angle]
            fcos
            fadd [accumulateY]              ;cosine of the angle times radius = Y
            fst [accumulateY]
            fistp [Y]
            ;----
            cmp ecx , 90
            jnz line6
            fld [angle]
            fstp [branchangle]
            fld [accumulateX]
            fstp [branchX]                  ;save coordinate for a side branch?
            fld [accumulateY]
            fstp [branchY]

    line6:

            ;-----
            cmp ecx , 200                   ;a greater value here lengthens
            jnb line5
            cmp ecx , 25
            jb line5
            add dword [colour] , 0990000h
            fld [accumulateX]
            fadd st0 , st0
```

```
        fidiv [divi]
        fadd [angle]                                    ;a semicircle
        fstp [angle]
        ;----
line5:
        call draw_pixel_xy                              ;Draw several pixels at XY.
         ;-----
        sub ecx , 1
        jnz line_loop   ;

        ret

anginc dq 0.02
angincrun dq 0.0
spiral dq 0.002
rcang dq 0

red_circle:
        fld [anginc]
        fstp [angincrun]

        push [colour]                                   ;push pop colour works
        mov [colour] , 0ff5555h
        fld [angle]
        fstp [rcang]
        mov ecx , 70                                    ;a small red hook shape with 40 to 70
rcloop:
        fld [angincrun]
        fadd [spiral]
        fstp [angincrun]

        fld [rcang]
        fsub [angincrun]
        fst [rcang]

        fsin
        fadd [accumulateX]                              ;sine of the angle times radius = X
        fst [accumulateX]
        fistp [X]
```

```
        fld [rcang]
        fcos
        fadd [accumulateY]              ;cosine of the angle times radius = Y
        fst [accumulateY]
        fistp [Y]
        call draw_pixel_xy
        dec ecx
        jnz rcloop
        pop [colour]
        ret

draw_pixel_xy:                          ;** pixels will only become visible when BitBlt runs.
        mov eax , [Y]
        mov edx , 700*4                 ;This assumes 700*4 is bytes-per-line in the Dibsection
        push ecx
        imul edx
        pop ecx

        mov [Yaddress] , eax
        mov eax , [X]
        add eax , eax
        add eax , eax                   ;times 4 when 4 bytes per pixel
        add eax , [Yaddress]

        mov ebx , [bitmap_address]
        cmp ebx , 0
        jz line4
        add ebx , eax
        add ebx , 700*4*350             ;get vertically nearly in the middle
        add ebx , 350*4                 ;get horizontally the center of the bitmap area

        cmp ebx , [bitmap_address]

        jb line4                        ;** Here jb prevents a crash, when it goes above top of window
        cmp ebx , [upper_limit_bitmap]
        jnb line4
        mov eax , [colour]

        mov dword [ebx] , eax           ;Here draws a 2x2 pixel dot
```

```
        mov dword [ebx+700*4] , eax
        mov dword [ebx+4] , eax
        mov dword [ebx+700*4+4] , eax
line4:
        ret


        ;--- The variables could all be moved into the data section, to avoid "writable" in CS.

divi dd 9000
accumulateX dq 0
accumulateY dq 0
X dd 0
Y dd 0
colour dd 0ffffffh
divisor dd 350                                          ; A larger divisor slows it ,
branchX dq 0
branchY dq 0
branchangle dq 0

Yaddress dd 0
angle dq 0
angle1 dq 0


;=========================
        ; To Save the Dibsection picture as a .BMP image file.

save_picture_file:

        call fill_headers       ;This should write bmp header over the start of the bitmap memory
        call copy_headers

        call get_open_file_name_txt             ;fill the ofn data structure
        invoke GetSaveFileName , ofn    ;This invoke asks the user to chose a file name

        invoke CreateFile , szTextPath , GENERIC_READ or GENERIC_WRITE , \
                        FILE_SHARE_READ or FILE_SHARE_WRITE , \
                        0 , 4 , 20h , 0
  mov [hcf] , eax
  cmp eax , -1
```

```
    jz errora

    mov ebx , [bitmap_address]                    ;************

    mov ecx , 700*700*4+54        ;700 pixels x 700 lines x 4 bytes per pixel
    mov esi , actual                              ;pointer to actual.

    invoke WriteFile , [hcf] , ebx , ecx , esi , 0
    invoke CloseHandle , [hcf]

    mov ebx , [actual]
    ret

errora:
    mov edx , _words7
    mov ebx , _words8
    invoke MessageBoxA , [h_Window] , edx , ebx , 0
    ret
_words7 db "error no handle " , 0
_words8 db " message box" , 0
;----------------------    To ask the user to chose a file name.
 get_open_file_name_txt:

 mov edx , sizeof.OPENFILENAME
 invoke RtlZeroMemory , ofn , edx
 invoke RtlZeroMemory , szTextPath , MAX_PATH

mov eax , sizeof.OPENFILENAME
mov [ofn.lStructSize] , eax
mov eax , [h_Window]
mov [ofn.hwndOwner] , eax
mov [ofn.lpstrFilter] , szTextFilter
mov [ofn.lpstrFile] , szTextPath
mov [ofn.nMaxFile] , MAX_PATH
mov eax , OFN_EXPLORER OR OFN_PATHMUSTEXIST OR  \           ;\ continued
OFN_HIDEREADONLY OR OFN_OVERWRITEPROMPT
mov [ofn.Flags] , eax
mov [ofn.lpstrDefExt] , szText
 ret
```

```
;=========================
copy_headers:
        mov ecx , 54
        mov ebx , bmf_header
        mov esi , [bitmap_address]
    copying:
        mov al , [ebx]                  ;* Copy the headers to create a .bmp file
        mov [esi] , al
        inc esi
        inc ebx
        dec ecx
        jnz copying

        mov ecx , [bitmap_length]
        sub ecx , 58
        add esi , 4                     ;Shift bitmap for adjust colors
    shifts:
        mov al , [esi]
        mov [esi-2] , al                ;-2 for colours. To make colours come out the same
        inc esi
        dec ecx
        jnz shifts
        ret


  ;============================== WindowProc
proc WindowProc hwnd , wmsg , wparam , lparam

    cmp [msg.message] , WM_COMMAND      ;WM_COMMAND means a menu item clicked on
    jnz .nocommand
    cmp dword [wparam] , 500            ;[wparam] and [msg.wParam] assumed exactly the same
    jz .wmdestroy
    cmp dword [wparam] , 501
    jz .bmp
    cmp dword [wparam] , 502
    jz .about

 .nocommand:
   ;---------------------------
```

```
        cmp     [wmsg] , WM_TIMER
    ;   jz .time
        cmp     [wmsg] , WM_CHAR
        je      .esca
        cmp     [wmsg] , WM_DESTROY
        je      .wmdestroy

.def:
        invoke  DefWindowProc , [hwnd] , [wmsg] , [wparam] , [lparam]
        ret

    .time:                  ;Time here either return quickly or call the drawing once each time
        ret
    .bmp:
        call save_picture_file
        ret
    .esca:
        mov eax , [wparam]          ;[wparam] and [msg.wParam] should be exactly the same
        cmp eax , 27                ;27 is the escape key. The Escape key was detected Here
        jz .wmdestroy
        jmp .def

    .about:
        invoke  MessageBox , [hwnd] , B1 , B2 , MB_OK
        ret

.wmdestroy:
        invoke  PostQuitMessage , 0
        xor     eax , eax
        ret
endp                                        ;the end of the procedure

;======================

endinga:                                    ;End the program.

            invoke GlobalFree , [pointing1]
            invoke KillTimer , [h_Window] , 300
```

```
            invoke ReleaseDC , [h_Window] , [hDC]
            invoke DeleteObject , [hBitmap]
            invoke DeleteDC , [hDC_Bmp]
            invoke FreeConsole
            invoke DestroyWindow , [h_Window]
            invoke ExitProcess , 0

;==========================
    object dd 0
    bitmap_length dd 0
    upper_limit_bitmap dd 0
    bitmap_address dd 0
                                            ;bmf is 14 bytes long.  Bmi is 40 bytes long.
bmf_header   BITMAPFILEHEADER     ; The two declared together do make a bmp file header
bmi      BITMAPINFOHEADER         ;The bmi header alone is enough for creating a dibsection
 rb 200                                     ;clear away a space to see it  uncluttered
;---=======================
    start_dibsection:

        call fill_headers                           ;Fill the header
        invoke GetDC , [h_Window]
        mov [hDC] , eax                             ;Device context of the window
        invoke CreateCompatibleDC , [hDC]
        mov [hDC_Bmp] , eax             ;device context for bitmap to be selected into

        mov ecx , bmi                   ;the address of the bmi header
        mov edx , bitmap_address        ;The invoke will write a new address = start
                                        ;Next create a Dibsection
                                                    ;middle 00== DIB_RGB_COLORS
        invoke CreateDIBSection , [hDC] , ecx , 0 , edx , 0 , 0

        mov [hBitmap] , eax
        invoke SelectObject , [hDC_Bmp] , [hBitmap]     ;Bitmap Selected into device context
        mov [object] , eax
        mov eax , [bitmap_address]
        add eax , [bitmap_length]
        sub eax , 700*12                            ;3 lines below ?  to not get too near
        mov [upper_limit_bitmap] , eax              ;use it for comparing
        ret
```

```
;=========================

    fill_headers:      ;fields in their order
            mov [bmf_header.bfType] , "BM"
            mov [bmf_header.bfSize] , 700*700*4+54              ;The file size
            mov [bmf_header.bfReserved1] , 0
            mov [bmf_header.bfReserved2] , 0
            mov [bmf_header.bfOffBits] , 54      ;54 bytes long when both parts. 14+40=54

    mov [bmi.biSize] , sizeof.BITMAPINFOHEADER              ;size of this = 40
    mov [bmi.biWidth] , 700
                                                            ;horizontal size in pixels
    mov [bmi.biHeight] , -700                               ;negative of vertical size in pixels
    mov [bmi.biPlanes] , 1                                  ;always 1
    mov [bmi.biBitCount] , 32                               ;32 bits per pixel
    mov [bmi.biCompression] , 0                             ;always 0
    mov [bmi.biSizeImage] , 700*700*4                    ;size of the picture in bytes
    mov [bmi.biXPelsPerMeter] , 2000                     ;not used here
    mov [bmi.biYPelsPerMeter] , 2000                                ;not used now
    mov [bmi.biClrUsed] , 0                                 ;always zero
    mov [bmi.biClrImportant] , 0                            ;always zero
    ;------------------------
    mov eax , 700*700*4
    mov [bitmap_length] , eax                                       ;save the length
    ret


            ;=====================
section '.idata' import data readable writeable

  library kernel32 , 'KERNEL32.DLL' , \
          user32 , 'USER32.DLL' , \
          gdi32 , 'GDI32.DLL' , \
          comctl32 , 'COMCTL32.DLL' , \
          winmm , 'WINMM.DLL' , \
          comdlg32 , 'COMDLG32.DLL'
```

```
    include 'INCLUDE\API\ADVAPI32.INC'
    include 'INCLUDE\API\COMCTL32.INC'
    include 'INCLUDE\API\COMDLG32.INC'
    include 'INCLUDE\API\GDI32.INC'
    include 'INCLUDE\API\KERNEL32.INC'
    include 'INCLUDE\API\SHELL32.INC'
    include 'INCLUDE\API\USER32.INC'
    include 'INCLUDE\API\WSOCK32.INC'

    import winmm , \                                      ; this one was not in the INCLUDE\API\
        waveOutSetVolume , 'waveOutSetVolume' , \
        sndPlaySound , 'sndPlaySoundA' , \
        PlaySound , 'PlaySound'

;end of program animation of bending lines, about 15 pages.
;=================================================
```

## About Procedures. And a DLL example.

As I hardly know anything about procedures, this writing is not going to be expert.
 In Windows programming there is something called a 'Procedure', and when I learnt basic assembly  language, there were no procedures in it.  So it was subject I did not know anything about.  And I still do not understand why they were invented? At first procedures seemed very difficult. But then you realise that creating a new procedure is not difficult, and you can really create one immediately by writing a few lines.
 Actually in reality, many of your programs only need to contain the single procedure, which is traditionally  called WindowProc. The main part of your computer programs can be quite separate from WindowProc and does not need to include any procedures.  You can also keep WindowProc quite short if you want to.


-------- Procedures
I am going to try to write a short explanation of procedures, but I think it's important that most of your program does not need a procedure.  They are not always necessary.

What is a procedure? A procedure is a section of a program, it's a kind of a routine or a subroutine which you call in a specific slightly unusual way, and there is a standard calling convention.

To start out writing a new procedure, you just write the word "proc" and then the name of the new procedure, and then, a series of a few words which stand for parameters, and which are separated with commas. All written on a horizontal line.
To end the procedure on its bottom line you just use the word "endp".
So to create a new procedure is simple with the flat assembler, one horizontal line to start it, and an endp to end it.
To call the procedure, you can write the word "stdcall", or sometimes the word invoke, followed by the name of the procedure you want to call, followed with a series of parameters separated with commas.
Those parameters, can be constants, can be registers, they can be the labels of variables either with or without rectangular brackets.
Usually write it all on a horizontal line. Writing the procedure and calling it should all be easy, but you can crash the computer by writing the wrong number of parameters. Any number of parameters is  right, except that you need to match exactly the same number of parameters in the line that calls the procedure as there is in the line which starts the procedure itself.

Both just have to have exactly same number of parameters, separated with commas, or else the computer crashes.
So for calling a procedure one uses the word stdcall, followed by the name of the procedure, followed by parameters separated with commas.

When it gets called, the procedure always assumes that just before the computer gets to it, the parameters or variables which were on that horizontal line have been pushed onto the stack, from right to left, which puts them onto the stack space, at offsets which are relative to the stack pointer.

A procedure assumes that parameters which communicate with it are mainly on the stack.
This seemed strange to me because I thought the stack should be mainly used for the return addresses of calls, which the "ret" pops back into the instruction pointer to return from a call.

Assemblers which are partly specialized for the Windows operating system seem to try to make it easy for a programmer to call procedures with the parameters pushed onto the stack easily, an easy way.
In the stdcall which calls a procedure, you put the parameters onto a horizontal line separated with commas, and the assembler automatically writes all the "push" instructions for you. You don't see the "push" instructions which the assembler writes, they are created automatically and you need a dissassembly to see them.

As you write the procedure itself, you start it with a horizontal line starting with the key word "proc" and the name of the procedure, and any names you like for parameters separated with commas.

The number of parameters has to be exactly the same as the number of them when you try to call the procedure.
But they don't need to be given the same names. It's important now that they do not need to be given the same names. But you can give them similar names to remind yourself what they are.
As you are about to call the procedure the names of the parameters are important if they refer to labels in your program, but in the first line that starts the procedure itself, the names don't matter and could be written anyhow.
I found that writing just letters a, b, c, d, e worked perfectly well as the names of five parameters in the top line which starts off a procedure, separated with commas. So the name of a parameter does not even need to be a word, it could be just one letter. And the assembler can automatically understand that when the computer begins running a procedure these parameters are assumed to be pushed on the stack at offsets just above the stack pointer.

Now a procedure assumes that before it is called, the parameters have been pushed onto the stack. But, you don't write the pushes which are necessary, as the assembler writes them automatically for you, and you don't even see the pushes.
As a procedure ends, it assumes that the stack pointer will be returned to exactly where it was before these pushes. But you don't write anything to return the stack pointer to where it was, since the assembler writes the instuction to do that automatically for you, and you don't even see this unless you use dissassembly.

What does a push/pop instruction do exactly? A "push" instruction such as "push eax" firstly decrements the stack pointer by the length of the data (eax is 4 bytes so -4 must get subtracted from the stack pointer.) And then the same instruction writes the data into the memory at the new address of the stack pointer. Like most computer data it is little-endian, which means the least significant byte is at lower memory, and the more significant bytes are above it.

A "pop" instruction such as "pop eax" takes the memory which is pointed to by the stack pointer, and copies it to the destination such as eax register. Then after that the stack pointer is incremented automatically by the length of the data, in the case of pop eax the stack pointer has +4 added to it. I have heard that to remember the direction people say "push down, and pop up". In many cases the integrated circuit on the computer chip is designed for speed, and goes a bit faster than other instructions. During a push the subtraction from the stack pointer goes first, while during a pop the adding to the stack pointer goes afterwards.

As you write your program inside your procedure, you refer to parameters by using the word you gave to the parameter as a name, (on the top line which starts out the procedure.)

When any data is on the stack it can be read either with the stack pointer or with the ebp register. For some reason it is safer to use the ebp register to read the parameters, and so the assembler automatically creates an instruction to load the stack pointer register esp into the ebp register.

And whenever you write loads inside the procedure using the names you gave to the parameters, the assembler must automatically create instructions which load the named parameters from the stack space, using the ebp register as a stack address register. You don't see the instructions which the assembler creates automatically, unless you do dissassembly. For example I tried using the free "Borg dissassembler".

For example I tried to dissassemble a very short procedure, which had only 4 lines, and this was it:

proc Dissassembly   a , b , c , d                                  ; A very short procedure

mov eax , [c]
ret
endp

The dissassembly showed that the assembler has turned that procedure into this:

push ebp                                                           ; Its dissassembly
mov ebp , esp
mov eax , [ebp + 10h]
leave
ret  10h

To call this very simple procedure, I wrote this:

stdcall  Dissassembly , 0, 1, 2, 3

The dissassembly showed that the assembler had turned this standard call into this:

push 03
push 02
push 01
push 00
call loc_00402026

When the load inside the procedure
mov eax, [c]
was converted by the assembler into the load
mov eax, [ebp+10h]

Why was the offset of parameter "c" equal to +10h? I think it's probably because, firstly in the call itself, the Instruction Pointer is pushed onto the stack, as a return address, and the stack pointer decremented by -4.

Next, you see the instruction "push ebp", so the stack pointer is decremented by another -4, making -8 after the parameters get pushed. The parameters were 4 byte size. This would cause parameter "a" on the left to be at [ebp+8]. And parameter "b" to be at [ebp+0ch] and parameter "c" to be at [ebp+10h].
I think that's probably the reason.

You understand that as the parameters are pushed, the stack pointer has more and more subtracted from it. As the stack pointer has the data length subtracted from it, the pushed data is above the stack pointer, and at offsets which are positive amounts such as +10h.
;==============================
A second dissassembly. I made another very short procedure, with 2 parameters:

 proc DissassemblyB , a, b

add eax , [a]
cmp eax , [b]
ret
endp

The dissassembly was:

```
push ebp
mov ebp, esp
add eax, [ebp +08]
cmp eax, [ebp +0Ch]
leave
ret 08
```

That was it. I think the automatically added push ebp, was what caused the parameter "a" to start at address [ebp+8] instead of being at address [ebp+4] ? (remembering that the call which calls the procedure pushes the Instruction Pointer after the two parameters were pushed.)

When I called the above small procedure with this line:

stdcall DissassemblyB, 0, 1

The dissassembly showed the call had been turned into:

```
push 01
push 00
call loc_0040203d
```

;============================
When I called it with this next line, using the edx and ecx registers:

stdcall Dissassembly, ecx, edx

Dissassembly showed that the stdcall been turned into this:

```
push edx
push ecx
call loc_0040203d
```
;==================
In another test I checked that the parameter on the right, which gets pushed first, is also
the parameter on the right in the top line which starts the procedure.
So both the procedure and the call which calls it have the same left to right ordering of parameters.
But in the top line which starts a procedure, the names of parameters are quite unimportant.
And it's the left to right ordering and having the same number of them, which matters a lot.


With the flat assembler you call your own procedures with stdcall. For example if you start out a procedure with this first line:

proc procedureA one, two, three

Then you have named it "procedureA" and you have given it three parameters assumed to be on the stack, named one and two and three.

When you call this procedure, you could call it with this line, or anything remotely like it:

stdcall procedureA, [label1], ecx, 100

As it calls the procedure, you should assume that in your procedure "three" will contain the number 100. And that "two" will contain the contents of the ecx register. And that "one" will contain whatever number was in the variable which has the label "label1".

Now if you write inside your procedure a load instruction like

mov eax, [three]

Then the assembler will automatically create an instruction which loads parameter you called "three" into the eax register, an instruction which uses [ebp+n], as it's on the stack space. And so when the instruction runs the eax register would contain the number 100, in this example.

Imagine that you create the procedure like this:

```
proc multiplies  one, two, three            ;The top line which starts the procedure.

mov eax, [three]                            ;imagine simple operations
mov edx, [two]
imul edx

ret                                         ;The ret is turned into a leave and a ret n instruction.
endp                                        ;The special word endp ends the procedure.
```

When the computer returns from calling it, the eax register would contain the product 100 times the number which was in ecx, if the procedure was still called by

stdcall multiplies, [label1], ecx, 100                          ;It didn't actually need [label1].

You see that in the top line which starts the procedure you don't have to use the same labels which you used when you called it, but you could use very similar looking labels just as a reminder to yourself of what they are coming from.

I suppose that in the first line which starts off a procedure, even simple labels like the letters a,b,c,d are practical, just separate them with commas and count how many.

When the computer is inside a procedure, theoretically this procedure could be running anywhere, and it could even have been transplanted into a DLL and running with someone else's program, theoretically.

Following this idea that the procedure might have been running somewhere else, you are supposed to follow a strict rule that inside the procedure you don't use labels which refer to things outside of the procedure.

If you want to follow this rule, you are supposed to assume that when the computer is running in the procedure it can't know anything of labels or things that are outside of the procedure, unless you have passed those numbers or those addresses to the procedure when you call it.

I had the impression that the Masm32 assembler forces you to follow the rule, and creates an error if you don't.

But luckily, the flat assembler does not force you follow this rule, and that makes it more flexible.

You only have to follow the rule if you think you are going to convert the procedure into a DLL, and it's obvious really that if the procedure is on its own, it can't know anything about labels to other parts of your program. If you want to follow that rule, on the inside of the procedure you must not refer to any labels which are outside of the procedure.

A little problem with ret.

When you write the instruction "ret" to make the computer come out of the procedure and return, the assembler automatically converts the ret into a "leave" instruction and then a "ret n" instruction which adds the right number to the stack pointer, which undoes the pushes. You see it only when you do dissassembly. It must return the stack pointer to where it was before the procedure was called. And return it to where it was before any of the parameters were even pushed in the stdcall.

But sometimes you might want to put a small subroutine inside a procedure. And you need to remember that when you want to write a normal ordinary 'ret' to end a small subroutine placed inside a procedure, then you should write "ret 0" instead of "ret", which tells the assembler not to turn it into that special leave with ret n. If you forget to write ret 0 instead of ret, at the end of any small subroutine in a procedure, the program will crash.

With some assemblers like Masm32, you are supposed to call your own procedures with the word "invoke", but the flat assembler wants you to use the word "stdcall", which I think stands for the standard call convention. If you are interested in procedures you should look up the "standard call convention" on the internet. And there is a different convention for 64 bit programs.

With the flat assembler there actually is a way of calling your own procedures with the word "invoke", if you want to, and you do that by writing the actual address of your procedure into a 4 byte variable and then invoking the label of the variable, which holds the address.

You write "invoke" followed by the name of the variable into which you have put the address.

I wanted to show an example of it further on. But I prefer to write programs without procedures.

Here is a very simple example of creating a procedure, and of calling it using "stdcall".

You start a procedure by writing the word proc. The following could be a complete procedure.

Proc Procedure1  one, two, three, four

mov eax, [four]
add eax, [three]

ret

endp

The above procedure can be called this way (but with any other parameters or registers used):

stdcall Procedure1, eax, ebx, ecx, edx

Because the line which started the procedure has been written with 4 parameters, the call to call it also must have 4 parameters.
You see that in this example call, the register edx would get pushed first because you wrote it on the right hand side, and pushes go from right to left, and the contents of edx will be in the stack space you have called "four" as the computer enters the procedure.

The procedure should simply add together fields three and four, and return with the result in the eax register. On return, eax should equal the sum of the edx register and the ecx register.
 You can use anything else for parameters. Using a label inside rectangular brackets means the contents of a variable, while using a label without any brackets, means the address of where the label is.
For example calling the same procedure by

stdcall Procedure1, [addess1], 0,0, text

Would firstly push the address of where the label "text" is within your program. It becomes [four].
It should then push two zeros, and then lastly it should push the "contents" of a variable which has label "address1". The contents will be pushed because of the rectangular brackets. This should become [one].

The assembler will automatically write instructions so that as the procedure is called, those 4 registers or any other parameters you specify are pushed in right to left order.

When the computer starts running the procedure, field "four" contains the contents of the parameter on the right. And the field "three" should contain the next pushed from right to left. As the procedure runs, the fields one, two, three, four are actually on the stack space, because they have been pushed.

------------

To call a procedure which has been made into a DLL, you always simply use the word "invoke" then the name of the procedure.
 So if you have made your procedure into a DLL file, then calling it is the same sort of thing as calling functions which are part of Windows operating system, you use invoke for calling them. But if a procedure is in your program, and is not a DLL, then the flat assembler wants you to use the word "stdcall". Unless you have loaded the address of your procedure into a variable, as you can then use the word "invoke" followed with the name label of that variable which holds the address.

 Obviously you don't see the pushes unless you do dissassembly. The number of parameters while calling, must be the same as the number of parameters on the horizontal line that starts off the procedure.
So the procedure and the stdcall or the invoke that calls the procedure, must fit each other by having exactly the same number of parameters.
Now it is necessary to show some examples of creating a simple procedure, and of calling the procedure, both using stdcall and using invoke. Because a few examples explain it very much more clearly than an explanation made of words.

When I did a little experiment, it was done in several stages.
I am going to show here several stages which I went through as I think one can find something interesting that way. To start the example, I began with a program that animated some pictures of bending lines. The animation happened to be called with a timer, "invoke SetTimer" was used.

The program first used invoke BitBlt as one way of erasing the picture to blackness, and then did the drawing.
And then it used invoke BitBlt to copy the drawing from the Dibsection to the visible window. Near the message loop, the part of the program which did the animation was at first called with this:

```
    invoke BitBlt, [hDC_Bmp], 0,0,700,700, [hDC_Bmp], 0,0, BLACKNESS          ;erasing the picture

    call draws_line1
                                                                              ;calling animation

    invoke BitBlt, [hDC], 0,0,700,700, [hDC_Bmp], 0,0, SRCCOPY                 ;copy to the window

    jmp msg_loop
                        ;back to message loop
```

This first erased the Dibsection memory to make blackness, then it called draws_line1, which draws the animated lines, and then it used BitBlt with the flag SRCCOPY to copy the Dibsection onto the window where you can see it. BitBlt uses two device contexts, the destination [hDC] on the left.

Next, these lines were converted into a procedure like this:

```
proc black one, two, three                                          ;Start line of new procedure

   invoke BitBlt, [hDC_Bmp], 0,0,700,700, [hDC_Bmp],0,0, BLACKNESS     ;erasing the picture

     call draws_line1
                                                                    ;calling animation

     invoke BitBlt, [hDC],0,0,700,700, [hDC_Bmp],0,0, SRCCOPY          ;copy to the window
     ret
  endp                                                              ;endp ends a procedure
```

With the flat assembler, it was easier to use "stdcall" rather than to use "invoke".
Now calling the procedure to make it work was firstly done with stdcall like this:

```
stdcall black, eax, ecx, edx
```

This ran the program, and the animation was as before, unchanged. You see the three parameters in registers were not actually used for anything at this stage. Note that though it was not used, register eax must have gone into the field named "one" in the stack space of the procedure, and register edx must have gone into the field named "three" of the stack space of the procedure. But it wasn't used at this stage.
Next the same procedure was called in this way:

```
stdcall black , 0, 0, 0
```

This worked equally well, and it called the procedure, the animation was the same. And in this case, the number zero must have been loaded into all three of the procedure's fields, but it was not used.

Next I tried calling the procedure with an "invoke" and when you are using the "flat assembler" you need to declare a labelled 32 bit variable, load the actual address of the procedure into the new variable, and then "invoke" with the "label" of the variable that holds the address, used as the function name. The label of the variable is used as the name of the function to invoke.

```
   mov eax, black                ;Load the real address of the procedure named black into eax
   mov [blackproc], eax             ;Save the address into the new variable.
   invoke blackproc, 0,0,0       ;Invoke with the name of the address-variable.  working!!
```

As well I had declared the variable which holds the address, like this:

  blackproc    dd 0                        ;

This worked equally well, and the animation was the same.

Important:
Now so far the procedure was written somewhat wrongly, because it was using 3 labels referring to things in my program.
It contained the labels of my 2 device contexts, which were   hDC and hDC_Bmp
and it also contained the label of my animation program which was "draws_line1".
This was at first breaking the important rule that labels of things outside of the procedure should never be used inside the procedure.

With the flat assembler, you are allowed to include labels to things in your program in your procedures, to break the rule when you put them in the procedure, which makes the assembler flexible.

But, if you are going to convert your procedure into a DLL you need to avoid completely using labels that refer to things in your program.
You need to follow a strict rule that inside of your procedure you will not use labels that are outside the procedure, because you need to remember that the computer running inside a DLL has no idea what the main part of your program is like, and cannot understand labels that refer to things in your main program.  And the DLL is assembled as a separate program.

So to follow a rule, I removed all the 3 labels from my procedure. And the removing of the labels makes it possible for the procedure to be later turned into a DLL.
Then the procedure became like this:

  proc black one, two, three          ;Now the 3 fields one, two, and three are actually being used

   invoke BitBlt, [one], 0,0,700,700, [one], 0,0, BLACKNESS          ;erasing the picture

   call  [three]        ;  Call the animation (OK even when the animation is separate from the DLL)

   invoke BitBlt, [two], 0,0,700,700, [one], 0,0, SRCCOPY    ;Copy the picture to the Window.
     ret
     endp                                          ;End the procedure

And now the procedure "black" was called with stdcall this way:

stdcall black, [hDC_Bmp], [hDC], draws_line1

This calls the procedure.  It worked, and the animation turned out the same.
The stdcall with its three parameters separated with commas, causes the assembler to automatically write push instructions which push the three numbers, pushing the one on the right first, going from right to left.
So the assembler must write first an instruction to push the real address of the label "draws_line1" (the address of where the animation program starts). This will go into the stack space field labelled "three". Then to push the Window's device context number "[hDC]", which becomes [two], and then to push the Dibsection's device context "[hDC_Bmp]", which becomes [one].

And when the procedure starts running, the three fields which are declared on the procedure's top line, one, two, three, should be the numbers pushed by the call. The procedure started with this top line:

proc black one, two, three              ;Top line shown again

So [three] should be the address of "draws_line1", and [two] should contain [hDC], and [one] should contain [hDC_Bmp]. And this must be what actually happened, since it worked.

It's important that the instruction "call [three] "  inside the procedure, correctly called my animation program, and that it did the same thing when the procedure was actually converted into a DLL. !
I tried the experiment of converting this procedure into a DLL, and then simply calling the DLL with one invoke. And it worked.

And now that the procedure is written without using any labels which refer to things in the main program, it should be possible to turn the procedure into a DLL.

Then I used the example of creating a DLL which came downloaded with the flat assembler. (In their folder called /EXAMPLES/.)
By following its pattern and rewriting its export section, it became quite easy to create a new DLL.
Then my program to test it, simply used the word invoke.

Invoke on its own simply calls programs in DLLs, as it is not necessary for yourself to load the address into a variable. When you have converted your procedure into a DLL you write "invoke" simply, the same way as you do for Windows functions which might be part of the operating system. Actually I think the flat assembler automatically loads the address of the DLL into a space and the space for it is reserved by the import section.

A DLL has something called entry point, but that's definitely not what you use for this. The socalled entry-point of a DLL is never where your program starts running the DLL. The place where the computer starts running in the DLL is the procedure name which is in the DLL, and you have to add that procedure name to the DLL's export section. I read that a DLL can have an optional entry point, but it might be better not to use it.

In this test I deleted the entry point, as the DLL does not need it.

The entry point of a DLL is a place which gets called automatically when the program first loads up or starts and loads up the DLLs, and it is called once again when the program shuts down and ends. When you use an entry point, it should go to a small procedure in the DLL with 3 fields, and it should end with load of number 1 into the eax register, and then ret. And endp. As it returns, the 1 in the eax register is a code that means OK.

But you don't need an entry point. To invoke any procedure in the DLL you use the name given to one of its procedures, and the procedure in it runs.

The name of the procedure has to be written in the "import section" at the bottom of your program.

This is the difficult part for me, you have to learn to add the name of the DLL and of the function in it which you want to call, to your program's import section, following the pattern which they use in their examples.

I think the DLL can contain any number of procedures, which can all work with your programs, but they have to be declared in the export section of the DLL. And also they have to be declared in the import section of your programs.

So there is an export section of the DLL, and there is an import section in your main program, and that's something which seemed difficult. Understanding the export section isn't so easy, but I suppose you have to see the pattern used in their examples, and then write in that way. It worked as I tried it. Maybe it's not as difficult as it seems?

I noticed the import and export sections follow a certain pattern.

I think the import section of programs can have a complete path and name for the DLL, or it can just assume that the DLL is in the same folder as the program?

I would like to show a complete example of creating this small DLL. Just to show how it could be tested.

Before showing the DLL's creation, this is an example of how it can be invoked.

The following DLL was used in a program by invoking it with this :

  invoke black3, [hDC_Bmp], [hDC], draws_line1           ;Working! ** with my trydll.dll

One interesting thing was finding that while the computer was running in the DLL it was able to call and run the whole animating part of the main program, the address of which it got from the third parameter of the invoke, (the label "draws_line1"), and which it actually called with the instruction "call [three]".

That is interesting. Also, in the import section at the lower end of the program, this was added:

In the library section, in the group of lines started by the word "library" the extra line was added:

```
    sides,'trydll.DLL'              ;The name of the new dll file. With to its left the label "sides"

    import sides,\                  ; the label sides again.
        black3,'black3'             ;The name of my procedure inside the dll. (The name must be written twice)
```

;--------------------------
Remember that this is the invoke which called the new Dll:

 invoke black3, [hDC_Bmp], [hDC], draws_line1

As a very simple test of making a Dll.
I had named the experimental DLL "trydll.asm" and as it was assembled with the flat assembler it was turned into a file named: "trydll.DLL". (You see its extension was .DLL instead of .EXE).

In the import section of the program I just happened to make a label "sides", I think in that place any label could be made up. And then the name of the procedure inside the DLL was black3. The name has to be written double, as usual. (the import section needs these double repeated names.)

* The following is a complete program for making a DLL. A very short and simple DLL.

The semi colons on the left show the parts which are Deleted, because they were not useful here.

;-------------------------- The start of the DLL program which was named "trydll.DLL"

```
  format PE GUI 4.0 DLL                            ;The word DLL must be there.

;;; entry DllEntryPoint

  include 'win32a.inc'

  section '.code' code readable writable executable

;; proc DllEntryPoint, hinstDLL,fdwReason,lpvReserved    ;Optional entry not used.

;;      mov     eax,TRUE
;;      ret
;; endp

  proc black3, one, two, three                     ;start of the procedure

      invoke BitBlt, [one], 0,0,700,700, [one], 0,0, BLACKNESS    ;erasing the picture to blackness
```

```
    mov ebx, [three]
    call  ebx                                ;Calling the animated drawing in the main program
 ;;   call [three]                         ;also worked when calling [three] this way

 invoke BitBlt, [two], 0,0,700,700, [one], 0,0, SRCCOPY       ;Copying the picture to visible window.
     ret
   endp
```

;=======

```
       section '.idata' import data readable writeable

 library kernel32,'KERNEL32.DLL',\
      user32,'USER32.DLL',\
      gdi32,'GDI32.DLL'
                                                  ;The pathways would need to be changed

   include 'C:\0 computer\INCLUDE\API\GDI32.INC'
   include 'C:\0 computer\INCLUDE\API\KERNEL32.INC'
   include 'C:\0 computer\INCLUDE\API\SHELL32.INC'
   include 'C:\0 computer\INCLUDE\API\USER32.INC'
```

;================

```
section '.edata' export data readable ; writable

    export 'C:\0 computer\TRYDLL2.DLL',\
    black3,'black3'                             ;The name of your procedure, in DLL, written twice.


section '.reloc' fixups data readable discardable    ;######  This reloc line was maybe essential?
                                                     ;Even though nothing is below it.
```
;==========================
;;===    This was the end of the DLL.  I have no idea why the line about section '.reloc' fixups was necessary to make it work?

I think, though I am not quite sure, that in the export section of a DLL, you need to use the Exact name of the DLL. Except that ASM is changed to DLL. For example in the export section just above, "TRYDLL2.DLL".

I think the only case when creating a procedure is interesting, is when you want to create a DLL program. It is apparently easy to convert a procedure into a DLL, and when you get the 'flat assembler' an interesting example of how to create a DLL is there in the folder called "examples". It's downloaded in the same zip file with the assembler.

This is a subject I don't know anything about, but I found that following their example it was easy to both create and then use a new DLL of my own. To test it again, another experiment which created a much longer DLL.
I had created a program which converts a floating point number into decimal text including a decimal point.
I mean, when you have a floating point number which is the result of some calculation, how do you show that as readable numbers on the screen?
Firstly converting the short program into a procedure was quite easy. And then turning the procedure into a DLL was not too difficult. With that procedure deleted from my program, the program could still work by invoking the DLL file.
There are certain ways of writing an import section and a DLL export section which follow a pattern which I don't understand, but if you try to copy the pattern of writing that you see in their example it can work.
When you create a DLL, your program still has the usual extension ".ASM" as usual, but the first line at the very top of the program has the word DLL added to it.
The assembler must act on that word.
Then at the lower end of the DLL creating program there should be the export section, and just below that, I found it was necessary to include a line which declares a relocation section "reloc" but I have no idea at all why this is absolutely necessary?

The DLL did not work at all unless this reloc fixups line was there at its end. I don't understand what it means. It was like this.

```
section '.reloc' fixups data readable discardable     :This was A necessary line.
;---------


;=====================
```

## How to rearrange WindowProc's start not to look like a Procedure.

Masm32 examples can give a wrong impression that you should build up your programs by creating many procedures. The flat assembler's examples did not give that impression.
When I started to teach myself Windows programming, I did not like procedures and so I tried converting several procedures into non-procedures, into ordinary subroutines or parts of a program. One of the things I tried was converting the special procedure called WindowProc into a form which did not look like a procedure.

Every Windows program contains WindowProc, and the operating system calls it many times automatically while it is creating a window. Then it gets called again with
invoke DispatchMessage, msg.
I am going to show how WindowProc can be changed so that it does not look like a procedure, yet the operating system can still call it properly.
This is for 32 bit mode. When the program was in 64 bit mode, the method was quite different, but even simpler.

;================

When you write a procedure, it is started off by its top line, and you write the word "proc" then the name of the procedure, and then the names of the parameters separated with commas.
The stdcall or the invoke which calls the procedure needs to push the same number of parameters onto the stack starting with the parameter on the right, going from right to left.

In starting off the procedure, the actual names you give to the parameters really does not matter to the assembler. What matters is the number of parameters, as there must be exactly the same number of parameters, separated with commas, in the stdcall or the invoke function which calls the procedure, as there is in the top line which starts the procedure itself.

The following is my example of how experimentally WindowProc can be rewritten so it doesn't look like a procedure, and still works as normal:

In the normal case, WindowProc was started with this line:

```
proc WindowProc hwnd, wmsg, wparam, lparam          ;Usual Start  of WindowProc

ret
endp                                                ; endp ends it
```

I made a note that even this procedure can be changed so that it does not actually look like a procedure. And (while the computer is in 32 bit mode), its start can be changed to be like this:

```
WindowProc:
pop eax                            ;I suppose this pops the return address
pop [hwnd]                         ;pop the 4 parameters into variables in the data section.
pop [wmsg]
pop [wparam]
pop [lparam]
sub esp,20           ; -20 from the stack pointer, it again points to its return address
;---------
( program instructions here)

invoke  DefWindowProc, [hwnd], [wmsg], [wparam], [lparam]    ;This function essential

ret                                ;Now it ends with just "ret", you can remove its "endp".
```

Because of the subtracting of -20 from the stack pointer, the stack pointer again points to the return address. The simple "ret" then returns the computer to wherever it was in the program, or inside the operating system, when it called WindowProc.

In the data section the 4 parameters had to be declares like this:

```
hwnd    dd 0
wmsg    dd 0
wparam  dd 0
lparam  dd 0
```

 The parameters were declared in the data section of the program. This did work.
If you try this, you will see the program still runs with WindowProc modified.

Of course the function "invoke DefWindowProc" is always essential since it does some default processing for the operating system.

When I tried this I found that I can leave all the program instructions which are in the procedure as they are, without having to change them.
;=====================

## Creating a typing cursor, and typing on normal memory.

I have done a lot of experiments to create a blinking typing cursor within an ordinary window. I mean a window that's not an edit control and so it's not automatic.

Firstly what is the simplest way to do typing onto an area of memory with your own program? You can try typing onto a big area of allocated memory, or instead onto a small area of memory declared in the data section of your program. You can then save your typing as a file, by saving the area of memory as a file.

While you are typing your words onto an area of memory, you have to make them visible on the window.

I tried 3 ideas to make the text visible onto an ordinary window:

1) Type into my program a complete 8x8 character pixels table, and use a subroutine to draw all the alphabetical characters pixel by pixel. The program started by creating a so-called device independent bitmap memory (Dibsection). Which is simply a memory area in which every 4 bytes make a pixel in an image, one byte for red, one byte for green, and one byte for blue. Plus one unused byte.

The good thing about a Dibsection is that Windows then lets you draw pixels using an address in an address register, which is called direct access.

When using this method with Windows, firstly a subroutine in the program has to draw all the alphabetic characters, by writing the pixels onto the Dibsection memory.

And then you copy that memory to the visible window using invoke BitBlit, which uses two handles, a source handle and the destination handle. The source handle is for the Dibsection, and the destination handle is to the visible window.

 The characters are tiny with 8*8 pixels, and this is not as good as modern larger sized lettering.

But there is a good thing about using a pixels table. Which is the striking thing is how easy it is to make a blinking on-off typing cursor, or even an additional copy cursor.

You can just compare addresses, and at the cursor's address the subroutine just inverts the binary bits which will be turned into pixels. Inverting binary bits means that for the character at your cursor, black becomes white, and white becomes black.

 This effect can be turned on-off a few times per second if you want to get the cursor to blink.

2) I tried using invoke DrawText and invoke TextOut.

They draw using a device context, and they can draw to the visible window directly.

 Or when you want it they can also draw text onto a Dibsection memory, as pixels.

And I had a lot of trouble with them at first, especially invoke TextOut, because though they worked very well for a few rows of text, they caused an annoying flickering whenever you try to fill a whole screen of text using them. It seemed to me that these two functions are faulty. They seem quite faulty when you try to draw too much of the screen at once. There was a decrease in the flickering if you call them once for each row of text doing but one row at a time.

There was also a decrease in flickering when firstly they write all the text onto a Dibsection memory, and the Dibsection is then copied to the visible screen. That is called "double buffering", as a well known way to decrease flickering with animations. And in this case the Dibsection has been called a "back-screen".

There was also a decrease of flickering if you call them using a Windows timer, I tried invoke SetTimer.

What I don't understand at all is why Microsoft did not make it easy to make a typing cursor using them? DrawText could have had an extra parameter, with the address of a cursor in that extra parameter. All they would need to do is to compare an address and invert pixels when the addresses become equal. That makes a typing cursor with such simplicity, so why didn't Microsoft do that? Maybe there is a function I don't know of.

Somehow later on I managed to fill the screen with text, using invoke DrawText and without too much flickering.

3) I tried an interesting experiment of "font capturing". Font capturing is really the best experiment, but maybe it is too long to include here.

In font capturing, as the program started it created a Dibsection. (To allow you to have access to the pixels with an address.) In order to capture the font, it drew a single letter at a time. With Windows it drew every alphabetical character as a single character, one at a time, on its own, in the natural alphabetical order of the ascii code.

And the single character was always in the exact top left corner of the Dibsection screen. At the same time it scanned all these alphabetical characters, one at a time, and wrote a character pixels table. This is all completed instantly.

This character pixels table was up to 24*24 pixels. And so much better sharper lettering compared with primitive 8*8 pixels. The experiment drew the characters pixels onto a Dibsection memory used as a back-screen, using loads with an address register.

And then invoke BitBlt copied the complete screen with text to the visible window.

The experiment went well, I could show a whole screen of text, always no flickering at all, and type and scroll the picture. And making a typing cursor was easy with nearly the same technique as used with the 8*8 pixel characters.

Drawing Characters.

Drawing alphabetical characters with a pixels table, involves 2 subroutines with several count-downs in each. One subroutine draws a single character, the second subroutine calls it many times to draw the whole text.

You always start with the pixel in the top left corner of the character. You then go from left to right across the character. And then jump back to the left hand side, and add "bytes per image width" value to the address to go one pixel vertically downwards, and then do the next horizontal line of pixels from left to right. This is repeated until the whole character is drawn.

You then recover the start address of the top left corner's pixel. And add an amount to move a letters space to the right, to get to the position of the next character's top left corner. (You can include proportional spacing.) After completing a row of text, you restart at the left and move down a row.

It becomes a bit more complicated when you are making the routine sensitive to the carriage return symbol 0dh. (the number 13 in decimal).

I made my program so that you could switch that sensitivity on or off, and compare the difference.

I got my program to font capture with several different font sizes. I also made it calculate which character was closest to the mouse cursor. Using X difference squared and Y difference squared, and using the formula that the actual diagonal distance is the square root of the sum of the squares.

And it caused the typing cursor to jump onto the mouse cursor, a function which is similar to the one you have in edit controls.


It was interesting, but it is quite long and would take so many pages, so instead of that I only want to go into the simplest method I found of typing onto an area of memory, and showing the text with invoke DrawText.

The next example of a typing program is intended to be as very short and simple as possible. It's not the best, but it's only intended to be simple. In the first version of it, you can only type one-way and the arrow keys won't work since they are not yet programmed to do anything.

The writing of how the address register is loaded, is slightly different depending on whether the memory you type on is in the data section, or whether it is a larger allocated area. In both cases it is risky to load anything outside of the safe area, and keeping the typing address in the safe area prevents the computer from crashing.

Firstly, in the data section the area that you can type on was marked this way:

```
section '.data' data readable writable          ;Start of the data section

space_for_typing rb  1000                       ;This line reserves 1000 bytes for typing
beyond_the_end db 0                             ;This line's label marks the end of the typing area.

insertion_point dd 0                            ;These were the main variables used.
save_one_character db 0
blink dd 0
tic dd 0
```

```
hDC dd 0
```

In the program's code section, this was called from the message loop at least once every time there is a WM_CHAR message, in [msg.message].

```
;====== Working simple typing one way
types:
    mov ebx, [insertion_point]
    cmp ebx, space_for_typing       ;Firstly make sure the address register is in range
    jnb type2
    mov ebx, space_for_typing
  type2:
    cmp ebx, beyond_the_end
    jb type3
    mov ebx, space_for_typing
  type3:
    cmp [msg.message], WM_CHAR
    jz type4
    ret
  type4:
    mov eax, [msg.wParam]           ;Read the character.
    mov [ebx], al                   ;One character typed from register AL.
    inc ebx
    mov [insertion_point], ebx
    ret
;=================================
```

This typing only worked one-way, it couldn't reverse as the left arrow key and the backspace key had not yet been programmed.

Notice that the labels "space_for_typing" and "beyond_the_end" are without brackets, this means "the address-of", or that is, the label's address gets loaded into ebx. (rather than loading the contents of a variable, for which you do have to use brackets).

In the alternative case that you allocate a big area of memory, not in the data section, then you would always have the start address of that allocated area, saved in a variable.

And you would have to record the ending address somewhere in another variable, so as to make an upper limit you don't go beyond.

And then the typing program would read these addresses by putting brackets around the variables names. For example, this would allocate 5 megabytes of memory:

```
        invoke GlobalAlloc, 0, 5000000
        mov [pointing1], eax                    ;The base address.
        add eax, 4000000
        mov [upper_limit], eax                  ;The address at an upper limit.
```

And the very short and simplest typing program would then have to put brackets around the labels [pointing1] and [upper_limit]. Since brackets mean "contents of" the variable.

```
                    ;====== Working simple typing for an allocated memory area.
  types:
        mov ebx, [insertion_point]
        cmp ebx, [pointing1]                    ;Firstly make the address stay in range
        jnb type2
        mov ebx, [pointing1]                    ;base address, space_for_typing
    type2:
        cmp ebx, [upper_limit]                  ;beyond_the_end
        jb type3
        mov ebx, [pointing1]
    type3:
        cmp [msg.message], WM_CHAR
        jz type4
        ret
    type4:
        mov eax, [msg.wParam]                   ;Read the character.
        mov [ebx], al                           ;Type one character from register AL.
        inc ebx
        mov [insertion_point], ebx
        ret
;=================================
```

The following program was for typing onto the small area of memory in the data section of my program. It is only a little bit more advanced, since it has a right and left arrow key function, and a delete key and a backspace key function. The up and down arrow keys can't work at all since they are still not programmed. The mouse is not programmed, so it is very simple typing. The carriage return symbol gets typed simply as a chararcter when you press the return key.

Firstly it uses a call to make sure the address is inside the safe typing area.
;Worked slightly more complex typing

```
staywithin_zone:                            ;keeps address inside typing area
    mov  ebx, [insertion_point]    ;
    cmp ebx, space_for_typing               ;*Label of beginning of the area
    jnb ty1
    mov ebx, space_for_typing               ;keeping address within the area
    jmp ty2
ty1: cmp ebx, beyond_the_end                ;**Label of upper end
    jb ty2
    mov ebx, space_for_typing
ty2: mov [insertion_point], ebx
    ret
    ;=========    You should Call types2 to do typing.
types2:
    call staywithin_zone                    ;A call which kept address within range.
    mov ebx, [insertion_point]
    cmp [msg.message], WM_CHAR              ;read the message for is there a character?
    jz ty3
    ret
 ty3:
    mov eax, [msg.wParam]                   ;read the character from [msg.wParam]
    mov [msg.message], 0            ;run only once??
    cmp al, 8                       ;compare to the backspace character which is no 8.
    jnz ty4
    ret                                     ;it should not type backspace letter
 ty4:
    call insert_for_type                    ;it shifts the string of text 1 space up.
    mov [ebx], al
    inc ebx
    mov [insertion_point], ebx
    ret
    ;--------------------------------------------
    ;

arrows1:
    cmp [msg.message], WM_KEYDOWN
```

```
        jz ty10
        ret
    ty10:
        mov ebx, [insertion_point]
        cmp [msg.wParam], VK_LEFT              ;Look for Left arrow
        jz ty11
        cmp [msg.wParam], VK_RIGHT             ;Right arrow key
        jz ty12
        ret
    ty11:
        dec ebx
        mov [insertion_point], ebx
        call staywithin_zone                   ;call here prevents a crash.*
        ret
    ty12:
        inc ebx
        mov [insertion_point], ebx
        call staywithin_zone
        ret

;---------------------------------------------------
    insert_for_type:                           ;worked

        push eax                               ;eax has character in it
        mov edx, beyond_the_end
        dec edx
    ty20:
        dec edx
        cmp edx, [insertion_point]
        jnb ty21
        pop eax
        ret
    ty21:
        mov al, [edx]
        mov [edx+1], al
        jmp ty20
;---------------------------------------------------
```

```
    back_space:                                 ;backspace key working

       cmp [msg.message], WM_KEYDOWN
       jz  ty40
       ret
    ty40:
       cmp [msg.wParam],08                      ;The backspace code
       jz ty41
       ret
    ty41:

       mov edx, [insertion_point]
       dec edx
       mov [insertion_point], edx
       jmp ty30                                 ;Jump to necessary test of upper/lower limit.
;------------------------------------------------------------
    delete_type:                                ;worked well
       cmp [msg.message], WM_KEYDOWN
       jz  ty33
       ret
    ty33:
       cmp [msg.wParam], VK_DELETE              ;Look for the Delete key
       jz ty30
       ret
    ty30:
       mov edx, [insertion_point]
       cmp edx, space_for_typing                ;lower limit
       jnb ty31
       ret                                      ;Return if going outside of safe limits.
    ty31:
       cmp edx, beyond_the_end                  ;upper limit and when to end
       jb ty32
       ret
    ty32:
       mov al, [edx+1]
       mov [edx], al                            ;shift the string of text down one space
       inc edx
```

jmp ty31

;----------------------------

The next program should use invoke DrawText to show the text onto the screen of an ordinary window. Together with a blinking character to show the typing cursor. To make it work it should preferably be called once when there is a character input, and called as well regularly using some form of a timing. Timing such as invoke SetTimer can work on its own, or instead using invoke GetTickCount with PeekMessage in the message loop?

It has an original way of showing a typing cursor. The typing cursor it creates is not perfect, but it is still usable.

```
  show_type_and_cursor:
      mov ebx, [insertion_point]              ;essential test for 0 or else crashes
      cmp ebx, 0
      jnz tim2
      ret
   tim2:
      mov al, [ebx]
      mov [save_one_character], al
;;;   mov byte [ebx], "-"                     ;"X"   ;X or use the - dash. Better without.
      inc [blink]
      and [blink], 7
      cmp [blink], 3
      jb tim3
      mov byte [ebx], "_"                     ;"Z"   ;Z or use the _ under dash, working

   tim3:
      call cls                                                ;clear screen white
      call typing_to_screen                   ;use DrawText with device context of screen
      mov ebx, [insertion_point]
      mov al, [save_one_character]            ;Replaces a character where it was.
      mov [ebx], al
      invoke ShowWindow, [h_Window1], SW_SHOWNORMAL           ;show window here
      invoke UpdateWindow, [h_Window1]
      ret
```

The above example created a typing cursor which can flash on and off clearly.
To make sure there isn't much flickering, there sometimes had to be a time delay of about 10 milliseconds added to the end of this routine. Add a short time delay?

Next This is called to draw the text onto the screen. It uses a device context of the normal window, [hDC] which my program gets once when it first starts running.

```
  cls:
     invoke BitBlt, [hDC],0,0,800,500, [hDC],0,0,WHITENESS    ;Erase screen to white
  ret

  typing_to_screen:                            ; DrawText is naturally sensitive to 0dh

     invoke SetTextColor, [hDC], 0             ;set text color to black
     invoke SetBkColor, [hDC], 0ffffffh        ;set background color to white
     mov [rect.top], 10
     mov [rect.bottom], 300                    ;DrawText needs a rect structure
     mov [rect.left], 0
     mov [rect.right], 900

     invoke DrawText, [hDC], space_for_typing, -1, rect, DT_NOCLIP
       ret
```

The RECT data structure had to be declared in the data section of the program with the two words:
rect RECT

The device context to the visible window had to be got once when this program first started running.

```
  invoke GetDC, [h_Window1]         ;Get the device context of normal window (Once)
  mov [hDC], eax
```

This was sometimes used in a message loop to call regularly every 50 milliseconds.

```
  invoke GetTickCount               ;Gets a continual counter of milliseconds in eax.

  cmp eax, [tic]                    ;Compare comtinuous counter to a saved number
  jb msg_loop                       ;jump to a PeekMessage at the top of the message loop
```

```
    add eax,50                      ;Add to time 50 milliseconds
    mov [tic], eax                  ;store counter plus 50
    call show_type_and_cursor
     jmp msg_loop
```

But I think invoke SetTimer is better than tick count.


; ==========================
Word processors sometimes need a combined carriage return symbol and line feed symbol, which is 0a0dh.
The 0a0dh should be in this order, with 0dh at lower memory than 0ah
This adds a small amount of complexity. You have to test for carriage return symbol 0dh just when you are about to type it.

When the 0dh is about to be typed, you change it to 2 bytes long 0a0dh, and when it's insert typing shift the string of text up 2 spaces instead of one.
The program should be able to detect when the typing cursor happens to be just in between the 0ah and the 0dh, so as not to separate them at the moment when you do more typing.

When the typing cursor is between them, the program should avoid typing the character in between the two, and instead type the character 1 position further along to avoid breaking up the 0a0dh into two separate symbols.
Your program then should also test to see whether there is an 0a0dh when you are deleting a space, and if there is, delete the two symbols spaces together instead of one.

In the past several different kinds of word processor used to crash whenever text is loaded into them, when the text is lacking a regular series of carriage return symbols, which needed to be at least one per 126 bytes. Some word processors accepted 0dh on its own, and others wanted 0a0dh. I don't remember which ones.

To make text which is compatible with these word processors, it was necessary to format the area of text with a subroutine which would make a regular pattern of at least one number "0a0dh" in every 126 or so bytes of memory.

When there is always at least one 0a0dh in every 126 bytes or less, the text is compatible with the older word processor. But if there is a stretch of memory where even a single 0a0dh is missing, the older word processors used to crash immediately.
This was apparently done to make it more difficult.
The presence of a binary zero, where there should be a blank character "20h", also used to crash some word processors.

So I used to make a subroutine which scans through the whole text area of memory, replacing binary zeros with blank character 20h, and also, looking for safe spaces in which to insert a carriage return and line feed as 0a0dh.

And it had to make absolutely sure there was at least one of them per 126 bytes of memory. In the past this used to be necessary to prevent these word processors crashing when they load up the file.

; =========================

## Setting a timer

You can set up a timer which gets the operating system to call places at regular times, over and over until you kill the timer.
It was a surprise that it was not difficult to set up and use a timer.
And it can be useful.
The only disadvantage of using a timer is that your message structure msg will frequently contain timer messages, but usually that wouldn't get in the way of anything.

A test was able to get a message posted at regular time intervals, and it can also call a new procedure, which can be very simple and easy to set up.
(A zero at the end tells the operating system to call WindowProc).
Two examples of starting up a timer.

Invoke SetTimer , [h_Window] , 300 , 16 , 0         ;Set it To call WindowProc every 16 milsec

or

Invoke SetTimer , [h_Window] , 300 , 16 , Time       ;To call proc Time every 16 milsec

While the first parameter should be a handle of the window, the second parameter can be any number at all that you want to use as a message ID,
it is a user-defined message identity.
300 is an example, of any number at all in that second parameter.

The 16 would get it to call every 16 milliseconds. 1000 would cause it to call every 1 second.
Both above examples should post a WM_TIMER message at every 16 milliseconds.

And whenever that message is posted, it should appear in
[msg.message] = WM_TIMER.

At the same time as that message, the user-defined ID of=300
in the example, should appear in
[msg.wParam]=300.

When its last parameter on the right is 0, then it should also automatically call WindowProc, whenever it posts a message. (A zero means it must call WindowProc.)

When its last parameter is the name of a proc , like "Time" , then it should automatically call the named proc regularly.
I mean SetTimer causes the operating system to make these
regular calls.
Setting up a proc edure called Time was very simple , you can set it up by just writing these few lines:

 proc Time  hwnd ,  wmsg ,  wparam ,  time

 (The program code to run goes in the middle here)
 ret
 endp

I ran a test which showed that the 4$^{th}$ and last parameter of the "proc Time" was filled with a timing number which was rapidly changing. It was definitely not filled by lParam.
I think it is the same as the message field [msg.time].
I suppose maybe the above example has something non-essential in it , since I find the even simpler way of writing this procedure here worked equally well.
I am not sure ,  is it Ok to write it with no parameters? I am not sure whether the simpler example below is safe?

 proc Time                           ;Maybe parameters here are not really necessary?

 (Program code to run goes in the middle here)
 ret
 endp

I also tried to set up a timer proc this way ,  which I am sure is safe:

 proc Time  a ,  b ,  c ,  d

 (program instructions here)
 ret
 endp

When I tried creating the simple procedure proc Time ,  it worked for me when there were either no parameters ,  or when there were 4 parameters. Other numbers of parameters badly crashed the computer.
Whenever you want anything to run at regular time intervals ,  you should put a call to call it , whatever it is,  in the procedure "proc Time ", and the call can go to anywhere else in the program ,

since of course if you are using the flat assembler it can go to call something outside of the procedure.

Another example, imagine you want a message ID of 100. The 50 miliseconds means 20 times per second:

Invoke SetTimer , [h_Window] , 100 , 50 , 0              ;To call WindowProc every 50 milsec

Timer messages appearing in the field [msg.message] , could be looked for with program code from any other places , such as you can look for it at the end of the message loop , or in WindowProc , or in the new proc set up like the example called "Time."
If you look for timer messages outside of the proc Time , and outside of WindowProc , then this instruction should find it:

    cmp [msg.message] , WM_TIMER
    je found_timer

If you erase the message after finding it , that will make absolutely sure something will not re-run unnecessary. It's sometimes necessary to prevent things from rerunning when you don't want them to. If you have set up several timers , you should give each timer a different timer ID , and look for the timer ID numbers in [msg.wParam] with something like:

cmp [msg.wParam] , 200              ;(assuming you have given one of the timers an ID of 200)

When the program all stops running , the timers needs to be stopped.
It was stopped with:
 invoke KillTimer , [h_Window] , 200
 invoke KillTimer , [h_Window] , 300

You see to stop the right timer it should have both the
handle to the window , and the number you chose as a timer
message ID.

    ;=======================================

## Creating a menu without pictures, and with them.

I have been creating menus for all of my programs. A menu is so useful because it lets you control the program with a mouse click on a menu item. I also think that a few months later on the menu reminds you of what the program was for.

As you make them up starting from scratch , they are at first a few words on the top border of a window. And as you mouse click on the word a drop-down rectangle with lines of words appears. Each line of words is a menu item. You give it as many items as you want , and a mouse click on any item triggers a WM_COMMAND message to be added to the operating system's message queue. Somewhere in the data section of your program you always have to declare the existence of the message structure called MSG , with the two words:

msg MSG

Somewhere in your program you always have a message loop with the function:

 invoke GetMessage , msg , 0 , 0 , 0

It causes the messages to be taken out from the operating system's internal message queue and placed into the MSG data structure.

The Fasmw assembler automatically knows the names of different parts of the MSG message structure , because the assembler looks for that information in the include file named "user32.inc". And to detect the mouse clicks on a menu item , you should test for WM_COMMAND in the field called [msg.message]. You can use the comapare instruction:

Cmp [msg.message] , WM_COMMAND
jnz no_command

And if you do find the WM_COMMAND , then you should test for the various message ID numbers in the field called [msg.wParam].

As you create a menu item , you yourself decide what number you want to use as a message ID. Any number at all can be used as a menu item ID, assuming that you test those 2 fields in their four bytes size.

When that menu item is clicked on with the mouse, a message is created by the operating system. When "invoke GetMessage , msg , 0 , 0 , 0" puts the message into the MSG data structure , then the [msg.wParam] field in this message contains your message ID number. (Identity).

You can test for the message and for the menu ID , from almost anywhere at all in your program. The usual place to test for it might be at the bottom of your message loop.

You can decide what number you want the message ID to be, when you create a menu, and then, whenever there is a WM_COMMAND message in [msg.message], you test for the ID in [msg.wParam]. If you find the ID number there, it means someone has mouse clicked on that menu item. Then your program can take action and call something because the menu item was clicked on. In some cases it's important to prevent the action from being repeated over and over, and one way to get it to run only once, is to erase part of the message after acting on it.

I avoided a type of menu which needs complex resources, because I wanted it to be simple, and the resources would make everything much too difficult for me.
(Obviously there is a level of difficulty which prevents people from wanting to do it, and Microsoft is faulty in having made many things unpleasantly difficult, when naturally they should most certainly be extremely simple.)

It is possible to create a perfectly good menu without using any resources at all.
To create a menu without any resources you only have to use 2 functions or invocations, which are called invoke CreateMenu, and invoke AppendMenuA.

I feel resources were much too difficult and too complicated. At first I read somewhere that a menu created without any resources is a system menu. That was not true. But at first when I created a normal menu without using resources, I thought it was a system menu.
But then I read on a Microsoft website that a true system menu is really something quite different, it is a small automatically created menu which you will see when you mouse click on a tiny symbol in the Top Left corner of a window border. It's created automatically without your programming.
(But you can add menu items to that real system menu as well, using nearly the same technique.)

I want to explain with an example how to create a normal menu of the kind that does not need resources. (But if you want to add pictures to it, then you need a simple form of resource section. Adding pictures to be explained further down.)

I think the right time to create a menu is immediately before you create your window. Creating even a long menu was easy, and you can add more and more to a menu and gradually build it up, make the menu as long and complicated as you need to.

When you create a window, a "handle" to your menu has to be used as a parameter of the function that creates the window. It is usually the function

invoke CreateWindowEx

Which creates a window (and the function has I think 12 parameters). So before you create the window you have to firstly get at least one menu handle, using invoke CreateMenu

Which returns the handle in the eax register. You have to save that handle from the eax register, and use the handle while creating the window. That is what connects the window and its menu together.
When you create the window, the handle to the menu should go in the 3$^{rd}$ parameter if they are counted from right to left.

The best time to create a menu is immediately before you create the window. But I noticed some part of my menu could be created after creating the window.
It's just that the first handle of the menu, has to be done first before you create the window, so that the first handle of the menu can be a parameter of
invoke CreateWindowEx.


;=================
The preliminary. I used the same code that you see in their short example programs, to make the very start of my programs.
Before starting to create the Menu, my Windows programs all started with

invoke GetModuleHandle , 0
mov [wc.hInstance] , eax

which returns with the handle hInstance in the eax register, and saves a copy of that not just as a variable but also saving it in a data structure called wc WNDCLASSEX.
And then
    invoke  LoadCursor , 0 , IDC_ARROW
    mov     [wc.hCursor] , eax

I don't know what that is for, but I know most programs crashed without it.
My programs all have to declare the existence of the WNDCLASSEX data structure with the writing of these two words somewhere in the data section of the program

wc WNDCLASSEX

Notice that the wc on its left is your label, and from then on The assembler will understand that where you write "wc." With a full stop, you mean a field of this WNDCLASSEX structure.
(If you write the name of a field in the data structure, within rectangular brackets, then, your label wc is on the left side of the full stop, and the field name is written in a recognized case sensitive way on the right hand side of the full stop.)

And then computer programs must do filling in of the WNDCLASSEX data structure.
It is essential to fill in some of the fields of this data structure , since you can't create a window without it , but you can just copy the method of filling it in from a simple example. And it should always work. It is not necessary to actually understand the data structure, since filling it in can be done the same way for all programs.

You see that there are really two different ways of filling it in with the essential fields. One of the methods uses the horizontal row of items, and then the order in which you put them matters a lot. The other method is sort of vertical, it uses lines like "mov [wc.hInstance] , eax" to fill fields of the data structure, and when you
use this method, the assembler automatically knows the right order. So you don't need to be at all careful with the order , as that ordering is done automatically.

As soon as WNDCLASSEX is filled in , all computer programs have to register the class of the window before creating it , with

invoke RegisterClass , wc

The little "wc" is the label of the WNDCLASSEX structure. The window class always has to be registered in that way , but I don't know why. You can do it the same way with every program.
One of the things that happen as you register a window class , is that this tells the operating system the address of the one special procedure which is called WindowProc.
And the operating system will call WindowProc several times now , as if testing whether it's there.
When the operating system calls WindowProc automatically , it is important that this one function should run within WindowProc , because it does default processing:

invoke DefWindowProc , [hwnd] , [wmsg] , [wparam] , [lparam]

Now it seems that the best time to create a menu is just after you register the class , but just before you create the window with invoke CreateWindowEx.
;-----------------------------------------------------------------------

The first step in creating a menu has been to run "invoke CreateMenu" several times , to collect and save handles. This invocation has no parameters , but it returns with a handle in the eax register.

How many handles do you need?
You need one handle for starting the whole menu and attaching it to a window , and then you need another handle for each drop down menu area you want to create.
That is , you need a handle for each small string of words which will appear on the top border of the window , and which when mouse-clicked on will drop down a menu with several items.

For example , when I want to create 2 drop down menus , I have to get 3 handles. And when I want to create 10 drop down menus , I have to get 11 handles , and so on. (One handle more than the number of menus.) I think you should get the handles before you create the window.
For example:

    invoke CreateMenu
    mov [h_menu1] , eax                             ;Save all the handles.
    invoke CreateMenu
    mov [h_menu2] , eax
    invoke CreateMenu
    mov [h_menu3] , eax

This collects 3 handles which can be used to create 2 drop down menus.
The first of these handles is special because I pass it to the invoke CreateWindowEx
(as the 3$^{rd}$ parameter from right to left in CreateWindowEx) when it creates the new window. That is , [h_menu1] is used as a parameter when the new window is being created , and that is what links the window to the menu.

When you count parameters from left to right , then it is the 10$^{th}$ parameter out of its 12 parameters.

Then in the data section you need to prepare several short strings of text.
And as usual , each string of text has a label on its left , and then the two letters db and then the text words in quotes , and then a comma and a binary zero. The binary zero is really necessary to tell the operating system where the text ends.

For example , in the data section , maybe have these labels and words

top_word1 db "Exit" , 0
top_word2 db "Menu2" , 0

item1 db "End the program" , 0
item2 db "Load File" , 0
item3 db "Erase" , 0

Now in the program , just after obtaining 3 handles ,

    invoke AppendMenuA , [h_menu1] , MF_POPUP , [h_menu2] , top_word1       ;exit

```
    invoke AppendMenuA , [h_menu2] , 0 , 501 , item1
         ;End program
;--------
    invoke AppendMenuA , [h_menu1] , MF_POPUP , [h_menu3] , top_word2      ;menu2
    invoke AppendMenuA , [h_menu3] , 0 , 502 , item2
    invoke AppendMenuA , [h_menu3] , 0 , 503 , item3
    ;---------------------------------------------
;
```

The invoke AppendMenuA has 4 parameters separated by commas.
The first parameter looking from left to right , is a handle.
The second parameter should normally be zero for any dropping-down item in a drop down menu.
But when you want to create the top menu words on the upper border of the window , then the second parameter has to be the flag MF_POPUP.
I have mentioned that the first of the handles , [h_menu1] is used as a parameter in invoke CreateWindowEx creating the new window , that was what links the window to its menu.

Just looking at an example of programming is probably much easier than reading a long description of it in words , a picture is worth a thousand words.

Invoke AppendMenuA can take several forms depending on what flags are in it.

So far I mentioned the form when there are no flags , as the 2$^{nd}$ parameter was 0.

In the case when the flag MF_POPUP is in it (as the 2$^{nd}$ parameter) , then the first parameter of AppendMenuA should be the first of the handles [h_menu1] , or that is the same handle used while creating the window.
And its 3$^{rd}$ parameter should be a handle you will use as a 1$^{st}$ parameter for all the next invoke AppendMenuA which make all the drop down menu items appear just below.

And its 4$^{th}$ parameter should be the address of the short string of text which you want to appear on the upper border of the window. And which will create a rectangular drop-down menu if you mouse-click on it. (To make the 4$^{th}$ parameter be the address , simply write the label without any brackets).

About the Flat assembler. When you simply write the label without brackets , then the assembler will automatically convert that label without brackets into the address of where the labeled data is. The data is something which you usually put in the data section of the program. So you just write the label of the text string as the 4$^{th}$ parameter , and that label is converted into the address of your short string of text.

Now you add to that menu as many drop-down items as you want, I think there is room for at least 40 items one above the other, and in the width of a window probably room for about 20 menus horizontally, if it is a large window.

And for each of the items in one particular drop-down you use the same handle in the 1st parameter of invoke AppendMenuA, so that each of those lines should appear together. (The second parameter can contain a zero).

You can make its second parameter zero, and you write in its 3rd parameter a number, any simple number which you would like to use as menu ID.

You decide to use what number you want as a menu ID. This number identifies the menu item. And later on, whenever someone mouse-clicks on the menu item, that number which you have chosen will appear in the [msg.wParam] field of a message, and at the same time WM_COMMAND will appear in the [msg.message] field. And it will also appear in WindowProc's [wmsg] field, exactly like [msg.message]. While also, [wparam] in WindowProc should contain exactly the same thing as [msg.wParam].

So it is simple to detect when someone has clicked on a menu item. This detecting can be done anywhere in your program. First test to see whether WM_COMMAND is in [msg.message]. And then if it is, test secondly for the number which you have chosen as a menu ID to see if it is now in [msg.wParam]. When the numbers are there you can be sure that someone has clicked on that menu item.

When your program has taken some action because of a menu click, there can sometimes be a risk of the action running again and again unnecessarily, and to avoid this rerunning one idea is to erase one of those 2 fields to zero. Sometimes something went wrong in my program until I erased one of them to make sure that a menu-triggered action only runs once.

When the computer is running within the special procedure which is often called WindowProc, I think there is normally the same number in the WindowProc field [wmsg] (which is often written as [uMsg], ) as there is in [msg.message]. And there is usually the same number in a WindowProc field which is often called [wparam] or [wParam] as there is at the same time in the message field called [msg.wParam].

(I think the difference is that the field [msg.wParam] can be detected from anywhere in the program, whereas [wparam] can be detected only from inside WindowProc.)

This is all assuming that somewhere in your data section you have declared the message structure by writing

  msg MSG

The small msg on the left is your label, and the capitals MSG is a word which is automatically recognized by the assembler, since the assembler is specialized for Windows and finds the format from an include file.

The flag MF_POPUP has numerical value 10h. So when you write the number 10h it should have exactly the same effect as writing the flag as a word MF_POPUP. The assembler should convert the words into the number anyway.

You can add small pictures to a menu, and doing that requires getting a handle to the picture. The main way to get a handle to a picture, is a resource, but it can be simple.

Showing a visible check mark.

A check mark on a menu lets you see which item has been selected, or clicked on.
Apparently it does not happen automatically and you need an invocation to create the check mark. To be able to create some check marks easily, it was essential that you make the menu ID numbers consecutive. If they are not consecutive numbers the method won't work well.

You can check one menu item with a little round spot, while at the same time unchecking a whole group of the menu items together, using this function.

   invoke CheckMenuRadioItem , [h_menu9] , 525 , 538 , 537 , 0

(In this example I just happened to have used the numbers 525 to 538 as a message ID, but they can have any consecutive values.)

In invoke CheckMenuRadioItem you write in 1$^{st}$ parameter (from left to right) the handle of the group of menu items, then the first ID number of a group of consecutive menu items to be "unchecked". Then the ID number of the last one in the group of consecutive menu items to be "unchecked".
 Then you write the ID of the one single menu item which you want to "check", that is create a little round check mark for it. And then in the last parameter the number 0 is   the flag MF_BYCOMMAND , which signifies that you are using your menu ID numbers.

You see in the example just above here, 525 was the ID of the first menu item to get unchecked (in a group), and 538 was the ID of the last item to get unchecked, and 537 was the ID of the single menu item you want the check mark in visibly.
 So it can work simply with a group of items.
Turning on a check mark for one item and turning off check marks in all the others.
 (They are grouped by giving them consecutive ID numbers.)

If the numbers were not consecutive it seemed a muddle, and many more invocations had to be used.

If instead you used the flag MF_BYPOSITION in its last parameter, (numerical value 400h) then the first 3 numbers have to be the position of the menu items instead of being the ID. I have actually only used the ID method, so I always put zero in the last parameter.


A menu was easy to create both with and without bitmap pictures.

I have created a menu with almost all of my programs, but the menus have only contained words. But I found out it is actually not very difficult to substitute bitmap pictures for the lines of words, and I did that in my program using the Flat assembler.
To use pictures instead of the words, you use the same

 invoke CreateMenu.

And you use the same

invoke AppendMenuA.

To do it you do not need any new functions apart from the

invoke LoadImage.

But the invoke AppendMenuA now needs the flag MF_BITMAP,
as its second parameter.
The second parameter which previously was a zero for the drop down part, or which was MF_POPUP for the topmost part of the menu.
Where previously the flag was zero, I just write MF_BITMAP for adding a picture.

And that by itself means that the 4th and last parameter of AppendMenuA, should now be the handle of a bitmap picture, instead of the address of text.

(So a handle to a bitmap picture replaces the address of text, in some of the items. And you just need the flag MF_BITMAP in the place of zero.)
This works easily enough to be practical.

 Wherever previously the flag was MF_POPUP,

to create the topmost part of a menu , the flag should now have MF_BITMAP as well , (When you want a picture to replace the words at the top border of the window). So you have MF_POPUP OR MF_BITMAP ,
the combination of both flags together in the second parameter , using the logical "or" between flags.

Then the fourth parameter should be a handle of the bitmap picture.
Use the 2 flags together only if you want the topmost part of the menu to contain bitmap pictures. When adding a picture to the drop down part of a menu just use one flag alone MF_BITMAP.

I found that when you include a bitmap picture in the topmost part of the menu , the upper border of the window , automatically widens to make it fit the picture.
A menu can be partially made with words , and partially with images. But if you need pictures that have a word written in them , then obviously you should use a picture that has the word.

Now the only problem is to obtain the handle to a bitmap picture.
I found that it is actually easy using invoke LoadImage. (But this worked with resources.)
Like this for example:

```
  invoke LoadImage , [wc.hInstance] , 1 , 0 , 100 , 100 , 0
    mov [bitmap_handle] , eax
```

If you look at this , the two parameters which I made 100 , 100 turned out to be the only thing that controls the size which the bitmap picture will have when it's inside the menu.
They are X and Y size of the picture. (4$^{th}$ and 5$^{th}$ parameters left to right). Apparently nothing else affects the size when it goes into the menu.

The number 1 is supposed to be a resource identifier. For example number 1 to 9 can be used if the resources section specifies 9 bitmap pictures. Replace the 1 with the resource identifier.

Though I do not understand resources and find resources a difficult subject ,
I found in this particular case with the Flat assembler it's not too hard to include bitmap pictures in a resources section. This is something that can be used in practice.

This idea of using a resources section causes the bitmap pictures to be permanently incorporated inside the executable EXE file , which is better than having to keep several bitmap files in the same folders as your EXE files when you run them.

Of course you do need to keep the bitmap pictures files in the same folder as your ASM file while you assemble it into an EXE file , unless you write in the resource section the complete path and file name of the bitmap pictures , to help the assembler to find the pictures.

This example of using "invoke LoadImage" , is in the form of it which you can use for resources.
In that form the first parameter has to be the handle to your running EXE program , and that is the reason why it is [wc.hInstance].
(Windows programs which I have seen in the flat assembler examples all start out with the function

invoke GetModuleHandle , 0
 and this returns with hInstance in the eax register. I think the hInstance is probably the handle to your running EXE program. You save it , and now you use it in invoke LoadImage.)

The second parameter , a number which I made a 1 , is a resource identifier , 1 for the first bitmap , is 2 for the second bitmap , is 3 for the third bitmap picture , and so on. It is a small integer number which identifies the bitmap picture addressed in the resources section of the program.

```
  invoke LoadImage , [wc.hInstance] , 1 , 0 , 100 , 100 , 0
    mov [bitmap_handle] , eax

 invoke LoadImage , [wc.hInstance] , 2 , 0 , 100 , 100 , 0
    mov [bitmap_handle_2] , eax
```

You just run this invocation as many times as you need to get a handle to each bitmap picture. With a different resource identifier each time. I mean a different $2^{nd}$ parameter each time , the small integer number which identifies the picture. Saving the handle each time.

The following example shows a resources section of my program , as it needs to be for the Flat assembler. This is a simpler than usual example of resources for the Fasmw. And it works. I would not understand a more complicated example.

I do not know why the resources section needs to be organized in certain ways , but , you can just observe that it has a certain pattern in the way it is written , and copy its pattern.

And then it should work. If you can copy the pattern which you see in a resources section , it may work when you try to change it or add to it.

Its purpose is to incorporate your BMP pictures into the EXE file and also to allow
invoke LoadImage
to to find a picture from the small integer number which identifies
the picture.

It should work with bitmap pictures of any size , and I think it is a good thing that the real size of a bitmap picture has no effect at all on its visible size when it goes in a menu to be a part of the menu.

Because only one thing , (the 4$^{th}$ and the 5$^{th}$ parameters) in invoke LoadImage , affects picture size in the menu , so the control of picture size is better and simpler than it would be if there were several factors.
You notice your EXE file getting much larger because images are included inside it.
I think maybe so as not to increase the size of the EXE file too much as many pictures get incorporated into it , it might be a good idea to use bitmap pictures which have a relatively small number of pixels , such as ten thousand pixels?
Anyway this is the example:

```
section '.rsrc' resource data readable          ;Start a resource section.
                                                ; resource directory

directory RT_BITMAP, bitmaps                    ;working

                                                ; resource subdirectories
resource bitmaps, \
      1, LANG_NEUTRAL, bitmap1, \               ;working
      2, 0, bitmap2, \
      3, 0, bitmap3, \
      4, 0, bitmap4

bitmap bitmap1, 'bitmap.bmp'                    ;working
bitmap bitmap2, 'picture.bmp'
bitmap bitmap3, 'f.bmp'
bitmap bitmap4, 'fly2.bmp'

;======================================
```

In this example which works in my program , the top line is necessary to
tell the Flat assembler that this is a resource data section.

You have to copy the first line exactly.
Next the resource directory is very simple in this case as it has only one line and one item. Unfortunately it can be horribly complicated in other kinds of programs.

Next the resource subdirectory.
You just have to look at the pattern of its writing and then copy the

pattern exactly whenever you add more to it.

Next my bitmap images are declared. For some reason you need to do this in a
certain pattern too. I think the resource data is operated on by Macros, and the
strange pattern that is necessary is for the Macros.
You can see the picture file names are there within quotes, and I think this assumes that the pictures are in the same folder as the ASM program.

If your pictures are in another folder, then it does work if you write in quotes the full path and file name going to the picture instead of just a file name.
You see I named one of my pictures 'bitmap.bmp' and the last one was a picture of a dragonfly, which I named 'fly2.bmp'
As an example of writing the complete path and file name, this worked:

bitmap bitmap5 , 'C:\fasmw17304\horn.bmp'
;----------------------------
Branches in a menu.
A menu can be given a branching shape. The following single line in the right place would cause a branching in the menu. This shows a line in the middle of a menu which uses the handle [h_menu3].

 invoke AppendMenuA , [h_menu3] , MF_POPUP , [h_menu2] , text1

A menu was already created with the handle [h_menu2]. And the branching causes it to branch out from a menu which uses the handle [h_menu3].
In the data section you need to put a few words with label text1.


;================

The kind of menu which I have been creating in my programs should not be called a system menu, though apparently it has been called that sometimes. So it's not a system menu. It's an ordinary menu.
I think a real system menu is when you click on the tiny little symbol in the very top left corner of a window. It has a different handle from other menus.

You know there is a tiny symbol in the very top left corner of most windows, sometimes it is a tiny icon picture.
And if you mouse click on that top left corner you get the system menu. A system menu is not created by your program, instead it is created automatically by the operating system with a window.

I found out by experiment that the true system menu can be given new lines of text and new menu items, with words or pictures in about the same way as a normal main menu. But there are a few differences. Firstly a system menu has a handle which you need to get with the invocation

invoke GetSystemMenu , [hWindow] , 0
mov [hSysmenu] , eax

The handle to the system menu is returned in the eax register and you need to save it. Then when you use invoke AppendMenuA to add lines of text or pictures to the system menu , you need to use the handle to the system menu [hSysmenu] as the first handle in invoke AppendMenuA.
With AppendMenuA you can as usual chose the ID number which identifies the menu item when someone clicks on it , exactly in the same way as you do with a main menu.

Note. The right time to add things to a system menu seems to be immediately after you create the window with invoke CreateWindowEx. The computer already has a system menu automatically and so you don't ever need to create it. This was different from my normal menu , my normal menu has to be created immediately before creating the Window , unlike a system menu which should be added to just after creating the window.

You may also add bitmap pictures to the system menu in the same way as with a normal menu.
In general with a system menu , whenever someone mouse clicks on a system menu item , the Windows operating system posts a different message.

It posts a WM_SYSCOMMAND message instead of the WM_COMMAND message. Normally your program has to have a message loop in it. In your message loop the
invoke DispatchMessage , msg
will as usual cause the procedure WindowProc to be called ,
and now inside WindowProc your program should test for the WM_SYSCOMMAND message as well as your ordinary testing for the WM_COMMAND message which was for the normal menu.
For the system menu only the WM_SYSCOMMAND message matters and needs to be detected.
The following is a small example of adding menu items to a system menu , which has a rather strange effect. It is not a complete example , but shows parts of it with a strange effect. It worked just After creating a window.

    invoke GetSystemMenu , [hWindow] , 0
    mov [hSysmenu] , eax
                                                ;a first line attaches a branch to the sysmenu

    invoke AppendMenuA , [hSysmenu] , MF_POPUP , [hpopmenu2] , A1
    invoke AppendMenuA , [hpopmenu2] , 0 , 501 , A2

```
;------------
    invoke AppendMenuA , [hSysmenu] , MF_BITMAP , 503 , [bitmap_handle3]
    invoke AppendMenuA , [hSysmenu] , MF_BITMAP , 504 , [bitmap_handle4]
    invoke AppendMenuA , [hSysmenu] , 0 , 505 , A3
```

This strange experimental example added a branching structure to the system menu. The first of the invoke AppendMenuA caused a complicated part of my main menu to branch out from the system menu.

You notice that it did that because the handle in its first parameter was [hSysmenu] returned by invoke GetSystemMenu , while its handle in the third parameter was the handle [hpopmenu2] returned by invoke CreateMenu , which was the handle I used to create my normal menu just before creating the window. So this linked together the system menu and the specification of the main menu , causing a branch.

The last 3 invoke AppendMenuA , just added 2 bitmap pictures and one line of text to the lower end of the system menu. You see for example it specifies the menu ID numbers 501 , 503 , 504 , 505 and any other numbers could have been used equally well for menu ID , and when WindowProc runs you can test for any of those numbers in [wParam] or in [msg.wParam].

And the test will show when any of the menu items was mouse-clicked on , whether it was text or bitmap image.

The following is a small part of WindowProc , merely showing that if you are using the special system menu , you should test for WM_SYSCOMMAND as well as your normal menu testing for WM_COMMAND

```
proc WindowProc hwnd , wmsg , wparam , lparam

        cmp     [wmsg] , WM_COMMAND                         ;numerical value 111h
        je      .wmcommand
        cmp     [wmsg] , WM_SYSCOMMAND                      ;numerical value 112h
        je      .wmsyscommand
```

I have read that in the special case of the system menu of the top left corner , and WM_SYSCOMMAND you should clear to zero the lowest 4 binary bits of wParam , by AND 0fff0h. Of course that is never necessary with the normal menu and WM_COMMAND.

  Notice that the tests do not really have to be done from inside WindowProc , I think you can do the tests anywhere else in your program , for example
cmp [msg.message] , WM_COMMAND.
Then
cmp [msg.wParam] , 504.

(If you had decided on a menu ID of 504.) When you test for menu item clicks in other areas of your program , it is sometimes a good idea to erase the [wParam] field to zero after testing it , so as to prevent the actions from wrongly being repeated again and again. For example maybe use
mov [msg.wParam] , 0
to erase it after some action was triggered by it.


;=====================


In most of my programs I have only used ordinary drop down menus , but I notice there is a way to create a menu which floats in the middle of the screen at XY coordinates which you specify.
Creating this kind of floating menu , is slightly different.
Firstly you have to create some handles using "invoke CreatePopupMenu" instead of using "invoke CreateMenu".
The Popup is important. Assume that you get a handle with:

invoke CreatePopupMenu
mov [h_popmenu4] , eax

When you create the normal menu , you also start to create the floating menu too , except that I think you need to omit from it the top row invoke AppendMenuA.
That is , you leave out the one that contained the flag MF_POPUP , and that also contained the first handle , such as [h_menu1].
Assume that you have **left out** the usual top row. This row was **not used** anymore.
  invoke AppendMenuA , [h_menu1] , MF_POPUP , [h_popmenu4] , T2

Assume that without that row, you run like this before creating the window:
    invoke AppendMenuA , [h_popmenu4] , 0 , 501 , Word2    ;ID =501 ;
    invoke AppendMenuA , [h_popmenu4] , 0 , 502 , Word3
   ;---
Now somewhere else in the program , at the moment when you want the floating menu to appear , you run the function or invocation ,

  invoke TrackPopupMenu , [h_popmenu4] , 2000h , 100 , 300 , 0 , [hWindow1] , 0

And this will cause a floating menu to appear anywhere in the window at the X , Y coordinate which you specify with its $3^{rd}$ and $4^{th}$ parameters.
In the above example the X , Y coordinate were 100 , 300.
The handle to the window is in its $6^{th}$ parameter.
(There is in the $2^{nd}$ parameter a flag of fixed value 2000h , and Zeros in $5^{th}$ and in $7^{th}$ parameter.)

As the floating menu appears anywhere , a mouse click on any menu item causes exactly the same system of message ID as you normally have with the normal menu.
So you can run invoke TrackPopupMenu in your program at the specific times when you want a menu to appear.

```
 invoke TrackPopupMenu , [hpopmenu2] , TPM_NOANIMATION , -50 , 300 , 0 , [hWindow1] , 0
```

Any number at all can be used as a menu item ID , (if in your program you firstly test [msg.message] for WM_COMMAND , and then test in full 4 bytes form [msg.wParam].)
But if instead you only test 2 bytes of [msg.wParam] , then you might be able to detect a mouse cursor hovering over a menu without actually clicking on it.

I have not used the popup menus , as the menus with simple text attached to the window upper border were enough.

```
 ;========================================
```

## Downloading a page from a website.

This is about an experiment. The experiment downloaded the first page from a website, and showed the web page as a form of text on the screen. I could not read it at all, since the text was in Html code. It worked for any website.

The web pages were downloaded onto an area of allocated memory.

And then the area of memory which had the web page downloaded onto it, was saved as a file, which had to have the file name extension ".htm"

When the file was saved as an .htm type of file, then browsers were able to load up the file and show it as a proper normal looking webpage.
The data did not need to be prepared in any kind of way, simply saving it as a file with the filename extension ".htm" was good enough, to make it compatible with a browser.

I tried some different Urls to get it to read the first page from some different websites.
The Url used was a part of the program, and to change the Url I had to type it into the program then reassemble the program with "run".

First to allocate memory:

```
    invoke GlobalAlloc , 0 , 1000000h
    mov [pointing1] , eax                    ;saved the address of the memory
    ;========================
```
To download the webpage, call here.

```
  Download_webpage:

                ; ; (InternetOpen  tells the internet dll to initialize and to prepare)

 invoke InternetOpenA ,  szAgent ,  INTERNET_OPEN_TYPE_DIRECT ,  0 ,  0 ,  0
     mov [hInternet] ,  eax
                                              ; 0 = failed
     cmp eax ,  0
     jz failed

                ; ; InternetOpenUrl  returns a handle to the Url ,  or a 0 if failed
```

```
        invoke InternetOpenUrlA , [hInternet] , szUrl , 0 , 0 , INTERNET_FLAG_RELOAD , 0

    mov [hFile] , eax
    cmp eax , 0
    jz close2
    mov ecx , 8
    mov [total_length] , 0                           ;*This loaded the whole web page.
    mov eax , [pointing1]
    mov [read_pointer] , eax                         ;A starting address was [pointing1]
  loopa:
    push ecx

    invoke InternetReadFile , [hFile] , [read_pointer] , 50000 , bytesRead    ;;runs several times

    pop ecx
    cmp eax , 0                                      ;0=fail.
    jz close
                        ;;InternetReadFile should fill [bytesRead] with an actual length
    mov eax , [bytesRead]
    add [total_length] , eax
    add [read_pointer] , eax
    cmp [bytesRead] , 0        ;** condition of bytes read=0 and eax=1 means finished?
    jnz loopa                                        ;Around another turn of a loop

  close:
    invoke InternetCloseHandle , [hFile]
  close2:
    invoke InternetCloseHandle , [hInternet]
  failed:
    ret
```

Just by chance I tried to get it to read 50000 bytes in one go. Any other number should work as well. Whenever the web page was longer than 50000, it should go round and round in a loop, and read more bytes of the web page with every turn.

You see how the [read_pointer] variable, and the [total_length], both get the [bytesRead] amount added to them in every turn.

In the experiment the ecx register counted down how many times the program can go around in a loop, running "invoke InternetReadFile" in each turn of the loop.

In that function there are no brackets around bytesRead because you are giving the function the address of the variable labelled bytesRead , and the function will automatically write an actual length value into the variable.
I read somewhere that when "invoke InternetReadFile" returns eax=1 plus also [bytesRead]=0 then the combination means it has finished reading the web page.


;--------------- Preferably in the data section declare several variables:

```
    pointing1 dd 0
    read_pointer dd 0
    total_length dd 0
    hInternet dd 0
    hFile dd 0
    bytesRead dd 0

    szAgent db "agent ?" ,  0
```

;---------------- The area of memory happened to be erased firstly to blanks with this:

```
   erases:    mov ecx , 200000
              mov ebx , [pointing1]
     eral:    mov byte [ebx] , 20h
              inc ebx
              dec ecx
              jnz eral
              ret
```
;-------------- The program asked me for a save file name. (Not shown here)
The program had a default file name extension of ".htm" because of this line in the data section , which worked together with  "invoke GetSaveFileName , ofn "

szTextFilter db "html Files" , 0 , "*.htm" , 0 , "All Files" , 0 , "*.*" , 0 , 0           ;Necessary for saving file

```
        szTextPath rb MAX_PATH
        szText db ".htm" , 0
```

The szTextFilter string above, makes it more easy to save the file as an htm type of file. The usual method which asks the user for a save file name, is explained in another chapter. As you see the code for reading the website page was simple, but two flags may need to be declared like this to tell the assembler their values:

;In the data section:

```
INTERNET_OPEN_TYPE_DIRECT = 1           ;
INTERNET_FLAG_RELOAD = 80000000h        ;7 zeroes ; download from server, not from cache

; INTERNET_NO_CALLBACK  = 0
;; INTERNET_FLAG_OFFLINE                ;= from cache only (did not want this flag)
```

;Some Urls which were tried , and I think they all worked

```
;  szUrl db "https://www.mangaeden.com/api/list/" , 0
   szUrl db "https://www.anguillesousroche.com/" , 0      ;* an url. end slash
;  szUrl db "https://www.crazyclearance.co.uk/" , 0       ;result read = <!DOCTYPE HTML>
;; szUrl db "https://www.amazon.co.uk/" , 0

   ;==================================
```

## Allocating Memory

Whenever you want your program to use a large area of RAM memory it has to ask the operating system for permission to use the memory, which is called allocating memory.
Writing onto memory at addresses that haven't been allocated crashes the programs.
Maybe this is partly because the operating system should prevent different programs from accidentally using the same area of memory and then accidentally erasing each other's work.

But if you run invoke CreateDIBSection it automatically allocates an area of memory ,
and gives you its start address , which means it might not be necessary to allocate more memory.


I have so far tried 3 different methods which all work.
I don't know why Microsoft has made several methods when one would have been enough.
And I don't know why all their methods seem a bit weird, when they should have been simple to understand?

    The 3 methods I tried were

    GlobalAlloc    (With Fixed And Movable flags)
    HeapCreate
    VirtualAlloc

By chance the first method I tried was GlobalAlloc, and as it worked I used it in all
of my programs.
It was easy to use, and it can probably give you all the memory you need.
But I tested HeapCreate and VirtualAlloc, and perhaps VirtualAlloc might be the best method.
Though the word 'virtual' sounds bad, the word virtual does not describe what the function really does, since all it does is to give your program memory.
A test with an experiment proved that it must have been working, and the test also showed that the clean-up when the program ends must have also been working properly.


## GlobalAlloc

GlobalAlloc, has two different forms, depending on whether a flag in it is number 0 or number 2.
If the flag is number 0 , it immediately returns with a pointer to the new allocated area of memory, in the eax register.
Such a pointer might be called a base address, or a 'start address'. I prefer start address.
This GlobalAlloc, was better with the flag of 0.

A simple test to discover whether the memory really has been allocated, is to try writing onto the memory. If the program does not crash immediately, then the memory has
probably been properly allocated.
The computer should crash when you write onto addresses outside of the allocated areas.
For example the completely harmless instruction "mov [ebx] , al" would crash the computer if [ebx] pointed to an area of memory that has not been allocated, and that is not part of the program's data section.

When you want your computer program to completely end, you are supposed to free any
allocated memory. That is you deallocate it, so that this memory is no longer reserved.

This was called 'cleaning up after',  on some websites.
I created a test to find out whether the memory was really being deallocated as it should be, to make sure it was possible to clean up properly.
The idea of the test was that if you deallocate memory and then reallocate it over and over again many times, while it goes round and round repeating the cycle you can look at the actual numbers of the handles or of the base addresses.

If the pointer to the start of allocated memory is the same every time, that would indicate that the memory had been deallocated properly just before being reallocated.

But if the pointer to the start of allocated memory keeps on increasing in value, it shows that the deallocation must not have been taking place.
As a test, every time I pressed on the keyboard, memory was deallocated and then reallocated in the same way, I could see the pointer and the handle numbers in hexadecimal on the screen.
The result of the test was that in some cases the address pointer stayed exactly the same all the time.

But that sometimes they alternated between two values. In both cases I assume deallocating worked. When deallocating didn't work, the address kept increasing every time higher and higher, proving it wasn't working, and the allocated memory wasn't being deallocated.
Quite often, if the method you try does not work, then after a while the program crashes.

The following is an example of simply allocating memory using invoke GlobalAlloc.

   invoke GlobalAlloc , 0 , 1000000
   mov [pointing2] , eax

In this method, its flag is a zero, which causes the process to be simple and
one step. The length of memory asked for, this time is 1 million bytes.

This does work. This immediately returns with a base address in the eax register.
If for any reason it fails, it is supposed to return with zero in eax.
You can ask it for hundreds of megabytes of memory too.

The method of deallocating memory as the program ends and stops running , was also working , like this:

invoke GlobalFree , [pointing2]

You see to deallocate in this case you can simply use the pointer. The pointer has to be exactly the same number which was returned by GlobalAlloc.
If you make the slightest change to that pointer number it won't work in deallocating.
The above way of deallocating is for the case that you have made the flag zero
during allocating with GlobalAlloc.

In the other case that you have made the flag = 2 , this 2 is supposed to mean 'movable' , the process of allocating becomes 2-step, and a bit more complicated.
The 2 step process gives you a handle to the memory area, as well as an address. Unless there is a reason why you want the handle, I assume that a flag of 0 is maybe better than a flag of 2?

The following is an example of allocating memory with a GlobalAlloc and a flag of 2.

```
invoke GlobalAlloc , 2 , 1000000        ;It returns with a handle in eax
mov [hAlloc2] , eax
invoke GlobalLock , eax                 ;The handle will be turned into a pointer
mov [pointing2] , eax                   ;The pointer is saved
```

  In the above example, it is asking for 1000000 bytes of memory, and because the
flag was the number 2,  instead of returning with an address in the eax
register,  it returns with a handle in the eax register. (A handle to the memory.)

Then you have to use the handle with invoke GlobalLock , [Handle] which is supposed to
"turn the handle into a pointer". It should immediately return with a pointer
or base address in the eax register.
In this example, both the handle and the pointer are being saved since they will be used.

In this case making the flag number 2 caused the process to be 2 step.
As its second step,  GlobalLock is used to turn the handle into a pointer.
In this case,  deallocating the memory when the program ends,  is supposed to be done

in 2 steps this way, but only the GlobalFree was necessary as I tried that:

  invoke GlobalUnlock , [hAlloc2]         ;seems ok with or without GlobalUnlock

  invoke GlobalFree , [hAlloc2]           ; This one maybe worked alone.


I have tried GlobalUnlock , [Pointer] and GlobalUnlock , [handle]. It did not matter or do anything.

I have read that for Clipboards, it is essential to use GlobalAlloc with the flag of 2.

I think it was maybe better to use a flag of 0, to make allocating a 1 step process. And to make the deallocating when the program ends, a 1 step process too.
A Microsoft page said GlobalUnlock simply decrements a lock count. When is that necessary??
Note that with my computer, GlobalUnlock did never seem to do anything. It wasn't necessary to use it.


;------------------------------------------

## HeapCreate

Next, the example of invoke HeapCreate.

    invoke HeapCreate , 0 , 2000000 , 0
    mov [hAlloc2] , eax

    invoke HeapAlloc , eax , 0 , 1000000       ;use 0 , an 8 did not work properly
    mov [pointing2] , eax

The above example worked well. Firstly "invoke HeapCreate , 0 , 2000000 , 0"
asks for 2000000 bytes of memory. Of course you can also ask for much more memory.
You see two of its parameters were 0. I think one should make them zero.

It should immediately return with a handle to memory in the eax register.
This handle is being saved, and this handle is also being used immediately
as the first parameter of invoke HeapAlloc. (In eax)

Then
invoke HeapAlloc , eax , 0 , 1000000

asks for 1000000 bytes of memory.
Invoke HeapAlloc should return with an address in the eax register,
the address should be the base address of the new allocated area of memory.

At first I thought I had read that the number of bytes asked for by HeapAlloc
should be a bit smaller than the number of bytes asked for by HeapCreate.
But a simple test showed that even when HeapAlloc asks for more memory than
the amount in HeapCreate, it still worked with no trouble. I wonder why?

HeapAlloc has a flag of zero. A flag of 8 should cause erasing to zeros of the
allocated memory, but, when I tried an 8 it did not work, it seems to malfunction
somehow. I could not use the automatic erasing, it malfunctioned.

In HeapCreate , its last parameter always had to be zero. I stick to flags which work ,
since using the wrong flags can stop it from working.
Look up on the internet "api Heapcreate" and Microsoft's website will explain these flags.
I made the first flag zero too, but a 40000h in the first flag could
mean that the allocated memory becomes "executable". I would try it if I wanted to make a program run there.

The following is how to deallocate the memory allocated with HeapCreate.
This is supposed to be important
when the program ends, as cleaning up, and when I tested this with many allocate/deallocate cycles, it worked
reasonably well but not always quite perfectly.

You see these two have to both run in this order. First HeapFree must run and then
HeapDestroy. HeapFree has both a handle and a pointer, and a flag of zero,
whereas HeapDestroy has only a handle. They had to both run in this order.

```
    invoke HeapFree , [hAlloc2] , 0 , [pointing2]      ;when alone , quickly crash
    invoke HeapDestroy , [hAlloc2]                     ;worked but maybe not perfectly?
```

They need to run only once when necessary, since running them again unnecessarily
crashes.

You can probably allocate many different areas of memory, and then deallocate
all of them when the program ends.

As a second example of HeapAlloc, this allocated 2 areas of memory using one HeapCreate with 2 HeapAlloc. Then after that it deallocated the memory:

```
    invoke HeapCreate , 0 , 200000h , 0
    mov [hAlloc2] , eax

    invoke HeapAlloc , eax , 0 , 100000h
    mov [pointing2] , eax                      ;Base address of first memory area

    ;---
    mov eax , [hAlloc2]                        ;** to load eax here.
    invoke HeapAlloc , eax , 0 , 100000h
    mov [pointing3] , eax                      ;Base address of second memory area

;---------- Below properly deallocated both memory areas with 3 operations

    invoke HeapFree , [hAlloc2] , 0 , [pointing2]
    invoke HeapFree , [hAlloc2] , 0 , [pointing3]

    invoke HeapDestroy , [hAlloc2]
```

One HeapCreate has to come first to get a handle to a heap. And then
several HeapAlloc can come after that, each of them using the same handle
returned by HeapCreate.
I found it wasn't necessary to make the length in HeapCreate greater.
In fact, the amounts of memory asked for by HeapAlloc, could be greater than the
amount in the HeapCreate, and it still worked Ok. But maybe it is not supposed to?

;-----------
A mistake with HeapAlloc

But I have noticed something wrong, which I can't understand.
My program was doing something wrong with HeapAlloc.
The computer seems to know whether a call which uses the allocated memory
areas comes from inside WindowProc or from anywhere else.

When the program which uses the allocated memory is called from the bottom of the message loop, or from some other part of the program, then it always worked with no problems.

But when the call which uses the Heap allocated memory, comes from inside WindowProc ,
then it only works if the Windows message in [msg.message] was one of the common messages you often use like for example WM_COMMAND or
WM_CHAR for example.
It was important to test for one of these common messages, and only call to use the allocated memory if one of those messages was there.
I wonder how does the computer know where the call comes from?
;------------------------------

## VirtualAlloc

The VirtualAlloc might be the best method? Here is an example of using it.
This will allocate
1 million bytes of memory. And it will return with a base address pointer in eax.

   invoke VirtualAlloc , 00 , 1000000 , 3000h , 40h       ;;The flags 3000h , 40h were essential.
   mov [pointing2] , eax

And for example this will deallocate the memory , and it should be run when
the program ends.

   invoke VirtualFree , [pointing2] , 0 , 8000h

When VirtualFree succeeds it returns with eax = 1 , and if it fails , eax = 0

Certain flags seem to be absolutely necessary , and I would always use these
flags without changing them.
Note that VirtualFree can only work when its length field is zero. (assuming you have the MEM_RELEASE flag in it)

A non zero length field will completely prevent VirtualFree from working.
VirtualAlloc should use the flags 3000h , 40h.
VirtualFree should use the flags 0 , 8000h

;----------- The values of these flags are in hexadecimal , with their names:

    1000h = MEM_COMMIT

2000h = MEM_RESERVE
40h = PAGE_EXECUTE_READWRITE
8000h = MEM_RELEASE

MEM_COMMIT OR MEM_RESERVE = 1000H OR 2000H =3000H
The 3000h combination might be always essential. (The Flags have the letter "h" at their right hand ends to show that they are in Hexadecimal).
;=====================


More examples of VirtualAlloc.
VirtualAlloc allows you to ask for memory at specific addresses , but it may refuse
to give you the memory if you ask for a difficult specific address.


An example of not asking for any specific address:

invoke VirtualAlloc , 00 , 42000000 , 3000h , 40h
 mov [pointing1] , eax


In this example I made the first parameter zero , which means that like the other two methods you let the operating system decide on the address of the allocated memory.

 VirtualAlloc is different from the other ways in that you can also specify in the first parameter the actual address of the memory area you want.  (But not always getting it. You won't always get it!).

The decimal number 42000000 in the second parameter is the length of the memory
you are asking for, in this example 42 megabytes.
The 3000h in its 3rd parameter is a combination of 2 flags:

The flag MEM_COMMIT = 1000h
And the flag MEM_RESERVE = 2000h
It's likely that one should always use 3000h for these two flags.
The 40h in the 4th parameter is another flag
40h = PAGE_EXECUTE_READWRITE
It is possible that the 40h flag value must always be used.
I saved the address pointer which it returns with in the eax register
with

    mov [pointing1] , eax                ;save the address pointer to the newly allocated memory

   (I happened to write the amount of memory as a decimal number ,  but the
   flags are numbers which should always be written as hexadecimal numbers ,  and so
   the flags end in the letter "h". h for hexadecimal.)

When your program stops running and you want to give the allocated memory back to the operating system ,  or clean-up ,  this can be done with one invocation:

   invoke VirtualFree , [pointing1] , 0 , 8000h

 It is therefore simple to clean up when the program ends.
 Its 1st parameter is the address of the memory area you want to give back to the operating system.
   (Within rectangular brackets the label of the variable in which the address was stored.)

I think the address for VirtualFree has to be exactly the same address as the one VirtualAlloc gave to you in the eax register.
VirtualFree's 2nd parameter must always be zero.
It won't work unless the 2nd parameter is 0. Its 3rd parameter has to be a flag, number 8000h.
I think it is probably always necessary for the two last parameters to always be a zero and 8000h written as 0 ,8000h
I did a good test to try to prove if the invoke VirtualFree was working.  It does work.

## Asking for specific memory.

Now an example of asking for memory of a **specific address which you want**.
  You can specify in its 1st parameter the actual memory address of an area you want the operating system to give to you.

(Example shows Address 100 million ,  length 1 million ,  and two essential flags)

     invoke VirtualAlloc , 100000000 , 1000000 , 3000h , 40h

When I tried that with a laptop and Windows 7 , specifying an address of 100000000 worked, but specifying addresses of 10000000 and below that did not work!
 I found, the Windows operating system always refuses to give my program memory below an address of about 100 million.
  When it fails to work ,  it should return with eax = 0 as a sign of failure.

So you can ask for a specific area of memory and its specific address, but it doesn't always work , depending on the address. Very often it won't give you the memory you ask for if you have specified the address.

But VirtualAlloc should be quite easy if you make the first parameter 00 and therefore you are not asking for a specific address.

 Probably it refuses to give you memory below an address of 100 million because the operating system is already using that memory. It can't give you an area which it is already using for some other purpose.

I know that the screen memory of many computers starts at the address 0c0000000h or at the address 0d0000000h. That is it may be zero "c" then 7 zeros , then the letter "h".

Unfortunately when I tried to allocate those areas of memory it always refused to.

If you can get access to that area,  you would write pixels directly onto the screen  which they call a desktop.


Microsoft's website with free information can be found by Google for
"Windows API GlobalAlloc"
"windows API GlobalLock".

;===================

## Crashing with Addressing Errors

What happens when you write something to a memory address just below the
allocated memory area? It can crash the program!
Unfortunately VirtualAlloc made the computer even more sensitive than usual to
that error.
Test that using a simple write onto memory like:

```
mov ebx , [pointing1]        ;The pointer returned by either GlobalAlloc or VirtualAlloc.
mov [ebx-10] , eax           ;Will writing -10 below [pointing1] crash the program?
```

When the memory was allocated by GlobalAlloc a write to an address
  of only -4 or -10h below the start of the allocated memory area did not
crash my testing program. But going a bit further down any write to an address of
 -20h below the start of the allocated memory area did crash
  the program immediately, even when allocated by GlobalAlloc. And of course lower below that crashed too.

But when the memory area was allocated by VirtualAlloc a write to an address
of just -1 below the start of the allocated area crashed the program immediately.

```
mov ebx , [pointing1]            ;The pointer returned by VirtualAlloc.
mov [ebx-1] , al                 ;This crashed the computer immediately
```

This always happened , it was a bad crash. It happened whether I had specified
  in VirtualAlloc the actual memory address I wanted to get allocated or not, that made no difference.
So if you use VirtualAlloc you have to be extra careful that the program
does not write anything onto an address below the start of the
allocated memory area.
I think the simplest way of being extra careful is to save a second copy of
the lower limit address number , adding something to that number to make the bottom
of your work less close to the dangerous borderline. If you are less close
to the border it becomes easier to avoid a mistake.


  For example ,

```
invoke VirtualAlloc , 00 , 20000000 , 3000h , 40h      ; asking for about 20 megabytes

mov [pointing1] , eax            ;save the pointer returned in eax for VirtualFree
add eax , 1000h                  ;add something to make a safe distance
                                 ;from the dangerous borderline
mov [used_pointer1] , eax        ;use this slightly increased number as a base address
```

For VirtualFree an unchanged copy of the start address has to be kept.

  Microsoft's website with free information can be found with Google searching for

    "Windows API VirtualAlloc"
;==========================================

## Loading and Saving Files, 32 bit and 64 bit.

Here are several examples of loading and saving a file. These are never complete programs, but are just a part of a program which should load or save.

First this was an example of loading a file with a predetermined file name into an area of memory. The area of memory into which it is loaded might be a big area, and in that case it has to be allocated first.

```
load_a_file:                                              ; 20h=archive flag

  invoke CreateFile , filename1 , GENERIC_READ OR GENERIC_WRITE , \
                    FILE_SHARE_READ OR FILE_SHARE_WRITE , 0 , 3 , 20h , 0
  mov [hcf] , eax
  cmp eax , -1                      ;minus 1 means an error
  jz endbad
  mov ebx , [pointing1]             ;The address of the area of memory to get loaded into.
  mov edx , [length1]               ;The length in bytes of the file to be read
  mov ecx , actual                  ;A pointer to where "ReadFile" can write an "actual length".

  invoke ReadFile , [hcf] , ebx , edx , ecx , 0

  invoke CloseHandle , [hcf]
  ret

  filename1 db '1Picture.bmp' , 0    ;Any File name ending with one binary zero
```

It wasn't actually necessary to load the parameters into registers as I have done above.
This should do the same thing:

```
  invoke ReadFile , [hcf] , [pointing1] , [length1] , actual , 0
```

In 32 bit programs, it does probably not matter which registers you use for the parameters while loading or saving files. And so any of the 5 registers ecx , edx , ebx , esi , edi can probably be used to hold parameters.
The register is without brackets if it already has in it the value you want.
But put brackets around it if it holds an address of the place where the parameter is saved. But maybe avoid register eax , because perhaps the assembler could write additional instructions which

change the value of eax. I think it did not matter which registers I happened to use when in 32 bit mode.

 But in 64 bit mode programs, the situation is so different from that, because in 64 bit mode it matters very much which registers you use.

Then the first 4 parameters must be in registers rcx , rdx , r8 , r9 in that order , from left to right in the proper order.

And in 64 bit mode trying to use other registers for the first 4 parameters , or the same registers but in the wrong order , will prevent it from working. And often that crashes the computer.

As 5$^{th}$ parameter in CreateFile there was the flag number 3.   3=OPEN_EXISTING

This opens the file if it's there. If the file is there , CreateFile should return with a handle to the file in the eax register.

 You need to use the handle for both reading the file and to close the file. If the file was not found , it should return with an INVALID_HANDLE_VALUE in the eax register , which is just the number minus -1.

The file name text might need to include a full pathway , which includes a drive letter then a colon , like this with drive C:

 filename1 db   "C:\pictures\1Picture.bmp" , 0

The right flag for this type of read a file , seems to be 3=OPEN_EXISTING. If you used the wrong flag , 2=CREATE_ALWAYS , then this would have the effect of instantly truncating the named file , which is reducing its length to zero making the file empty though it still would be listed in your directory.

Perhaps flag 4=OPEN_ALWAYS would also be used safely , but as it creates a file if the file is not found as already there , the flag 4 would maybe make it harder to see whether the file already existed? But I think the flag 4 is often Ok.

You get the details and explanation of the flags in detail if you look up on the internet "windows API createfile"

;==========================

This is an example about saving an area of memory as a file , with a predetermined file name which is written in the program. Of course the program can also change the file name.

This might not be the best way of doing it , but it worked in my program.

```
    save_a_file:
                                                            ; 20h=archive
    invoke CreateFile , filename1 , GENERIC_READ OR GENERIC_WRITE , \
                        FILE_SHARE_READ OR FILE_SHARE_WRITE , 0 , 2 , 20h , 0
   mov [hcf] ,  eax
   cmp eax , -1                            ;minus 1 means an error
```

```
    jz endbad
    mov ebx , [pointing1]           ;The address of the area of memory to be saved.
    mov edx , [length1]             ;The length in bytes of the area of memory to be saved
    mov ecx , actual                ;A pointer to where it can write an actual length.

    invoke WriteFile , [hcf] , ebx , edx , ecx , 0

    invoke CloseHandle , [hcf]
    ret

    filename1 db '1Picture_00.bmp' , 0      ;Any File name ending with one binary zero

    filename2 db "C:\folder3\filename" , 0              ;Any path and file name

    hcf dd 0
    actual dd 0

    room db 600h dup (0)
    ;------
```

The file name text could have included a pathway starting with the drive letter, like C: for example. In CreateFile the 5$^{th}$ parameter happened to be the flag 2=CREATE_ALWAYS, but a number 4=OPEN_ALWAYS should work as well. A number 2 had the disadvantage of immediately truncating the file to zero length, but the WriteFile which comes immediately after it should give back to the file a real length.
 I wonder if Number 4 could be a better flag since it did not truncate?

In this, you notice the label filename1, as 1$^{st}$ parameter of CreateFile, which did not have brackets around it. The flat assembler automatically converts any label without brackets into the address of where the label is. So the assembler converts it into the address.
 In this way you give it the address of your file name.

Its Second parameter is the combination of the two very common flags,
GENERIC_READ OR GENERIC_WRITE
This is the 2$^{nd}$ parameter, and for some reason it is very common for people to use those two flags together in general.
There is a comma, and the slash tells the assembler that the invoke is continued on the
next line. Next there is the very common combination of the two flags,
  FILE_SHARE_READ OR FILE_SHARE_WRITE

Which is commonly used in general for this 3rd parameter.

The next 4 parameters are there separated by commas, and they are, 0, 2, 20h, 0
I had made the 4th and the 7th parameters zero. I have always made them zero.

The 5th parameter, is supposed to be the "creation disposition flag".
2=CREATE_ALWAYS. The number 4=OPEN_ALWAYS might be better creation disposition?
The older file with the same name will be over-written.
If you write the words CREATE_ALWAYS the assembler will directly convert those words
into a number 2.
You can look up the complete list of creation dispositions on Microsoft's website by searching "Windows api createfile"

The number 20h in its 6th parameter means "FILE_ATTRIBUTE_ARCHIVE", and it should cause a mark of number 20h to go into the files directory, meaning that the saved file is an archive file. Perhaps most ordinary files should be archives?
As an alternative flag, an 80h in its 6th parameter would mean "FILE_ATTRIBUTE_NORMAL", but I had the feeling
that the 20h was ok.
Now the invoke CreateFile should return with a handle to the new file in the eax register. (normally most functions return numbers in eax).
The new handle to the file is saved, and I happened to call it "hcf". It was declared in the data section of the program by the line:
hcf dd 0

If there was an error CreateFile should return with
eax=-1, which means something went wrong. There is a test for the number minus -1.
Now assuming the handle was valid, there is

```
    mov ebx , [pointing1]       ;The address of the area of memory to be saved.
    mov edx , [length1]         ;The length of the area of memory to be saved
    mov ecx , actual            ;pointer to where it can write an actual length. (no brackets)

    invoke WriteFile , [hcf] , ebx , edx , ecx , 0
```

In this example just above, the variables have been loaded into registers and registers are used as parameters.
But of course instead of writing it that way it can work equally well if the parameters are specified in "invoke WriteFile" as labels with rectangular brackets around them. The parameters are stored in

memory, usually in the data section and each one is given a label, and in the functions like invoke WriteFile, you put the labels within rectangular brackets.
This is exactly equivalent,

invoke WriteFile, [hcf], [pointing1], [length1], actual, 0

You don't have to use the registers at all, as you can just use the labels which are variables names in brackets. But use no brackets for actual, since the purpose of the label "actual" is to give the function the address.
The system is quite flexible in that you can write the parameters either as names within brackets, or load them into registers and use the registers.
I have double checked that it works when written either way.

You see for the flat assembler a variable name without brackets gets converted into the "address of the variable", rather than an instruction to load "the contents" of the variable.
(In the example of WriteFile, the first 3 parameters are contents of the variables, while the 4$^{th}$ parameter is an address of an empty variable, into which the computer will write an actual length.)
As it runs invoke WriteFile is should return to you an actual length number, by writing the actual length into the memory at the address which you give it, in its 4$^{th}$ parameter.

It's interesting that both WriteFile and ReadFile can be do work in stages, rather than loading the whole length of the data all at once. If you make the length parameter small, these functions will read/write a small part of the file at a time. And they will advance an internal pointer, pointing to the next part of the file, allowing you to read or write a file in several stages by making your program go around in a loop.
I assume that their internal pointer is only erased if you close the file.
(The way of writing most functions is more flexible when the computer is in 32 bit mode. In 64 bit mode the situation is quite different, since in 64 bit programs the first 4 parameters have to be written with these 4 registers:
rcx, rdx, r8, r9 always in that specific order.)
 But even in 64 bit mode you can use the names of variables within the rectangular brackets instead. If you put a label in brackets rather than use rcx, then the second parameter has got to be in rdx, like before.

Invoke WriteFile probably will assume that the default folder is the folder which your running program is in. So if you don't specify the folder it should write the area of memory as a file, stored on the hard drive in the same folder as the running program. Unless you write a complete path and file name for the file name. The file can then be saved anywhere you want on the hard drive, or with a different drive letter it can be saved to another drive.
Next there should be:

invoke CloseHandle , [hcf]

The file should be closed as soon as you have finished with reading or writing it. It has only one parameter , which is the handle returned in eax by invoke CreateFile.
;=======================
Should you read a long file all at once , or in parts?
Invoke ReadFile uses an internal byte pointer which points to the file on the hard drive or in some other memory like a memory stick or a dvd. While a file is being loaded , the internal pointer moves along it.
If you read only part of the file , (because you made the length parameter too short) the internal pointer will be left pointing to the position in the file which is just beyond the last byte actually read. It points to the next byte to be read.
You can then call invoke ReadFile again , and again , each time reading part of the file until finally the whole file is read.

I think that with modern computers it is probably always possible to read long files in one go , but that very long ago the computer hard drives were less reliable , and it used to be necessary to read a really long file in bits at a time. This worked simply , and I did it.

I remember having a much older computer where the long files had to be read by turning round and round in a loop. Invoke ReadFile was run in every turn of the loop.
Every time a part of the file is read , the internal pointer is automatically moved by the right amount. But you must advance forward your own address pointer , which points to your RAM memory , by the amount that has been read.
So I wonder , should one always try to read long files in one go , or should you make the computer go round in a loop , with invoke ReadFile reading part of the file with every turn?

Each time a part of the file has been read you can keep track of how much by adding the returned "actual length" number to a length counting variable , if you want to.

I think that when the invoke ReadFile has been called many times , and at last it has read the whole file , it automatically zeros the "actual length" variable , and you can test for that to find out when the whole file has been read. This worked when I tried it in the example below.
Of course there is an alternative of obtaining the file length another way , but you probably don't need it , if you just test "actual length" for zero.

I tried the going around in a loop method of reading files , and just to be sure I made the amount of the file loaded in every turn very small. But it did work.
 Now the amount read , and the amount you move your pointer forward , obviously have to be the same number.

The following is an example of reading a file by going around in a loop. Each turn loads 10000 bytes. But normally, I suppose you would want to read at least 100K bytes in every turn. (invoke CreateFile has to come before this.)

```
  Mov edx , [pointing1]              ;The address to which the file should be loaded.
  Mov ecx , 300                      ;count down max turns in the loop , can be more
loop_reads:
  push ecx
  push edx
  invoke ReadFile , [hcf] , edx , 10000 , actual , 0
  pop edx
  pop ecx
  add edx , 1 0000
  cmp [actual] , 0
  jz Done1
  dec ecx
  jnz loop_reads
Done1:
  invoke CloseHandle , [hcf]
```

;==============

invoke WriteFile also has an automatic internal file pointer, like ReadFile.
In reality I think you can always write a file in one go. But perhaps some older computers have a limit to how much they can write in one go? I have not tested this question.

Below is an example of a similar looping experiment for Writing a file to the hard drive.
Normally the looping is not necessary. But this experiment did work.
(CreateFile has to come before it.)

```
  Mov edx , [pointing1]
  mov ecx , [save_length]
wr1:
  push ecx
  push edx
  cmp ecx , 10000
  jnb wr2
  invoke WriteFile , [hcf] , edx , ecx , actual , 0           ;one final time?
```

```
      jmp wr3

wr2:
   invoke WriteFile , [hcf] , edx , 10000 , actual , 0      ;repeats writing more of the file
wr3:
   pop edx
   pop ecx
   add edx , 10000                                          ;move your memory pointer forward
   sub ecx , 10000
   jb Done2
   jnz wr1
Done2:
   invoke CloseHandle , [hcf]
;======================
```

Asking the user for a file name.

This is a small part of a program which is tested and definitely works. I tried it with windows XP and windows 7.

The program should ask you to chose a file name for either loading or saving.
When you want to load a file you usually get the dialog box which asks you to look for the file name , or to type in the file name. That dialog box is created by the

invoke GetOpenFileName , ofn

This function obviously does some quite complicated things automatically. It does a lot of work automatically , and it was easy to use. And there is also

invoke GetSaveFileName , ofn

The letters "ofn" are the label of the OPENFILENAME data structure , and you always declare the existence of this data structure in the data section , usually with these two words ,

ofn OPENFILENAME

Your program has to fill in several parts of this data structure , before running invoke GetOpenFileName.

The most important two fields of the OPENFILENAME data structure were the pointer
to your "filter string", which in this example happens to have a label of szTextFilter in your data section.
 And there is a pointer to the important blank space, into which the user-chosen path and file name is automatically copied to.
In the example it happens to have the label "szTextPath", and the path and file name which will be copied into it will be used a moment later in running the "invoke CreateFile". These two fields were filled in with these instructions:

   mov [ofn.lpstrFilter] , szTextFilter
   mov [ofn.lpstrFile] , szTextPath

In these instructions, the part within brackets is case sensitive and has to be written exactly, as they are the names of fields in this data structure.
It's the flat assembler that wants these field names to be case sensitive, and the assembler checks it because it actually finds the specification of the OPENFILENAME structure in an include file.
On the right hand side, there are your labels in your data section, which can be written however you want.
The program creates the common dialog box which asks you the user to chose a file name.
In the example filter string here, a default file name extension is ".txt". And it gives the user a choice of looking for all files instead. Obviously you can change the default file name extension here to any other.

```
 section '.data' data readable writeable    ;This one line was the start line of the data section.
                                                             ;The filter string
  szTextFilter db "txt Files" , 0 , "*.txt" , 0 , "All Files" , 0 , "*.*" , 0 , 0    ;Ends in two zeros

  szTextPath rb MAX_PATH              ;The reserved space for full path and file name
  szDef  db ".txt" , 0                ; Default extension needs a full stop.
  ofn OPENFILENAME                    ;Declaring of the ofn data structure for the assembler
  save_file_signal db 0
```

Notice a filter string:

szTextFilter  db  "txt Files" , 0 , "*.txt" , 0 , "All Files" , 0 , "*.*" , 0 , 0

The sections of a filter string always have to be separated with one binary zero, whereas the whole filter string has to be ended by 2 binary zeroes together. This is unusual. Remember one binary zero to separate the parts, and two binary zeros to end it.

The special dialog box that asks you to chose a file name, has the main purpose of placing the path and file name which you chose into a small empty zone of memory which is going to be used for invoke CreateFile.

The word MAX_PATH is only a constant number with a value of 260 which the flat assembler finds automatically in the include file:

INCLUDE/EQUATES/KERNEL32.INC

MAX_PATH = 260

The assembler will automatically turn those words into the number 260. And you do not need to write the word, since you can write the number yourself. But it doesn't have to be 260, since a larger number would be equally OK. Declared in the data section of the program:

```
    szTextPath rb 260           ;The space to be filled with the chosen file's path and file name
```

Now the circumstances. In the code section of the program, the way I happened to call the program (for get save file name and save the file), was for it to be triggered by a mouse click on a menu item, and the click being detected in the procedure WindowProc.

(As usual, a way to detect the mouse click on a menu item is to find the constant WM_COMMAND in [mg.message] and then to find at the same time the Menu ID number in [msg.wParam].)
That detects a mouse click on a menu item.

As you create the menu you decide on what menu ID numbers you want. As the right menu ID number was detected, it could have made a call to the program which will save the file while inside the procedure called WindowProc.

And it would work equally well that way, but instead, in the case that it detected a menu click from inside WindowProc, it happened to set a number in a variable as a signal. The signal was then detected by my program as it went to run at the bottom of the message loop by this compare instruction:

```
    cmp byte [save_file_signal] , 2        ;2 used as a signal to save memory to a file
    jnz no7
    mov byte [save_file_signal] , 0        ;turn off the signal so it does not keep rerunning.
    call saving_text                       ;The call to save the memory area as a file
    jmp msg_loop                           ;back to the top of the message loop
```

;This is called to ask the user to chose a file name, and then to save an area of memory as a file.

```
saving_text:
    call ofn_structure      ;Call to fill in the OFN "open file name" data structure

  invoke GetSaveFileName , ofn            ;The operating system creates a dialog box to ask you
  cmp eax , 0                             ;to chose a file name , writes that into szTextPath.
  jz error1                               ;If there was an error, do not try to create the file

        invoke CreateFile , szTextPath , GENERIC_READ or GENERIC_WRITE , \
                    FILE_SHARE_READ or FILE_SHARE_WRITE , 0 , 2 , 20h , 0

    mov [hcf] , eax       ;Saving the handle to the file
    cmp eax , -1          ;Minus 1 is INVALID_HANDLE_VALUE
    jz error2

    mov ebx , [start_address1]          ;The address of memory to be saved as a file ,
    mov edx , [saves_length]            ;The length of data to be saved in bytes.
    mov dword [actual] , 0              ;erase actual length field

    mov esi , actual   ;(No brackets) pointer to where the actual length will be written

 ;;  ( invoke WriteFile , [hcf] , ebx , edx , esi , 0       ;Alternative. Writes the file.)

 invoke WriteFile , [hcf] , [start_address1] , [saves_length] , actual , 0       ;Writes the file.

    invoke CloseHandle , [hcf]                              ;You have to close the file

   mov ebx , [actual]                   ;The actual length was filled by invoke WriteFile
   ; cmp ebx , [saves_length]           ;Was the intended length saved?
   ; jnz error3
   ret

      error3:
         mov edx , words6
         jmp boxe
      error1:
         mov edx , _words7
```

```
        jmp boxe

    error2:
        mov edx , _words8                   ;I am Not sure the message box worked now
  boxe:
        invoke  MessageBoxA , [hCreatedWindow] , edx , _words9 , MB_OKCANCEL
        ret

  words6 db "Not right length" , 0
  _words7 db "no file name " , 0
  _words8 db " error no handle " , 0
  _words9 db "    " , 0
;------------------------------;ofn
  ofn_structure:                   ;You create the same structure for loads as for saves

  invoke RtlZeroMemory , ofn , sizeof.OPENFILENAME
  invoke RtlZeroMemory , szTextPath , MAX_PATH              ;Erases the area to zeros

  mov [ofn.lStructSize] , sizeof.OPENFILENAME
  mov eax , [hCreatedWindow]
  mov [ofn.hwndOwner] , eax
  mov [ofn.lpstrFilter] , szTextFilter
  mov [ofn.lpstrFile] ,  szTextPath
  mov [ofn.nMaxFile] , MAX_PATH
  mov eax , OFN_EXPLORER OR OFN_PATHMUSTEXIST OR OFN_HIDEREADONLY \
  OR OFN_OVERWRITEPROMPT

  ;;   OFN_EXPLORER might not be right?

  mov [ofn.Flags] , eax
  mov [ofn.lpstrDefExt] , szDef      ;szDef is a starting extension with a full stop
  ret
;==============================

  ;FILE_SHARE_WRITE == 02 ;;FILE_SHARE_READ = 01.
```

Notes: The flag you see in [ofn.Flags] called OFN_OVERWRITEPROMPT is interesting because it causes Windows to ask you whether you still want to save the file, when another file with the same file name already exists.
 It prompts you on whether you want to overwrite.
You see that usually in the data section of your program you have to declare the existence of the important OPENFILENAME data structure by once writing the two words:

ofn OPENFILENAME
These two words declare the data structure for the flat assembler.
Then the data structure had to be filled in. After filling it in, two invocations can use it,

invoke GetSaveFileName , ofn
or
invoke GetOpenFileName , ofn

You see the small label ofn will later be turned into the address of your ofn data structure, because when it assembles, the flat assembler converts the word ofn into the address of where that structure is.

These should both create the very common dialog box which you are very used to using with Windows. That is the kind of dialog box which asks you for a file name.
When you see this dialog box open up you normally type or look for a file name.
This should automatically fill the path and the file name into the area of data which in this example is labeled "szTextPath"  It Should fill in the area labeled as szTextPath with the chosen file name.
(I noticed that some people like to start these labels of strings of text with the letters "sz" though that's not necessary, the "s" stands for string, and the "z" is to remind you that the text string has to be ended with one binary zero.)


The "flat assembler" seems to automatically know all the fields of the data structure called OPENFILENAME, but really it gets the information from an INCLUDE file.
(The assembler always looks through include files when it assembles your program, to find information about constants and data structures.)

```
  cmp byte [save_file_signal] , 3   ;3=temporary signal to Read a file
  jnz no8
  mov byte [save_file_signal] , 0   ;turn off the signal stops rerunning.
  call load_text              ;This call asks you to type a file name and then loads files.
  jmp msg_loop
```

;==========================
load_text:
        call erasing                    ;this was there and erased the memory
        call ofn_structure            ;get_open_file_name_txt

    invoke GetOpenFileName , ofn     ;It asks the user for a file name.
    cmp eax , 0                   ;it should return 0 when any error. Does it?
    jz errord

 invoke CreateFile , szTextPath , GENERIC_READ , FILE_SHARE_READ , 0 , 3 , 20h , 0

                                     ;3=open existing for read ,
    mov [hcf] , eax              ;it should return only −1 when an error
    cmp ax , INVALID_HANDLE_VALUE     ;invalid = −1
    jz error

    mov ecx , 20000h           ;The length in bytes , or any greater length?
    mov esi , actual           ;place in which it writes an actual length number.
    mov dword [esi] , 0

    invoke ReadFile , [hcf] , [start_address1] , ecx , actual , 0
    invoke CloseHandle , [hcf]

    call length          ;A subroutine to find the length of text
    ret
returns:
    ret

The loading and saving in 64 bit mode programs.

This is a program which I wrote then tested and it definitely works.
 It asks the user for a file name , and then it saves a length of memory as a file with the chosen file name. It happened to be called in this way: A mouse click on a menu item was detected , it happened to be detected in WindowProc (but could instead have been detected from  somewhere else).
As the mouse click on a menu item was detected , it set a number in a signal variable , and then , the number was detected by a part of the program at the bottom of the message loop , triggering a call to the label 'saving_text:'.

Instead of setting any signal from WindowProc, it should work as well by detecting menu clicks from the message loop. To detect menu clicks from the message loop you should test [msg.message] for WM_COMMAND, and then test [msg.wParam] for a menu ID number.

The 64 bit program started like this at its top, for the Fasmw assembler,

```
format PE64    GUI 5.0              ;declare 64 bits. with Gui there was no black rectangle,
entry start

include 'win64a.inc'

section '.data' data readable writable              ;A data section begins

    szTextPath rb MAX_PATH
    szTextFilter db "TXT Files" , 0 , '.TXT' , 0 , "All Files" , 0 , "*.*" , 0 , 0

    szDef db ".TXT" , 0                ;This default 3 letter extension starts with a full stop

    ofn OPENFILENAME <>                ;declare the ofn data structure for the assembler
```

64 bit mode differed from 32 bit mode in two important ways:
Firstly in invoke functions, the first 4 parameters are supposed to be or have to be in these 4 registers, rcx, rdx, r8, r9, in that order. It often matters a lot that you use those 4 registers in the right order.

Secondly, in 64 bit mode, and using the Fasmw assembler, the lowest 4 binary bits of the stack pointer had to be 0000, or else the program might crash!

A call pushes the 8 byte instruction pointer, which changes the stack pointer, by 8.
(An 8 bytes push would change its lowest 4 binary bits from 0000 to 1000 in binary.)
And so, to make sure that the lower 4 binary bits of the stack pointer remain 0000, I added a push/pop of an 8 bytes register on either side of the "Call" instruction.
I don't know why but this stack pointer adjustment seemed to be essential when in 64 bit mode.

```
    cmp byte [save_file_signal] , 2              ;2=save drawing
    jnz no7
    mov byte [save_file_signal] , 0              ;turn off the signal so it does not keep rerunning.
```

```
        push rcx                    ;**** odd number of pushes before call to keep rsp bits 0-3 =0
        call saving_text
        pop rcx
        jmp msg_loop

saving_text:
        push rcx                    ;odd number of pushes before call to keep rsp bits 0-3 =0
        call ofn_structure
        pop rcx

    invoke GetSaveFileName , ofn
    cmp eax , 0
    jz error_1
    invoke CreateFile , szTextPath , GENERIC_READ or GENERIC_WRITE , \
              FILE_SHARE_READ or FILE_SHARE_WRITE , 0 , 2 , 20h , 0

    cmp eax , -1                ;minus 1 is error called INVALID_HANDLE_VALUE
    jz error_2
    mov [hcf] , rax             ;Must try rcx , rdx , r8 , r9 in that order

    mov rdx , [start_address1]
    mov r8 , [saves_length]
    mov dword [actual] , 0

      mov r9 , actual           ;[r9] * is a place in which the invoke writes an actual length.

    invoke WriteFile , [hcf] , rdx , r8 , r9 , 0
    invoke CloseHandle , [hcf]

    mov rbx , [actual]
;   cmp rbx , [saves_length]            ;Not necessary
;   jnz error_3
            ret

    error_1:;
        mov rdx , worda1                ;Not necessary
        jmp message_box
```

```
error_2:;
        mov rdx , worda2
        jmp message_box
error_3:;
        mov rdx , worda3
        jmp message_box

message_box:
    mov r8 , corner
    mov r9 , 0

    mov rcx , [hCreatedWindow]
    invoke MessageBoxA , rcx , rdx , r8 , r9          ;not necessary

    ret
worda1 db "No file name" , 0
worda2 db "No file creation" , 0
worda3 db "Not saved right length" , 0
worda4 db "Saved OK" , 0
corner db "Error" , 0
```

Filling in the data structure for get file name

```
ofn_structure:      ;64 bit working

mov edx , sizeof.OPENFILENAME
invoke RtlZeroMemory , ofn , edx
invoke RtlZeroMemory , szTextPath , MAX_PATH

    mov [ofn.lStructSize] , sizeof.OPENFILENAME
    mov rax , [hCreatedWindow]
    mov [ofn.hwndOwner] , rax
    mov [ofn.lpstrFilter] , szTextFilter
    mov [ofn.lpstrFile] , szTextPath
mov [ofn.nMaxFile] , MAX_PATH
mov eax , OFN_EXPLORER OR OFN_PATHMUSTEXIST \
```

    OR OFN_HIDEREADONLY OR OFN_OVERWRITEPROMPT

 mov [ofn.Flags] , eax
 mov [ofn.lpstrDefExt] , szDef
 ret


Loading a file in 64 bit mode:

This is a program I wrote which I tested and it worked.

It was called from the bottom of my message loop , and in order to make sure that the lowest 4 binary bits of the stack pointer remained 0000 , I added 1 push/pop of an 8 bytes register to either side of the "Call" operation. This is something which is only necessary in 64 bit mode.

Also in 64 bit mode , you have to remember that the first 4 parameters of any invoke function should be in these 4 registers: rcx , rdx , r8 , r9 , in that order , and in some functions that matters very much.

This happened to be the way it was called
 no7:
  cmp byte [save_file_signal] , 3   ;3=read drawing
  jnz no8
 mov byte [save_file_signal] , 0  ;turn off the signal so it does not keep rerunning.

 push rcx  ;**essential. odd numbered pushes before call to keep rsp bits 0-3 =0
 call load_text
 pop rcx
 jmp msg_loop

 load_text:  ;the call must have 1 push rcx either side of the call to make rsp ok
  call erasing
  push rcx  ;odd numbered pushes before call to keep rsp bits 0-3 =0
  call ofn_structure  ;Writing the structure , load/save use the same one.
  pop rcx

  invoke GetOpenFileName , ofn
  cmp eax , 0
   jz error1
   mov rcx , szTextPath
   invoke CreateFile , rcx , GENERIC_READ or GENERIC_WRITE , \
   FILE_SHARE_READ or FILE_SHARE_WRITE , 0 , 3 , 20h , 0

```
                                                    ;3=open existing for read.
            cmp eax , -1                            ;-1 is invalid handle value
            jz error2
            mov [hcf] , rax
            mov rdx , [start_address1]
            mov r8 , 20000h                         ;r8 = the length to be loaded
            mov r9 , actual                         ;[r9] is a place to write an actual length.
            mov dword [actual] , 0

            invoke ReadFile , [hcf] , rdx , r8 , r9 , 0    ;try rcx , rdx , r8 , r9 in that order
            invoke CloseHandle , [hcf]
            mov rbx , [actual]

            call length                             ;find length of loaded text
            ret
    error1:

    error2: ret


;------------------------
```

For proper detailed information about CreateFile, look on Google for [Windows API CreateFile]

The common combination of flags was written in words "GENERIC_READ OR GENERIC_WRITE"
GENERIC_READ  = 80000000h     (8 with 7 zeroes and h)
GENERIC_WRITE = 40000000h     (4 with 7 zeroes and h)
Since the numbers are so big it must be best to write these two flags as Words.
I have always used these two flags without understanding what they are for.

Another usual combination of flags is "FILE_SHARE_READ OR FILE_SHARE_WRITE"
The numeric value of FILE_SHARE_READ = 01 and of FILE_SHARE_WRITE = 02
So the common combination of the two flags can be written as the number 03.
The two flags should cause subsequent open file operations to succeed?
I did not try FILE_SHARE_DELETE = 04

I have used in my program the FILE_ATTRIBUTE_ARCHIVE flag. Its numeric value = 20h
I used the value 20h for reading and writing all normal text files.
For the same parameter , one can use instead , FILE_ATTRIBUTE_NORMAL = 80h.

I read "if dwShareMode = 0 then subsequent open operations fail unless handle is closed firstly."
The flags:         (with their numeric values)
CREATE_NEW        = 1        Means Create only if it does not exist yet , otherwise fail
CREATE_ALWAYS     = 2        Means create always so it overwrites files of the same name.
OPEN_EXISTING     = 3        Mean open only if it already exists , error if did not exist.
OPEN_ALWAYS       = 4        Means Open , or create the file if it is not already there.
TRUNCATE_EXISTING =5         Means decrease the file length to zero , which must erase it?

The Parameters of function invoke CreateFile ,  listed from left to right.
LPCSTR lpFileName                  Address pointing to file name , or to a path and file name
DWORD dwDesiredAccess     GENERIC_READ OR GENERIC_WRITE is most common desired access.
DWORD dwShareMode                          FILE_SHARE_READ OR FILE_SHARE_WRITE = 3 = common flags.

lpSecurityAttributes  =0          A long pointer , but I always made this Zero.
DWORD dwCreationDisposition      how to create , for example 3 = OPEN_EXISTING
DWORD dwFlagsAndAttributes       I made this FILE_ATTRIBUTE_ARCHIVE = 20h
HANDLE hTemplateFile  =0  a handle to a file with attributes to copy. Always made it 0

Note: When dwShareMode is Zero , the handle needs to be closed before next create file
Note: in dwFlagsAndAttributes there are Many other flags which I did not use

The effects of flags in the 5th parameter of invoke CreateFile

| The Flag | Its Number | The file existed | The file was not there |
| --- | --- | --- | --- |
| CREATE_ALWAYS | 2 | Truncates to zero | Creates |
| CREATE_NEW | 1 | Fails | Creates |
| OPEN_ALWAYS | 4 | Opens | Creates |
| OPEN_EXISTING | 3 | Opens | Fails |
| TRUNCATE_EXISTING | 5 | Truncates to zero | Fails |

    ;====================================

## Sending emails by Assembly language and SMTP

An experiment.

I wanted to find out how an assembly language program, just assembly, can send an email?

Emails are often sent by something called SMTP, which I think stands for Simple Mail Transfer Protocol. I wrote a program which has been able to send emails.

I read somewhere Microsoft approved of something called Mailkit, and something maybe better than it came before it? I have not tried to use these things yet, since what I wanted was to know about plain assembly language.

On the internet you can read about the specification of SMTP. This is the name of one of the documents which were interesting: RFC 5321 and RFC 2821.

I spent nearly 2 weeks looking up SMTP on the internet, and writing program experiments. It took me that long to create a program which can send an email, and I tested my program by sending lots of emails to myself. The emails were addressed to go to either my Gmail inbox, or to Hotmail or to my Yahoo.com inbox.

When I sent emails to my Gmail account, at first the emails went to my inbox in less than a second. And then it stopped working. And then later it started working again.

It was probably because the header section of emails is important. My header section is poor. Certain shapes of the header prevent the emails from being received by Gmail.

When I sent my email to Hotmail, it arrived instantly, but it usually went into the trash emails section, as it was considered Spam. The header section can determine whether it gets there at all, but Hotmail was different from Gmail. Then sometimes the emails only arrived after a few minutes.

When I send my email to my Yahoo account, it takes between 1 and 40 minutes for the email to arrive, and it immediately went into Spam. And when the Yahoo mail took so long to receive, it made me feel uneasy and wonder whether a human might have the job of inspecting faulty emails and deciding whether to let them pass into my spam?

A week later I tried sending emails to Yahoo again, and this time they went properly to my inbox, not to spam. I had changed the header section of the emails somehow.

I noticed that for Yahoo, emails went to my inbox only when the "From:" part of the header was absent. If the email to myself had any From: section at all, it made the email go to Spam.

I still do not know the right way of making an email header, and all the headers in my experiments might be wrong somewhere.

The experiment was interesting for its own sake, sending an email by pure assembly language, but not very practical. It wasn't practical because my test emails did not all reliably get there. Often they went into Spam, and this might be because I was only capable of using an old-fashioned kind of authentication.

My emails to myself as experiments were relayed through the server of a company called Twilio SendGrid. Your computer can instantly contact the SendGrid servers from any distance. And there is another similar company called Smtp2go, which you could try using.

Perhaps because people have used these companies to send advertising which was spam, Yahoo.com might be automatically suspicious of an email that is relayed through these companies? So the problem might not just be the header section of the emails.

SendGrid did not charge anything. I had to sign up and get a free user name and password. The user name and password had to be entered as two permanent lines in the computer program.

So in order to send emails with the following program, you have to get a user name and a password with SendGrid, and put the user name and the password into the program. As your computer contacts their server, it instantly checks the user name and password, but they don't charge money. They would only charge money if you sent thousands of emails.
You could try exactly the same thing with the Smtp2go company.

I did not know the meaning of the word authentication until I looked up SMTP.
Authentication seems to be proving that your identity is not false. I read that email companies such as Gmail and Yahoo, have made it much more difficult because of the fight against Spam, and to prevent Spam there are difficult and secret methods of authentication.

As I looked up SMTP on the internet, the first thing was finding a way to connect the computer to an 'Smtp server'. An Smtp server is a kind of software which can relay an email from your computer to an email inbox. When you look up 'Smtp servers' on Google you can find some examples of server addresses and then see if it's possible for your computer to connect with them.

An interesting thing is that your computer normally starts an electronic conversation with a distant server in an Smtp language. This is mostly simple, since there are only a small number of Smtp commands. You just need to send a few Smtp commands to the server, and then you receive immediately replies in English from the server.

That was the first thing my experiments did. The replies from the server are mostly in english language, and some things are easy to read.
Starting the electronic conversation with a server, I got the conversation to print on my screen in 2 different colors. There was a color for my output I sent sent to the server, and a different color for

the replies from the server.  The examples of conversations with a server which you find on the internet ,  start each line of text with C: for client ,  and S: for server ,  for clarity. But these letters are not actually in the electronic conversation.

 Replies from the server can include some useful English words when you make mistakes ,  so it looks as if at some stage in the design of the SMTP system somone wanted it to be easy for computer programmers and so they included things that could help computer programmers.

I had in my programs a line of text ending with a binary zero ,  which specified the name of the server. The binary zero marks the end of it.
 This line with the name of a server ,  is the only thing in the program which specifies which server you connect to. Trying to connect to a wrong server can crash the program since the computer gets stuck somewhere. Contacting a suitable server is almost instantaneous.

On Google I looked up "SMTP servers" and tried to find servers which do emails. What server should you connect to if you want to send an email?
I read on several websites that in order to get an Smtp server to relay your email ,  you have to prove your identity so the system can avoid Spam and avoid unwanted emails.
The process was called Authentication.

The oldest system of Authentication was simple ,  you just had to convert your user name and password to a code called base64 encoding ,  and send your encoded user name and password to the server. The server would then tell you that authentication was successful ,  and it would relay your email to an inbox.
The older system of authentication by servers is called 250-AUTH PLAIN and 250-AUTH LOGIN.
When you send a server an EHLO command ,  it replies to you by sending you a message in English , and when these words are in its reply ,  they are written in english in block capitals. The two are very similar and I have been using the one called LOGIN.
I tried the other one ,  and it worked as well ,  but was a bit more difficult.

Unfortunately because of the severe problems people have had of spam and unwellcome  emails , modern email companies like Hotmail and Yahoo ,  refuse absolutely to use AUTH LOGIN and instead they all use a much more difficult and complex method of authentication. One of them is TLS ,  which stands for Transport Layer Security.

I think that when you send emails through the SendGrid company's server ,  the system of authentication is automatically converted to TLS as it goes relayed from their server to the email company.

When you send them the EHLO command ,  the servers send back to you words including
250-STARTTLS which means the modern system of TLS can be used.

I have never tried the modern authentication, as it was obviously too difficult.

What it means is that unfortunately, the simple experiments of programming cannot use most servers, and cannot use the servers of Hotmail and Yahoo mail accounts. Since their servers use the TLS system which is much too difficult.

Instead of that, it is necessary to use an email relaying company like for example SendGrid, which still accepts the older system of authentication called LOGIN.

The email relaying company can relay your email to an inbox with Gmail or Hotmail or Yahoo. But it usually goes into the Spam section. The header which you give to your email has a strong effect, and perhaps some of my difficulties were caused by a poor header.

As my computer program starts the electronic conversation with a server, the first thing you need to do is take an input to find out whether the server is connected. Then you have to send the server the EHLO command.
The following is a list of the SMTP commands which I used in the experiment.
 EHLO
 HELO
 DATA
 RCPT TO:
 MAIL FROM:
 STARTTLS
 AUTH LOGIN
 NOOP
 QUIT

They are not case sensitive and can be written in lower case, or partly lower case, partly capital.

In general you can send to a server the SMTP commands by writing these commands in English, as a short string of text within quotes, ending with the numbers, 13, 10, 0 separated like that with commas. (Which stand for Carriage Return, Line Feed, Zero.)

SMTP commands themselves are not case sensitive, and can mix upper and lower case letters. But internet addresses are very case sensitive in this system. I read that you should be very careful of the case in your email address.
For example sending a DATA command I used this text string with a label to its left:

 data1 db "Data", 13, 10, 0                    ;The Data command for a server is in quotes.

You can send that command to the server using:

```
mov ecx ,7                          ;The length of the text in bytes going into the ecx register
mov edx ,  data1                    ;the address of the text going into the edx register
invoke send , [sock] , edx , ecx , 0    ;invoke send can send any command to a server.
```

Because you are supposed to include the exact length of the text, it is useful to have a subroutine which will automatically count out the length, going up to the binary zero at the end, and putting that length into ecx. Otherwise mistakes happen.

To read a message from a server, or read any information from a server, you can use this invocation:

```
invoke recv , [sock] , input_buffer , 200 , 0       ;'recv' tries to input 200 bytes
```

The place in which to read the input information could be declared as:

```
input_buffer rb 300
```

The length in function recv can be longer than the actual length, as in the example I asked for 200 bytes all the time, though a lot of the inputs were much shorter.

It's interesting that the actual sending and the actual receiving is so simple.

The EHLO command is like saying hello. It causes the servers to immediately return to you a hello message which included some lines of important information. You have to arrange an experiment so you can read this information on the screen. I noticed that to properly read it you must try to input at least 190 bytes , since something can go wrong if you try to input less.

The server information comes as lines separated with carriage return symbols , and so you have to use something sensitive to them like invoke DrawText to be able to see the information neatly lined up with the left hand edge. (The carriage return symbols have to somehow restart the text to the left edge.)

The important thing to look for on the screen is the number 250 then capitals words LOGIN.

If you can see LOGIN, then this means the server will accept authentication in the very old-fashioned form which consists of just a user name and a password encoded in the base64 encoding.

This is what I did while I tried out lots of server names. Separately from that, some sever names can cause a crash in the program, or make you wait a long time.

Almost all of the server names I tried used only the modern system of authentication which is too difficult. When you send them the EHLO command, they reply and their reply does not contain the word LOGIN.

But, the server of the SendGrid company, did send the word LOGIN. And that's why I decided to use it.

SendGrid company lets you sign up for a free account, and I am not sure but I don't think you have to pay anything. To set up your account, you create a user name and a password, and from then on the SendGrid servers will automatically accept the user name and password as authentication, and relay your emails to any inbox.

Obviously this is not really practical, it's simply interesting as a computer program.

I enjoyed that some of my emails got quickly to my Gmail inbox, and that the emails can get to the spam section of the Hotmail account. I notice that the way an email header is composed has an effect on whether the email gets there, and something you can work on is trying to improve the header.

The electronic conversation between your computer and a server was interesting.

You find on the internet many short examples of the electronic conversation, many of them simplified. In the examples on the internet they usually begin each line with the letters C: for client, and S: for server. You are the client. The letters C: and S: are not actually part of the conversation, they are to help make the examples clear.

Getting the computer ready.

To get ready for sending an email, several things are necessary. With the Fasmw assembler, there needs to be 2 extra lines in the 'import section' of the program, which is usually at the end of your program.

Where the import section declares library items, you need the line:

```
wsock32 , 'WSOCK32.DLL'
```

and you also need to add one line which is to load an include file like this:

```
include 'INCLUDE\API\WSOCK32.INC'
```

That is enough for the import section?

To start the emails program, I needed
somewhere in the data section of the program:

```
wsaData   WSADATA              ;this declares a data structure
sin       sockaddr_in <>       ;this declares another data structure , sockaddr


szServer db "smtp.sendgrid.net" , 0      ;The name of the server to connect to
```

```
sock dd 0                                      ;A variable to hold a socket specification.
input_buffer rb 400                            ;A space for the input data.
;------------------------------------------------
Send_an_email:                                 ;Call the program here

invoke RtlZeroMemory , wsaData , 50            ;erase the data structure.

invoke WSAStartup , 101h , wsaData             ;Startup Returns 0 when Successful in this case.
cmp eax , 0
jnz error

invoke socket , AF_INET , 1 , 0       ;Last parameter= Protocol, 0=service decides the protocol
  mov [sock] , eax                    ;save a handle which was called a socket specification?
  cmp eax , -1                        ;If an error, eax would be returned as number -1 ?
  jz error

invoke RtlZeroMemory , sin , sizeof.sockaddr_in    ;Erase the space for the data structure.
  mov [sin.sin_family] , AF_INET                   ;write a flag into the data structure.

invoke htons , 587             ;2525 ;465 ;25; The socket number. 587 was best.
mov [sin.sin_port] , ax        ;Write the returned value from htons into the data structure.

      invoke gethostbyname , szServer          ;Important: this finds a server.
      mov eax , [eax+12]           ;A pointer in eax and +12 reads a second pointer
      mov eax , [eax]              ;With the second pointer read a third pointer
      mov eax , [eax]              ;With the third pointer read the number

      mov [sin.sin_addr] , eax     ;Write into the data structure

invoke connect , [sock] , sin , sizeof.sockaddr_in   ; Connecting with a server.
      cmp eax , 0                                   ;A 0 means connected OK.
      jnz error                                     ;in this case zero is success
;----------------------------
```

This above code creates the connection with a server. It seems to work easily, and it forms a connection with a server hundreds of miles away. The only thing that decides on which server will be contacted, is the line with the label szServer, and most servers would reject my program. This is the line I used mainly for the server:

szServer db "smtp.sendgrid.net" , 0

When the connection with the server was made , the first thing to do was to take one input from the server, with "invoke recv". I happened to erase the buffer before input into it.

  invoke RtlZeroMemory , input_buffer , 190        ; ** 140 bytes was not enough to see clearly
  invoke recv , [sock] , input_buffer , 190 , 0           ;Input from a server

The second thing to do was to send to the server an "ehlo" command. To send the command I only needed "invoke send". This simple "invoke send" did all of the sending , for both commands and data. The edx register contained the address of the data to be sent , while the ecx register contained the length of the data in bytes.

  invoke send , [sock] , edx , ecx , 0

After sending commands , you need to input. The input was always received with simple

  invoke recv , [sock] , input_buffer , 190 , 0

And the first of the inputs was sometimes like this:

220 SG ESMTP service ready at ismtpd0001p1l0n1.sendgrid.net

The program grew into something more complicated, because I had to see everything sent and received on the screen, and it used "invoke DrawText" to show all of this on the screen.

The next command after sending "EHLO", was the "Auth Login" command to do authentication. (In the less secure way).
(This area of the program which does sending and receiving, was worked by loading into the edx register the address of whatever I wanted to send to the server. And then by doing my call "call send_then_receive."
This firstly sends using just

"invoke send , [sock] , address , length , 0" ,       and then it receives using just
"invoke recv , [sock] , address , length , 0".        The length field is actually a number.)

The program had to convert both my user name and my Sendgrid password into some code I think called "base64" encoding. In order to do that , I looked up the specification of the Base64 table , and made my program write that table in the memory. Then the table works in the program which does conversion to the base64 code. And then it sent the user name and the password in the encoded form with two more of call send_then_receive.

The server replies with "235 Authentication successful"
Next the program sends the commands for "MAIL FROM: my email address"
And the server replies with "250 Sender address accepted"
Then the program sends to the server "RCPT TO: receiver_email_address".
And the server replies with "250 recipient address accepted".

With two more call send_then_receive. Next the program sends the Data command, with one more call send_then_receive.
The server replies to DATA with "354 Continue".

From then on the program sends my email text. But using send only.
The program must not try to receive anything from the server until after the end of the email text data. I notice that if it tried to receive anything before signalling the end of the text data, it would go wrong.
The end of the email text data is normally signalled by a line containing absolutely nothing
but a "." a single full-stop, which must have the carriage return and line feed symbols on either side of it. Like this for example ,

fullstop db 13 , 10 , "." , 13 , 10 , 0

After sending all the email text, and ending it with the special full stop, another "receive" is needed. When it gets the full stop, the server replies with a message somewhat similar to this:
"250 OK queued on xbxbgsgshsgs" ;(The Queue as some Unreadable letters and numbers.)

Then the program sends the server a "QUIT" comand , with call send_then_receive , and it receives a message from the server which is
"221 See you later".
My message text was of varying lengths , and all the main text came out properly in my received emails. But my email headers were always in some way faulty , they made a big difference. What a pity most emails sent in this way go into Spam, or sometimes don't get to the inbox. It was nice when my Gmail inbox worked.

I added to the program an edit control window. And any text typed into the edit control window went to the email as body text. This works , but I will be showing below here only the email area of the program , this is not a complete program.

When you send the server your user name and password, and they are supposed to be in base64 code, the server sends you two lines of specific letters and numbers which are not readable but which are supposed to help you to check your program code for encoding into base 64 code.

These two lines of letters, are specifically what the exact words "Username:" with a colon, and "Password:" with a colon, should turn into when you turn them into the Base64 code.

334     VXNlcm5hbWU6     ;This is the exact word "Username:" turned into the code.
334     UGFzc3dvcmQ6     ; This is the word "Password:" in the code.

When you actually send your user name or your password, you must not add a colon to them. I don't know why they put a colon in this test. The purpose of this is to help you check that you are encoding right. It doesn't change.
And it was useful to check that the base64 encoding was working.

The following program is the experiment

## This is the complete program code of an Email experiment

Below here is a complete program experiment which can send emails. To get it working you need to set up a free account with an email company like Twilio SendGrid , or Smtp2Go , which relay emails without requiring the more modern types of authentication.

You need your user name and your password with the account you set up with SendGrid. And you have to enter your user name and your password as permanent part of the program, where I had entered mine.

The program has a menu which gave me a choice of sending emails to my own inboxes with Yahoo, or Hotmail, or Gmail.

The program creates two windows. You can type your email message in the smaller window on the right. But the header part of the email is fixed in the program itself. The header must have errors in it, and it should be changed to improve it.
On the larger window on the left, the program shows details of its automatic conversation with a server.

The server is contacted instantly with no trouble ever. But emails do not always go to the inbox, and if they get there, they often go to the spam section.

```
format PE                    ;*******************
entry start
include 'win32a.inc'   ;

section '.data' data readable writeable          ;Start of the data section

hInstance dd 0

_title db 'Window' , 0                           ;word appearing in top left
_class db 'normal' , 0
h_Edit_Window dd 0
window_address dd 0
_title2 db "space for email text" , 0
_edit db "EDIT" , 0
```

```
pointing1 dd 0
;------
h_menu1 dd 0
h_menu2 dd 0
h_menu3 dd 0

hDC dd 0
h_Window dd 0

h_font dd 0

T1 db " Exit" , 0
W1 db "End program" , 0                          ;500

T2 db " email   " , 0
W2 db " Hello server alone " , 0   ;
W3 db " Send an email to hotmail  " , 0          ;502
W4 db " Send an email to gmail  " , 0            ;503
W5 db " Send an email to Yahoo  " , 0            ;504
text_buffer db 1024 dup 20h

 rect RECT
;-=
 wc WNDCLASSEX
 msg MSG
  ;==================

section '.code' code readable writable executable        ;later remove "writable!"


;===========
  start:

        invoke  GetModuleHandle , 0       ;But it was working without get module handle
        mov [hInstance] , eax
        ;========================
        mov dword [wc.cbSize] , sizeof.WNDCLASSEX            ;size = 30h
        mov    [wc.hInstance] , eax
        invoke  LoadCursor , 0 , IDC_ARROW
```

```
    mov    [wc.hCursor] , eax
    mov [wc.style] , 0
    mov [wc.lpfnWndProc] , WindowProc
    mov [wc.cbClsExtra] , 0
    mov [wc.cbWndExtra] , 0
    mov [wc.hbrBackground] , COLOR_WINDOW+1          ;background +3=black +1=white
    mov [wc.lpszMenuName] , _class
    mov [wc.lpszClassName] , _class
    ;------------
    invoke  RegisterClassEx , wc   ;


    ;==============
    invoke CreateMenu                                ; several menu handles
    mov [h_menu1] , eax

    invoke CreateMenu
    mov [h_menu2] , eax
    invoke CreateMenu
    mov [h_menu3] , eax


;----------------------------------------------

    invoke AppendMenuA , [h_menu1] , MF_POPUP , [h_menu2] , T1        ;exit
    invoke AppendMenuA , [h_menu2] , 0 , 500 , W1                     ;End program
 ;--------
    invoke AppendMenuA , [h_menu1] , MF_POPUP , [h_menu3] , T2

    invoke AppendMenuA , [h_menu3] , 0 , 501 , W2        ;hello to the server alone
    invoke AppendMenuA , [h_menu3] , 0 , 502 , W3        ;send an email to hotmail
    invoke AppendMenuA , [h_menu3] , 0 , 503 , W4        ;send an email to gmail
    invoke AppendMenuA , [h_menu3] , 0 , 504 , W5        ;send an email to Yahoo
     ;---------------------------------------------
                                            ;Creates a normal window
     invoke  CreateWindowEx , 0 , _class , \
     _title , WS_OVERLAPPEDWINDOW or WS_VISIBLE , \ ;
     1 , 1 , 850 , 800 , 0 , [h_menu1] , 0 , 0

     mov [h_Window] , eax
```

```
        invoke ShowWindow , [h_Window] , SW_SHOWNORMAL
     ;=========================
        invoke GetDC , [h_Window]
        mov [hDC] , eax                          ;The word "edit" seen by the OS
     ;=============                              ;Creates an edit control window
        invoke  CreateWindowEx , 0 , _edit , \
        _title2 , ES_MULTILINE or ES_AUTOHSCROLL or ES_AUTOVSCROLL or \
        WS_OVERLAPPEDWINDOW or WS_VISIBLE , \ ;
        615 , 1 , 400 , 400 , 0 , [h_menu1] , 0 , 0 ;

        mov [h_Edit_Window] , eax

        invoke SetWindowLongA , [h_Edit_Window] , GWL_WNDPROC , WindowProc
        mov [window_address] , eax
;==================
    ;To allocate memory
        invoke GlobalAlloc , 0 , 1000000h
        mov [pointing1] , eax
        ;--------------
        call font_start  ;??


;======================

  msg_loop:

        invoke  GetMessage , msg , 0 , 0 , 0
        cmp     eax , 1
        jb      ending
        jne     msg_loop

        invoke  TranslateMessage , msg

        invoke  DispatchMessage , msg
        cmp word [msg.message] , WM_CHAR
        jnz no1

  no1:

        jmp    msg_loop
```

```
    ;======================

font_start:
    invoke CreateFont , 13 , 7 , 0 , 0 , 40 , 0 , 0 , 0 , 0 , \
            0 , 0 , 0 , 0 , \
            fontname                            ;address of fontname

    mov [h_font] , eax                          ;this mov makes text larger size font
    invoke SelectObject , [hDC] , eax

    invoke SetTextColor , [hDC] , 0ffffffh      ;white
invoke SetBkColor , [hDC] , 0101010h            ;grey **it was to set background colour
            ret

    fontname db "Verdana" , 0

 ;==================
proc WindowProc hwnd , wmsg , wparam , lparam

 cmp [msg.message] , WM_COMMAND         ;It means a menu item has been clicked on
 jnz .nocommand
 cmp dword [wparam] , 500       ;[wparam] and [msg.wParam] should be exactly the same
 jz .wmdestroy
 cmp dword [wparam] , 501
 jz .ehlo_server_n2
 cmp dword [wparam] , 502
 jz .send_hotmail
   cmp dword [wparam] , 503
 jz .send_gmail
   cmp dword [wparam] , 504
 jz .send_yahoo
  ;-------------
.nocommand:
    cmp     [wmsg] , WM_CHAR
    je      .char
    cmp     [wmsg] , WM_DESTROY
    je      .wmdestroy
.def:
```

```
.defwndproc:

    mov edx , [h_Edit_Window]       ;Go One or the other depending on which window handle.
    cmp edx , [hwnd]                ;For edit control windows , also needed SetWindowLongA
    jnz .def2
    invoke CallWindowProc , [window_address] , [hwnd] , [wmsg] , [wparam] , [lparam]
    ret

    .def2:                          ;;For normal windows , default message processing
       invoke  DefWindowProc , [hwnd] , [wmsg] , [wparam] , [lparam]

       ret

.ehlo_server_n2:    call only_hello_server
      ret

.char:
       mov eax , [wparam]
       cmp eax , 1bh                ;The Escape key
       jz .wmdestroy
       jmp .def

  .send_hotmail:

      mov dword [wparam] , 0
      call send_an_email_hotmail
      ret

.send_gmail:
      mov dword [wparam] , 0
      call send_an_email_gmail
      ret

.send_yahoo:
      mov dword [wparam] , 0
      call send_an_email_yahoo
      ret

.wmdestroy:
```

```
        invoke  PostQuitMessage , 0
        xor     eax , eax
        ret
    endp

;==============================

ending:
                invoke closesocket , [sock]
                invoke WSACleanup
                invoke GlobalFree , [pointing1]
                invoke DeleteObject , [h_font] ;
                invoke ReleaseDC , [h_Window] , [hDC]
                invoke FreeConsole
                invoke DestroyWindow , [h_Window]
                invoke DestroyWindow , [h_Edit_Window]
                invoke ExitProcess , 0

;================================

  input_buffer rb 800h

ehlo db "EHLO <danielrosenthal66@yahoo.com>" , 13 , 10 , 0
quit db "QUIT  " , 13 , 10 , 0
sock dd 0

wsaData  WSADATA                          ;immediately recognized.
rb 100h

  sin    sockaddr_in <>
  rb 100h

; invoke lstrcpyn , buff2 , buff , 20     ;this invoke can run should contain size ,  not 20
;  invoke lstrcmpi , buff2 , OK1          ;??? ;this invoke can run
  ;--------------------

  only_hello_server:                      ;Does nothing but send ehlo then quit to a server

        call start_connection_to_server
```

```
        cmp ax , "er"                          ; on error jump to cle2 exit
        jz cle2
        ;-----------------------------
        mov [Ycoordinate] , 4
        ;------------------ is it much better not to start with an recv in?

        call receive
        ;------------------
        mov edx , ehlo                  ;*The words get reflected back
        call  send_then_receive
        add [Ycoordinate] , 40          ;*reply from EHLO was nearly 140/
        ;------------------
        mov edx , quit
        call  send_then_receive

    cle2:
        invoke closesocket , [sock]
        invoke WSACleanup
        ret

start_connection_to_server:
        invoke RtlZeroMemory , wsaData , 50
        invoke WSAStartup , 101h , wsaData                ;Returns 0 when Successful ,
        cmp eax , 0
        jnz eo                  ;It suddenly worked when STREAM was replaced with 0.

        invoke socket , AF_INET , 0 , 0        ;; 0 , 0 and 1 , 0 both work ,  1=sock-stream
    ;;  invoke socket , AF_INET , 1 , 0        ;This also worked and might be better??
        mov [sock] , eax
        cmp eax , -1
        jz eo

        invoke RtlZeroMemory , sin , sizeof.sockaddr_in
        mov [sin.sin_family] , AF_INET
        invoke htons , 587                                ;2525;;465;25;587;465 tried
        mov [sin.sin_port] , ax

        invoke gethostbyname , szServer
        cmp eax , 0
```

```
        jz eo
        mov eax , [eax+12]              ;With a pointer+12 read another pointer
        mov eax , [eax]                 ;with the second pointer read a third pointer
        mov eax , [eax]                 ;with the third pointer read the wanted number
        mov [sin.sin_addr] , eax

        invoke connect , [sock] , sin , sizeof.sockaddr_in
        cmp eax , 0                     ;eax=0 when OK !
        jnz eo
        ret
 eo:    mov ax , "er"                   ; only test for ax= "er" for error when it returns.
        ret

send_an_email_hotmail:
        mov eax , MailToh
        mov [which_mail_to] , eax
        jmp se1

send_an_email_yahoo:
        mov eax , MailToYahoo
        mov [which_mail_to] , eax
        jmp se1

send_an_email_gmail:
        mov eax , MailTog
        mov [which_mail_to] , eax
se1:
        invoke BitBlt , [hDC] , 0 , 0 , 500 , 500 , [hDC] , 0 , 0 , WHITENESS

        call encoding64         ;this call encodes my SendGrid account user name and password
        call show_the_encoded   ;(My user name and password become base64 encoded)
        call copy_the_encoded   ;
        call start_connection_to_server
        cmp ax , "er"
        jz cle


        ;-----------------------------
        mov [Ycoordinate] , 25          ;Start the height of text on the screen (0=the top)
        ;-------------------
```

```asm
        call receive                    ;receive the first reply from the server , is necessary
;-------------------
        mov edx , ehlo                  ;send the EHLO command to a server
        call send_then_receive          ;**The text Data from EHLO could be even 200 bytes

;-------------------
        mov edx , auths1                ;Send the authentication command. Then receive
        call send_then_receive
;===============================
        mov edx , tosend                ;Send My Twilio Sendgrid login name
        call send_then_receive          ; then receive the server's reply

        mov edx , tosend2               ;Send my Sendgrid login password
        call send_then_receive          ; then receive the server's reply.
;--------------------------------
        mov edx , mail_from1            ;Send the "Mail from" command ,
        call send_then_receive          ;then receive server's reply

;--------------------------------
        mov edx , [which_mail_to]       ;Send the "RCPT To" command , with mail address
        call send_then_receive          ;This determines where the email is sent to.
;--------------------------------
        mov edx , data1                 ;Send The DATA command
        call send_then_receive          ;then receive the server's reply.

;-----------------------------------

    mov edx , header_from       ;Presence of a from: field caused yahoo to send to spam

;; mov edx , sub_
    call send_alone             ;Send only , must not try to receive.
;----------------
    mov edx , header_separator      ;a completely empty line separates header from text

   call send_alone2             ;Absolutely must not try to receive here
;----------------------------------

    call load_edits_text        ;Load text from an Edit control window.
; ;; mov edx , text_2;
```

```
        mov edx , text_buffer        ;point to text body which comes from the edit window
        call send_alone
        ;--------------------------------
    mov edx , fullstop2        ;send a full stop & carriage return and line feed either side of it.
    call send_then_receive          ;send and get the server's reply.
                                 ;;(A fullstop with no spaces is a sign to end the text.)
    ;--------------------------------
    mov edx , quit              ;send the Quit command.
    call  send_then_receive         ; receive the server's reply. It was "221 See you later".

 cle:
        invoke closesocket , [sock]       ;Close the socket necessary when finished
        invoke WSACleanup             ;this essential cleanup.
        ret
;==========================
  load_edits_text:           ;***This should get the main text from an edit control window.

    invoke GetWindowTextA , [h_Edit_Window] ,  text_buffer , 180       ;length 180??
        mov ebx , text_buffer                    ;eax=0 in error
        add ebx , eax           ;**Returned eax=length, not including terminating 0

        mov dword [ebx] , 0a0dh        ;CR/LF at end of text.
        ret


 ;----   Text lines which need to be sent to the server, or emails.


                        ; ;Do auth login then user name and password ,  in base64.
 Ycoordinate dd 0              ;screen Y coordinate
 auths1 db "AUTH LOGIN  " , 13 , 10 , 0
 rb 100
 mail_from1 db "MAIL FROM:<danielrosenthal66@yahoo.com>" , 13 , 10 , 0

 MailToh db "RCPT TO:<danielrosenthal@hotmail.co.uk>" , 13 , 10 , 0

 MailTog db "RCPT TO:danielrosenthal36@gmail.com " , 13 , 10 , 0

 MailToYahoo db "RCPT TO:<danielrosenthal66@yahoo.com>" , 13 , 10 , 0   ;Yahoo

 which_mail_to dd 0      ;This variable is for a choice of either hotmail or gmail or yahoo
```

```
    noop db "NOOP" , 13 , 10 , 0
    data1 db "DATA" , 13 , 10 , 0
    header_from db "From:         " , 13 , 10
    sub_    db "Subject:  Test to Yahoo    " , 13 , 10 , 0
    header_separator db 13 , 10 , 0            ;must not have a blank space character
 ;; ender db    13 , 10 , 0
 fullstop2 db 13 , 10 , "." , 13 , 10 , 0
    rb 100
                            ;; ;Needed a free account with a user name and password
    szServer db "smtp.sendgrid.net" , 0
;   szServer db "mail.smtp2go.com" , 0 , 0    ;*** different company ,  maybe like sendgrid?


;------------------------------
  lengths:
        push edx
        mov ecx , 1
  lenes:
        cmp byte [edx] , 0
        jz lened
        inc edx
        inc ecx
        cmp ecx , 5000
        jb lenes
  lened:
        dec ecx ;need
        jnz lin2
        inc ecx
   lin2:
        pop edx
        ret


;-----------------------------------------------------
    send_alone2:              ;* Sends only ,  does not show the sent text

        call lengths          ;Get text length in ecx
        cmp ecx , 0
        jnz rec1
        ret
```

```
rec1:
    invoke send , [sock] , edx , ecx , 0        ;** This sends to a server
    ret

send_alone:          ;*Shows the text it's about to send , and then sends it
    push edx
    call see_the_sent
    pop edx
    call lengths                    ;Get text length in ecx
    cmp ecx , 0
    jnz rec2
    ret
rec2:
    invoke send , [sock] , edx , ecx , 0        ;** This sends to a server
    ret

send_then_receive:
    push edx
    call see_the_sent
    pop edx
    call lengths
    cmp ecx , 0
    jnz rec3
    ret
 rec3:
    invoke send , [sock] , edx , ecx , 0        ;**This sends to a server
 receive:
    invoke RtlZeroMemory , input_buffer , 190       ;erases input_buffer
    invoke recv , [sock] , input_buffer , 190 , 0    ;** "recv" receives from server.
    mov ebx , input_buffer
    mov ecx , [Ycoordinate]                 ; DrawText is sensitive to no 13.
    push ebx
    mov [rect.top] , ecx
    invoke SetTextColor , [hDC] , 0101010h
    invoke SetBkColor , [hDC] , 0ffffffh
    mov [rect.bottom] , 900
    mov [rect.left] , 10
    mov [rect.right] , 400
    pop ebx
```

```
        invoke DrawText , [hDC] , ebx , -1 , rect , DT_NOCLIP

        call count_13_in_buffer_input_buffer        ;count 13=0dh
        add [Ycoordinate] , edx                     ;downward next row on screen.
                                        ;Want spacing to depend on number of 13's.
        ret

count_13_in_buffer_input_buffer:            ;call to count carriage returns after receiving
        mov esi , input_buffer              ;carriage returns counted to make a vertical space
        mov edx , 15
        mov ecx , 120
    nood1:
        cmp byte [esi] , 13                 ;count 13 = carriage return symbols
        jnz nood
        add edx , 15                        ;edx increased every carriage return.
    nood:
        inc esi
        dec ecx
        jnz nood1
        ret


        ;===============
    see_the_sent:                           ;call with texts address in edx
        push edx
        invoke RtlZeroMemory , input_buffer , 190
        pop edx

        mov ecx , 190
        mov ebx , input_buffer
    sees:
        mov al , [edx]                      ;copy what was sent to a buffer to view it.
        mov [ebx] , al
        inc ebx
        inc edx
        cmp al , 10
        jz stopc  ;??;//
        cmp al , 0
        jz stopc
        dec ecx
```

```asm
        jnz sees
stopc:
        mov ecx , [Ycoordinate]
        mov [rect.top] , ecx
        invoke SetTextColor , [hDC] , 010ffff00h      ;chose a different color for the sent
        invoke SetBkColor , [hDC] , 00eeeeeeh
        mov [rect.bottom] , 900
        mov [rect.left] , 10
        mov [rect.right] , 400
        mov edx , input_buffer
        invoke DrawText , [hDC] , edx , -1 , rect , DT_NOCLIP

        add [Ycoordinate] , 18
        ret
;===========================
write_table:                                    ;Write a table which works for translate to base 64
        mov esi , base64_alphabet
        mov al , "A"
fo1:
        mov [esi] , al
        inc al
        inc esi
        cmp al , "Z"
        jnz fo1
        mov [esi] , al
        inc esi

        mov al , "a"
fo2:
        mov [esi] , al
        inc al
        inc esi
        cmp al , "z"
        jnz fo2
        mov [esi] , al
        inc esi
        mov al , "0"
fo3:
```

```
        mov [esi] , al
        inc al
        inc esi
        cmp al , "9"
        jnz fo3
        mov [esi] , al
        inc esi
        mov byte [esi] , "+"
        mov byte [esi+1] , "/"
        ret

  base64_alphabet db 0            ;a space of exactly 100h bytes for the new table
    rb 100h
;--------
source db "my user name" , 0 , 0 ;************ Must be my sendgrid account user name
rb 200h
encoding_output rb 200h           ;space for output of encoded user name

source2 db "my password " , 0 , 0      ;*** make it my sendgrid account password

rb 200h
encoding_output2 rb 200h          ;space for output of encoded password

sourcelength dd 27
tosend rb 100h                    ;user name when prepared for sending
tosend2 rb 100h                   ;password when prepared for sending
dd 0
;; source3 db "Username:" , 0  ;correct smtp test , real name must not have a colon
;; source4 db "Password:" , 0   ;correct smtp test , real password has no colon

show_the_encoded:                 ;Only shows the 2 encoded  words on window
    mov ebx , encoding_output             ;user name
    mov ecx , 500
    call showit
    mov ebx , encoding_output2            ;password
    mov ecx , 530
    call showit
    ret
showit:
```

```
        push ebx                            ; DrawText is sensitive to 0dh.
        mov [rect.top] , ecx                ;Words height on the screen was in ecx
        invoke SetTextColor , [hDC] , 0101010h
        invoke SetBkColor , [hDC] , 0ffffffh
        mov [rect.bottom] , 900
        mov [rect.left] , 0600              ;at rect.left is the start of the check
        mov [rect.right] , 900
        pop ebx
        invoke DrawText , [hDC] , ebx , -1 , rect , DT_NOCLIP

        add [Ycoordinate] , 50              ;Move Y down on the screen.
        ret

copy_the_encoded:
        mov ebx , encoding_output
        mov esi , tosend                    ;tosend is ready to be sent to the server
        call ji1
        mov ebx , encoding_output2
        mov esi , tosend2                   ;tosend2 is ready to be sent to the server
        call ji1
        ret

    ji1:
        mov al , [ebx]                      ;The point of copying was to add the 0a0dh
        cmp al , 0
        jz ji2
        mov [esi] , al
        inc ebx
        inc esi
        jmp ji1
    ji2: mov dword [esi] , 0a0dh
        ret
;==========================
;One table of base 64 alphabet= binary 0=capital A , binary 26 is lower case a
;binary 52 is ascii 0 , binary 61=9; 62="+" and 63="/" simple regular.
;0-25 = A-Z , ; 26-51 = a-z ; 52-61 = ascii 0-9.
;other table for urls: 62 and 63 can be "-" and "_"
;Wiki: 3 bytes of 8 bits , are replaced with 4 bytes of 6 bits.
;its input must be considered binary side , output as 6 bit numbers which are letters.
```

```
encoding64:                        ;Call to here

  call write_table
  invoke RtlZeroMemory , encoding_output , 50
  invoke lstrlen , source
  mov [sourcelength] , eax
  mov esi , source
  mov edi , encoding_output         ;encoded user name used for sendgrid account

  call base64a
  invoke RtlZeroMemory , encoding_output2 , 50
  invoke lstrlen , source2
  mov [sourcelength] , eax
  mov esi , source2
  mov edi , encoding_output2        ;output2 is encoded sendgrid password
  call base64a
  ret

 base64a:                           ;call base64a encodes my user name and my password
  xor eax , eax
  cmp [sourcelength] , 1
  jnz by1
  mov al , [esi]                    ;source ptr esi +1
  inc esi
  mov ecx , 2
  mov edx , 3d3dh                   ;padding = 2 bytes
  sub [sourcelength] , 1
  jmp by3
  ;----------
by1:
  cmp [sourcelength] , 2
  jnz by2

  mov ax , [esi]                    ;source ptr esi +2
  add esi , 2
  mov ecx , 3                       ;bytes to output =3
  mov edx , 3dh                     ;padding = 1 byte
  sub [sourcelength] , 2
```

```asm
      jmp by3
  ;------------
  by2:
      mov eax , [esi]
      mov ecx , 4                    ;bytes to output =4
      xor edx , edx                  ;padding = 0 byte
      add esi , 3                    ;source ptr +3 (4-1)
      sub [sourcelength] , 3
  by3:
      xchg al , ah
      rol eax , 16
      xchg al , ah

  by4:
      push eax
      and eax , 0FC000000h           ;get the highest 6 bits
      rol eax , 6                    ; into AL
    ;=============
      add eax , base64_alphabet
      mov al , [eax]
  ;=================
      mov [edi] , al
      add edi , 1                    ;write AL to destination
      pop eax
      shl eax , 6
      dec ecx
      jnz by4
      cmp [sourcelength] , 0
      jnz base64a
      mov eax , edx                  ;add padding and null terminate
      mov [edi] , eax
      add edi , 4
      ret


  ;According to IANA's documentation , the PLAIN Authentication is defined in RFC 2245
  ;=======================


  section '.idata' import data readable writeable
```

```
library kernel32 , 'KERNEL32.DLL' , \
     user32 , 'USER32.DLL' , \
     gdi32 , 'GDI32.DLL' , \
     comctl32 , 'COMCTL32.DLL' , \
     winmm , 'WINMM.DLL' , \
     comdlg32 , 'COMDLG32.DLL' , \
     wininet32 , 'WININET.DLL' , \
     wsock32 , 'WSOCK32.DLL'

;------------------
   include 'INCLUDE\API\ADVAPI32.INC'
   include 'INCLUDE\API\COMCTL32.INC'
   include 'INCLUDE\API\COMDLG32.INC'
   include 'INCLUDE\API\GDI32.INC'
   include 'INCLUDE\API\KERNEL32.INC'
   include 'INCLUDE\API\SHELL32.INC'
   include 'INCLUDE\API\USER32.INC'
   include 'INCLUDE\API\WSOCK32.INC'
```

## About stop starts with animation

Preventing the program from freezing, and then restarting.

When I wrote programs to do a moving picture or animation , they often suddenly stopped moving and seemed to be stuck motionless after a only few seconds.
Then when that happens, if you move the mouse or if you press on any key, the program starts moving again for a second, but then stops again in a second.
This is a common thing, and I wondered how do you get the picture to keep moving? And another question, I thought if a computer program does a lot of processing, you can get an error called 'not responding'? The not responding error might be caused by you not running "invoke GetMessage" often enough? Because the operating system's message queue becomes over filled?

The stop-start rather than continual running is usually caused by the message loop.

invoke GetMessage , msg , 0 , 0 , 0

can block the flow of the computer by waiting, and not doing anything but waiting when there are no messages. How do you prevent an animation from freezing?

I think in the case of a program which has to do a lot of processing, one can use the

invoke PeekMessage , msg , 0 , 0 , 0 , 0

to find out whether there are any messages. Because it does not block the computer, and it should return quickly with eax=0 if there are no messages.
And then the computer can go to the message loop only when there is a message, and avoid going there when there isn't.
By avoiding the message loop at times when there are no messages, it is prevented from getting stuck motionless. It did solve the problem.

I found 3 different things which could make an animation keep moving.
They were:
    PeekMessage
    SetTimer
    InvalidateRect

Either of them is enough to make the program run continually. The function GetMessage very often caused the computer to wait for a message, and that blocks the running of the program until another message comes.

If you have set a timer, messages come regularly at the time intervals you have set. If you have not set a timer, they only come when you move the mouse or move the keyboard.
The function invoke GetMessage is absolutely necessary since the operating system
posts messages and it is essential for the program to remove them from the queue and read them.
Of these three ideas, SetTimer causes the lightest load on the processor. Apparently the processor does less work, and its temperature cools down.

## Peek Message

The idea of using invoke PeekMessage.
It can find out whether there are any new messages, without getting in the way of anything.
Also you can put it at the top of the message loop, just above the invoke GetMessage.
PeekMessage will not block the running of the program when there are
no messages.
Instead, PeekMessage should return immediately with eax=0 if there are
no messages.
You test for eax=zero, and when that has shown there are no messages then skip over invoke GetMessage. This means that
invoke GetMessage will never block the running of the program.
I was using PeekMessage like this to skip over GetMessage whenever there was no messages:

```
invoke PeekMessage , msg , 0 , 0 , 0 , 0
and eax , eax
jz skip_over
```

This lets the program run continuously. Notice the 4 zeros in it.
Its only disadvantage was that the processor works at maximum power.

I mean that when I used the free software called "Core Temp", I see that if the computer is continually running PeekMessage in a small loop, the processor starts running at higher power, and there is a rise of at least a few degrees centigrade in temperature.
I suppose that sometimes an older computer might overheat a little, perhaps as when they are old the cooling system is a bit dusty?
I only noticed that when I downloaded the free software called "Core Temp" for measuring the processor temperature, and continuously showing it to you.

## Set Timer

I tried "invoke SetTimer". The SetTimer was surprisingly easy to use and seems really useful because it worked so well.

It is interesting that SetTimer decreases the load on the processor, and it can lower the temperature of the processor by at least a few degrees.
You only need to set a timer once to get continuous regular calling of your program.
You set the timer one time specifying milliseconds, and over and over again the operating system calls whatever you want it to call.

That goes on until invoke KillTimer stops it, as it should do when the program ends.
If the last parameter of invoke SetTimer is zero, the zero specifically means that the operating system will call the special procedure WindowProc at the regular times.

 It calls WindowProc regularly from then on with a WM_TIMER
message in the field called [msg.message] , (and the same thing is in [wmsg]) and with any  timer  ID which you specify. This timer ID appears in [msg.wParam]. (and the same thing in [wparam].)

If the last Parameter of invoke SetTimer is not zero, that last parameter should be a label without brackets, meaning the address of a procedure which you want the operating system to call regularly , instead of WindowProc.
I was surprised at how easy it was to use that function,
the procedure which the operating system calls can be set up so easily, and it gives me no trouble which is surprising. I noticed that to create a small animated drawing, a timer time of
16 milliseconds seemed to work better than 15 milliseconds for some reason.

This is an example of SetTimer:

　invoke SetTimer , [h_Window] , 300 , 16 , 0

In that example I decided that the number 300 would be the message ID,  and that the timing would be every 16 milliseconds. The message ID can be any number you like.
At the right end the 0 means the operating system will call WindowProc. (Remember the address of WindowProc is given to the operating system when a new window is registered or created.)

In this next example of SetTimer, the operating system has to call regularly a procedure called Time.

　invoke SetTimer , [h_Window] , 300 , 16 , Time　　　;timer ID, milliseconds,  call proc Time

Setting up the procedure called Time was easy ,  this worked:

　proc Time　　a , b , c , d　　　　　　　　　　　;declare the start of a procedure
;　　cmp [msg.wParam] , 300　　　　　　　　　　　;*Unnecessary cmp
;　　jz re

```
;  ret
; re:
   call moving_drawing              ;call to any animation.
   ret                              ;end running in the procedure
   endp                             ;end the procedure with "endp"
```

A test for the message ID is absolutely unnecessary in this example as it works equally well without it. (You would need the ID only if more than one timer is set up at the same time).

Though the procedure Time could be more complicated I think that is not necessary. It worked when the upper line "proc Time" has either no parameters , or had 4 parameters.

If it had any parameters , the number of them had to be 4 , as a different number of parameters crashed the computer completely.  It must be safest to include 4 parameters. If I wrote them as

proc Time a , b , c , d

I did a test to find out what happens. A , b , c , d must be reserving 4 spaces on the stack, and when the procedure is called by the automatic timer , something should be in those spaces at offsets relative to the stack pointer. My test found that
a=[h_Window]
b=[msg.message]
c=[msg.wParam]
d=[msg.time]

Notice that "d" did not contain [msg.lParam] since it was [msg.time] instead.
I looked at [msg.time] and I saw in it a timing number which is running quickly.

When the program ends, the timer should be stopped with invoke KillTimer ,
which should have **both** a handle to the window and the timer ID which you have set.

   invoke KillTimer , [h_Window] , 300

In my program for example there was an animation on a device independent bitmap memory area (DIBSection). The Dibsection gives you direct access to all the pixels using any address register,  but the picture is not visible until you use "invoke BitBlt" to copy it to the visible window.

 And "invoke BitBlt" was used twice, the first time to erase the memory to blackness, and the second time invoke BitBlt ran, it copied the Dibsection memory to the visible window, which is so essential to make the picture visible.

It always uses 2 handles to device contexts in each case. It was only necessary to get the handles to device contexts a single time, at the time when the Dibsection was being created.

The direction of the copying depends only on these handles, the handle on the left is the destination, the handle on the right is the source. "Call drawing" was creating an animation.

The BLACKNESS flag is for erasing it. (There is also a WHITENESS flag when you want to erase the screen to white). Erasing worked if source and destination are the same.

Of course you can erase a Dibsection using an address register, to load zeros to make blackness, and so invoke BitBlt was just a slightly shorter way of erasing. Using an address register would be better ingeneral.

```
rectangle1:
    invoke BitBlt , [hdcMem] , 0 , 0 , 600 , 600 , [hdcMem] , 0 , 0 , BLACKNESS
    call drawing

    invoke BitBlt , [h_DC] , 0 , 0 , 600 , 600 , [hdcMem] , 0 , 0 , SRCCOPY      ;To visible screen.
    ret
```

The only problem with using invoke SetTimer was when I wanted to look at the Windows message structure MSG with a hexadecimal viewing of its numbers, because you mainly see the timer messages. The other messages are then hard to see, since timer messages keep coming so often. If you wished to study the other messages, the timer would need to be turned off for a while.

## InvalidateRect

I think invoke InvalidateRect, is a strange function which seemed to me hard to understand. This is not about how InvalidateRect is supposed to be used, not about the right way of using it, but something else, how it can be used to prevent an animation from freezing.

In a test I found that a single line like this:

 invoke InvalidateRect , [hWindow] , 0 , 0

If I put it near the bottom of the message loop, it prevented the animation from being stuck motionless.

It works if it is put in the message loop in such a way it runs whenever there is a WM_PAINT message, but it also seems to work if it runs whenever any message has come. The animation part of my program was called from the same place. This allowed the animating program to go on running. The problem was solved so simply in some cases but in other programs it was difficult and hard to get it working.

In theory InvalidateRect means that part of a window is "invalidated" which means it needs to be redrawn by the operating system, or by your program, and it means that the operating system posts a WM_PAINT message when the message queue is empty.

If you place "invoke InvalidateRect" in the message loop in such a way that it runs once each time there is a WM_PAINT message, then this sequence is self-perpetuating..

The self-perpetuating effect was what kept an animation going. And it only needs to be started off by one extra InvalidateRect placed somewhere above the start of the message loop, to be run before the computer drops into the message loop. Once started off, a single InvalidateRect at the bottom of the message loop will continue posting messages to itself. An animating program can be called from the message loop as well.

I tried InvalidateRect placed in such a way that whenever there actually is any message, it will run once. And I think that worked too.

If instead of placing it at the bottom of a message loop, it is placed somewhere in the procedure called WindowProc, then that sometimes worked, but I had trouble with it there as often it did not work there at all. It can cause some malfunction if it is put in WindowProc the wrong way.

Putting invoke InvalidateRect into WindowProc often went wrong, but the following way at the ending of WindowProc at least sometimes worked?

```
    invoke  DefWindowProc , [hwnd] , [wmsg] , [wparam] , [lparam]
    push eax
    invoke InvalidateRect , [h_Window] , 0 , 0
     pop eax
    ret
```

The value in "eax" when "ret" is reached , had to be conserved as it was important.

In WindowProc , whenever there is a WM_PAINT message , then the computer should always process it somehow , or at least run this function to process it (in WindowProc)

 invoke  DefWindowProc , [hwnd] , [wmsg] , [wparam] , [lparam]

Which is intended as a default way to process miscellaneous messages for you.

I read that in theory InvalidateRect causes the system to post a WM_PAINT message, but an unusual thing about the way it posts this message, was that this message is not posted or acted on until the message queue is empty of other messages.

Maybe that is useful by helping to make sure that it won't interfere with other things. Posting an unnecessary message regularly could interfere with other things , but invoke InvalidateRect should not get in the way of anything.

A WM_PAINT message can always be detected by

```
cmp [msg.message] , WM_PAINT
jz label
```
From anywhere else in the program. Or from inside WindowProc it could be detected by

```
cmp [wmsg] , WM_PAINT
jz label
```

You need to arrange for invoke InvalidateRect to run once when there is that message, and sometimes you should erase the field [msg.message] once your program has read it, so as to prevent an unwanted rerunning.
 I remember sometimes having trouble with it and it was better from the message loop.
 The result should be that messages keep coming and un-blocking invoke GetMessage , making the program keep moving.


### WaitMessage

I tried adding "invoke WaitMessage" to the message loop. It has no parameters.
Its main purpose is to stop your program at times when there are no messages , so it is very much blocking at times when the operating system does not post any messages such as keyboard or mouse messages.
It did not block the program at all while the animation was working with the Timer
which was started by invoke SetTimer.
Without the timer WaitMessage completely blocks everything when there are no messages. But it never blocks what the timer does.

WaitMessage has an effect of allowing the processor to work less hard , and sometimes you see the processor quickly lowering in temperature and cooling off.

I saw that with the free software called "Core temp" which shows temperature.
A typing program worked with WaitMessage in the message loop, when I arranged for the WaitMessage to only be running at times when you did not type on the keyboard for at least 10 seconds. After 10 seconds without typing anything , WaitMessage ran and the processor cooled down several degrees.
Though it normally completely blocks the program until there are messages, when invoke SetTimer had been used then WaitMessage did not block timer messages at all.
;=========================================

## Saving to the clipboard.

I did some experiments for saving on the clipboard, but I still don't know if the way I did it is the right way.
When my program had put text into the clipboard, edit-paste in a word processor recovered the text. And when my program had put a bitmap picture into the clipboard, edit-paste copied the image onto an Open Office page, plus paste-image also worked in the Fast Stone Image Viewer.

The Microsoft website was weird in saying that they had made the clipboard much more difficult than it should be. It should be extremely simple, but they have made the system strange.

Below is my three successful clipboard tests:

1) Text from an area of memory goes into the clipboard.
2) Text from the clipboard goes to an area of memory.
3) A color picture goes into the clipboard (from a Dibsection area of memory).

Text clipboard test. It worked for both directions, equivalent to copy and paste.
Program "32 typing one type of cursor Clipboard test 2 AL bit.asm"
I have checked that the code is working.

```
text_into_clip:                      ;Call Here to copy text into the clipboard.

    call get_clipboard_ready         ;essential, without it clipboard it can't repeat

    mov ecx, 200000                  ;ecx = max length of text being copied for clipboard.
    mov ebx, [pointing1]             ;*** the address of the text was [pointing1]
    mov esi, [pointing5]             ;area [pointing5] will become clipboard data

copy_text:
    mov al, [ebx]                    ;Maybe should test al for zero?
    mov [esi], al                    ;Copying the text to another area
    inc ebx
    inc esi
    dec ecx
    jnz copy_text
    mov word [esi], 0                ;One binary zero shows where the text ends.
```

```
        invoke OpenClipboard , [h_Window]              ;if it fails eax=0
        invoke SetClipboardData , CF_TEXT , [hMemory5]  ;eax becomes a handle ,

                                                        ;or eax=0 if it fails
        invoke CloseClipboard              ;It is Necessary to close the clipboard.
        ret
           ;----------This sequence was necessary to get clipboard working

get_clipboard_ready:
        pushad      ;
        invoke OpenClipboard , [h_Window]     ;These steps are all necessary
        invoke EmptyClipboard                 ;Empty clipboard is necessary
        invoke CloseClipboard
        mov ecx , [pointing5]
        cmp ecx , 0
        jz fi1
        invoke GlobalUnlock , [hMemory5]      ;Unlock did not do anything
        invoke GlobalFree , [hMemory5]        ;Free and then reallocate every time.
   fi1:
        invoke GlobalAlloc , 2 , 310000    ; 2=GMEM_MOVEABLE is used for clipboard
        mov [hMemory5] , eax               ;(With 200000 bytes or any length to be sent)
        invoke GlobalLock , eax            ;GlobalLock converts the handle into pointer.
        mov [pointing5] , eax
        popad
        ret

    pointing5 dd 0                            ;3 extra variables declared.
    hMemory5 dd 0
    hclip dd 0
;------------------------------------------
 This got text from the clipboard and copied it to an area of memory.


    from_clip:                                 ;Call it Here.  This was working

    invoke OpenClipboard , [h_Window]
    invoke GetClipboardData , CF_TEXT          ;It should return a handle in eax
```

```
        mov [hclip] , eax
                                    ;*** The return handle should never be freed or left locked.
        cmp eax , -1
        jz err_end
        invoke GlobalLock , eax                     ;gets a pointer in eax
        mov ebx , eax                               ;Pointer into ebx
        mov ecx , 200000                            ;ecx is the max length of the text
        mov esi , [pointing1]
        cmp ebx , 0
        jz err_end
copy_back:
        mov al , [ebx]              ;copy the text which came out of the clipboard
        mov [esi] , al
        inc ebx
        inc esi
        cmp al , 0                  ;* Test al for 0 prevented crashing of the program
        jz end_copying              ;without the test large ecx made it crash.
        dec ecx
        jnz copy_back
end_copying:
        invoke GlobalUnlock , [hclip]               ;'should not leave it locked'
err_end:                            ;Maybe GlobalUnlock did nothing with my computers??
        invoke CloseClipboard       ;
        ret
        ;=================
```

I don't know why, but every time I sent data to the clipboard it was necessary to de-allocate memory and then to re-allocate it. The de-allocation and then reallocation let the clipboard work over and over again. Whereas if I tried to avoid de-allocation, the clipboard would only work a single time and then stop working.

Above is the experiment with text going in and out of the clipboard.
I did a different experiment which put color pictures onto the clipboard, from a so-called Dibsection area of memory.

In this experiment I had drawn color pictures onto a so-called Dibsection memory. I had a system of drawing pictures roughly based on Mandelbrot. (Not shown here).
The Dibsection memory was created with "invoke CreateDIBSection" which automatically gives you the memory area and which then tells you its starting address.

(The Dibsection was where you have direct access to the color pixels as bytes in memory. There were 4 bytes for each pixel, one for red, one for green, and one for blue. The 4th byte seems unused. And the Dibsection is also called a back-screen while the visible window is a front-screen.)
I transferred to the clipboard one big area of memory, which was prepared to contain 2 things: firstly a bmi_header went exactly to the start of that area of memory, and then the Dibsection memory with all its pixels data went right after the headings.
This bmi_header is exactly the same as the one which you need when you use invoke CreateDIBSection, which creates the dibsection.
As the picture was put into the clipboard, word processors such as Open Office, can paste the pictures onto a paper page.

I mentioned a whole bmp heading, it includes the part which you don't need when sending to the clipboard. The heading of a picture file which has the file name extension .bmp, is of 2 parts stuck together as one, and in this particular case of sending pictures to the clipboard only the 2nd part of the whole header is written or at all used.
The first part is left out, and not written for the clipboard.

 If you're making a BMP picture file, then one way to write the header is firstly declaring the following two data structures, one following right after the other, so they are naturally combined.
 bmf_header    BITMAPFILEHEADER   ;Is 14 bytes long. And has 4 fields (checked)
 bmi_header    BITMAPINFOHEADER   ;Is about 40 bytes long. And has about 11 fields.

The first of these two, must not be used with the clipboard, you only include the bmi.
Only the second of these 2 parts needs to be written, either to create a Dibsection, or to send the image to the clipboard. I have confused this a bit by mentioning the 1st part which is only used when creating a BMP picture file.

 These declarations would just tell the assembler to reserve a really small memory space which is used for writing a header, and then you have to fill in its fields. The assembler then automatically looks for the specification of the header names and lengths in an include file, and the assembler produces error message if you use a wrong name for the fields. They are case sensitive.
The header, or in this case only the 2nd part of it, can be filled in using the names of the fields recognized by the assembler.
 Or instead a different way, the fields can be filled in using an address register with their offsets, if you have written down their offsets, on a piece of paper.

You need to have at the start of an area of memory the second header and then all the picture data.

 I confused something by writing both parts of the header. Some of my experiment happened to write the two parts of this header by calling the label "bmp", and then +14 was added to an

address to go on to copy the 2$^{nd}$ part only , onto the exact start of a memory area which was to be sent to the clipboard. (really it was not necessary to write the unused 1$^{st}$ part , as the 2 parts together are only necessary when you want to create a complete .BMP picture file.)
 The fields of the data structures can be filled in by several techniques , and there is an example of it somewhere else.

I have checked the code was working.

```
    Bmp_To_Clipboard:

        call get_clipboard_ready_2      ;A sequence to get the clipboard ready.
        call bmp                        ;call bmp wrote a bitmap header.
        mov ebx , [pointing1]           ;ebx reads the header
        add ebx , 14                    ;Skip over the unwanted 1st 14 bytes.
        mov esi , [pointing5]           ;memory for clipboard
        mov ecx , 40                    ;exact length of header to be copied
    copy_header:
            mov al , [ebx]
        mov [esi] , al
        inc ebx
        inc esi
        dec ecx
        jnz copy_header


        mov ebx , [BitmapMemoryAddress]     ;The address of my Dibsection.
        mov esi , [pointing5]
        add esi , 56                        ;+56 perfect colors , it affects color
        mov ecx , 1300*930*4                ;The length copied must not exceed allocated length

    copy_pixels:                            ;To copy all the pixels in the Dibsection or bitmap
            mov al , [ebx]
        mov [esi] , al
        inc ebx
        inc esi
        dec ecx
        jnz copy_pixels
```

```
        invoke OpenClipboard , [h_Window]

        invoke SetClipboardData , CF_DIB , [hMemory5]        ;Use flag  CF_DIB
        invoke CloseClipboard
        ret
```

;Note: the assembler finds the value of flag CF_DIB = 008   in the file Kernel32.inc
; To get the clipboard ready every time ,  it was essential to open/empty/close/deallocate memory
; And then re-allocate memory. All this sequence seems essential.
             ;---------------------------

```
  get_clipboard_ready_2:                          ; Essential to get the clipboard ready first.
        pushad      ;
        invoke OpenClipboard , [h_Window]
        invoke EmptyClipboard
        invoke CloseClipboard
        mov ecx , [pointing5]
        cmp ecx , 0
        jz fi12
        invoke GlobalUnlock , [pointing5]         ;Deallocate and then Reallocate.
        invoke GlobalFree , [hMemory5]     ;
  fi12:
        mov ecx , 1300*930*4                      ;Length in bytes = 1300 times 930 times 4
        add ecx , 80                                      ;And add a bit more
        invoke GlobalAlloc , 2 , ecx              ; 2 = GMEM_MOVEABLE  that is necessary.
        mov [hMemory5] , eax           ;
        invoke GlobalLock , eax                   ;convert handle into pointer.
        mov [pointing5] , eax
        popad
        ret
```

 The above test immediately copied a picture which I could see on the screen to the clipboard. And then I tested it and found that the picture could be pasted onto a word processor page ,  (Using Edit-Paste) ,  or onto an image with the Fast Stone image viewer. (Using Paste-image).
Though in this particular example the size of the Dibsection image was 1300*930 pixels ,  you have to adjust those numbers for different sizes of Dibsection images.

There is a question of whether one should use GlobalUnlock. Somewhere Microsoft said it should be used once for every GlobalLock. But whenever I tried out GlobalUnlock, it never seemed to do anything. I had tried GlobalUnlock with a handle and with a pointer, but it never did anything.

All the other steps were definitely necessary.
The whole sequence of first deallocating memory and then reallocating it, seems essential since without it the clipboard only worked once and then stopped working.
So the whole sequence of first deallocating and then reallocating might be essential?

Obviously Microsoft has made it complicated, and its complexity is quite wrong. Because what you want to achieve with a clipboard is so simple, they could have made the whole process very much simpler.

Below is the call bmp which I actually happened to use to write the BMF and BMI headers, though only the BMI header was used, and the BMF not used.
Of course the values for the size of the image in horizontal and vertical pixels, often needs to be changed.

The BMF header was at the start, and the BMI header was at offset +14
picture width in pixels was 1300, picture height in pixels was 930
When you use an asterisk, the assembler does a multiplication.

```
bmp:
    mov esi , [pointing1]  ;

        mov word [esi] , 4d42h                  ;The 2 letters "BM"
        mov dword [esi+2] , 1300*930*4 +54      ;File length , not necessary now
        mov dword [esi+6] , 0                   ;two reserved zeroes
        mov dword [esi+10] , 54                 ;size of both parts of header together

    ;------------------------ BMI = bitmapinfo
        mov dword [esi+14] , 40                 ;size of this bmi header in bytes = 40.
        mov dword [esi+18] , 1300               ;image width in pixels
        mov dword [esi+22] , 930                ;image height in pixels
        mov word [esi+26] , 1                   ;always fixed 1
        mov word [esi+28] , 32                  ;binary bits per pixel. 32 for me
        mov dword [esi+30] , 0                  ;zero for no compression

        mov dword [esi+34] , 1300*930*4         ;total data length
```

```
        mov [bitmap_length] , 1300*930*4          ;write the same length

        mov dword [esi+38] , 4000                 ;Not used now. Horiz Pixels/meter
        mov dword [esi+42] , 4000                 ;Not used now. V pixels/m?
        mov dword [esi+46] , 0                    ;always zero?
        mov dword [esi+50] , 0                    ;always zero
        ret
```

The alternative way of creating exactly the same BMF and BMI headers:

```
;------------------An alternative Declaring the data headers for the assembler.
  bmf_header    BITMAPFILEHEADER        ;14 bytes long.
  bmi_header    BITMAPINFOHEADER        ;40 bytes long. the bmi header alone is enough


;==========================
  ;*I think the assembler knows the structure from the file
   ;;     INCLUDE/EQUATES/GDI32.INC  ;there was no GDI64.

  whole_bmp_header:

;Unused first part

        mov [bmf_header.bfType] , "BM"
        mov [bmf_header.bfSize] , 1300*930*4+54         ;the file size
        mov [bmf_header.bfReserved1] , 0
        mov [bmf_header.bfReserved2] , 0
        mov [bmf_header.bfOffBits] , 54                 ;54 bytes long when both parts.
;----------------------------------------------------------------------
  bitmap_image_header:
        mov  [bmi_header.biSize] , sizeof.BITMAPINFOHEADER       ;=40
        mov  [bmi_header.biWidth] , 1300

        mov  [bmi_header.biHeight] , 930
        mov  [bmi_header.biPlanes] , 1                  ;planes always 1
        mov  [bmi_header.biBitCount] , 32               ;bits per pixel is 32
        mov  [bmi_header.biCompression] , 0             ;Flag BI_RGB=00
```

```
    mov  [bmi_header.biSizeImage] , 1300*930*4+40
    mov  [bmi_header.biXPelsPerMeter] , 4000
    mov  [bmi_header.biYPelsPerMeter] , 4000
    mov  [bmi_header.biClrUsed] , 0
    mov  [bmi_header.biClrImportant] , 0
         ;----------------
    mov [bitmap_length] , 1300*930*4            ;essential to save the length here
    ret
```

;===============================

## Something about edit controls.

A window in which you can automatically type something was called an Edit Control.
I am sorry that some of this writing might be unclear.
In the examples I have seen of Edit controls, it was made into a child window, and it was stuck onto the normal window. I did not know that method and have tried something different, which is not necessarily right.

You create a window so that it becomes an edit control, and then if you have clicked on the window so that the focus is on it, as soon as you type anything the typing appears in the window.
So the edit control is a window in which typing works automatically.

When the typing is not automatic, then of course you can arrange for typing to work in some other way.
One way was to use invoke TextOut, but this works faultily and flickers a lot if you try to draw many lines at once. Another way that was more interesting, was to create a character pixels table and draw all the alphabetical characters onto a bitmap memory (a DIBSection memory). You have to write a subroutine which draws the letters pixel by pixel.

The subroutine goes through a turn of a loop for each horizontal row of pixels in one character, starting at the top left corner of a character, scanned left to right and then downward. It goes through a larger loop once for each complete character. And the higher routine calls the subroutine over and over, once to draw every letter, counting down the rows of text, and resetting itself to the left edge of the screen when it reads a carriage return symbol. Clutter may have to be erased too by erasing what's left of the text row. One advantage of this, was that it is then very easy to create a flashing typing cursor.

Instead of all that which is rather complicated, an edit control window does typing automatically. What is it that causes the new window to be an edit control?

It is that the Windows Operating system recognizes the text word "edit" at the moment when it is creating the window. When it detects the word "edit" when it creates the window, then it makes it an edit control.

So somewhere in the data section of your program, you need to write something like this

    _edit db "edit" , 0            ;The Windows operating system sees this word "Edit"

Any label on the left, and the two letters db, and in quotes the word "edit" and then a comma and a binary zero to show where it ends. The operating system should recognize the word "edit" in it.

Then at the moment when you create the window with 'invoke CreateWindowEx' , you include your label which points to the text word "Edit" as the second parameter (2$^{nd}$ from left to right).
In this example the label _edit would be the second parameter from left to right.

When invoke CreateWindowEx creates the new window , it will be an edit control , and you should see typing working in it automatically.

But I noticed that unfortunately , the edit control window had at first lost the ability to receive normal Windows messages , and it had lost the ability to have a working menu.

So I thought I had to find out how to give back to the window the ability to have a working menu and to receive normal messages.
This is done with a new function

  invoke SetWindowLong , [h_Edit_Window] , GWL_WNDPROC , WindowProc
   mov [lpWindProc] , eax


This was for 32 bit mode programs.
For 64 bit programs , it worked with a slightly different function

  invoke SetWindowLongPtr , [h_Edit_Window] , GWL_WNDPROC , WindowProc
   mov [lpWindProc] , rax


You notice that with 64 bit programs there should be the extra 3 letters Ptr. (In the function name.) Together with this one extra function , there has to be another extra function inside the special procedure which is usually called WindowProc. The extra function is:

  invoke CallWindowProc , [lpfnWndProc] , [hwnd] , [wmsg] , [wparam] , [lparam]
   ret

If you don't have this new function (running inside WindowProc) , there may be difficulties in creating the windows and the whole process of creating a window would be faulty.

And there has to be a test , a nessesary test with a compare instruction in WindowProc , to test whether the windows message is coming for the edit control or coming for your normal window. (Assuming that messages from both windows go to WindowProc).

Whenever a message was coming for or from the edit control , then this function

i
 invoke CallWindowProc , [lpfnWndProc] , [hwnd] , [wmsg] , [wparam] , [lparam]
has to run. It has 5 parameters. If the message was for an ordinary window ,  then only this function

invoke  DefWindowProc ,  [hwnd] ,  [wmsg] ,  [wparam] ,  [lparam]

should run. And it is very important. It has 4 parameters. So one or the other must run.
Therefore there should be a test which compares a window handle to the field [hwnd] ,  and the test decides which one to run. (Assumes that WindowProc always has a field called [hwnd])

The procedure WindowProc is usually started by this top line:

proc WindowProc hwnd , wmsg , wparam , lparam

Whenever the procedure WindowProc is called ,  its field [hwnd] does contain the same number as the message field [msg.hwnd] and it should be the handle of the window involved with the message.

While its field [wmsg] should contain the message type ,  identical to [msg.message].
So lower down I am giving an example of the test which should decide which of these two functions has to run ,  by comparing [hwnd] to [h_Edit_Window] or to [h_Window] the handles.
(They are the handles to the windows ,  which you must have saved when the windows were created.)
;---------------------
A normal non-edit control window does not do typing automatically ,  but of course you can arrange for typing to happen in an ordinary window.

When you have made an edit control window two functions are often used to copy the text you are seeing to an area of plain memory ,  but there is also a way to get direct access to the text.
The two invocations which are necessary to copy the text in an edit control to an area of plain memory ,  are these:

invoke SetWindowTextA , [h_Edit_Window] , [pointing1]

 invoke GetWindowTextA , [h_Edit_Window] , [pointing1] , 50

SetWindowTextA works in direction of memory to edit control. It has 2 parameters.
GetWindowTextA works in direction of edit control to memory. It has 3 parameters.

You give them the handle to the edit control window, and you give them the address of the area of memory. When the direction is to the memory, you also give it a length in bytes as a 3$^{rd}$ parameter. In the above example that was 50 bytes.

You see that in the other direction there is no length parameter. I think there is no length parameter because a binary zero must be used to signal the end of the text.

When I tried it, the invoke SetWindowTextA copied the text from memory into the edit control, up to the first binary zero. So binary zero stops it.

You just use an address to the memory area, which can be just a string of text or a buffer area in the data section of the program, or which can be a long allocated area of memory, for example.
;--------------------

There is a second and different method of getting access to the text inside an edit control.

```
    edit_point:                          ;It Got a pointer to edit window text.

    invoke SendMessage , [h_Edit_Window] , EM_GETHANDLE , 0 , 0
    mov [handle] , eax         ;
    invoke LocalLock , eax               ;LocalLock turns a handle into a pointer.
    mov [pointer] , eax                  ;the pointer was working.
    mov ebx , eax              ;



    unlo:
    invoke LocalUnlock , [handle]        ;Unlock after you have finished using it.
    ret
```

The pointer obtained by invoke LocalLock, is an address of the edit control window's real text. When this pointer is loaded into an address register, such as ebx, you can use it to read and write bytes of memory into the edit control.

Mov dword [ebx+100] , "ABCD"

For example, wrote the letters "ABCD" into the edit control, at a position of 100 characters beyond its start. But I noticed that often,
the letters written into the edit control, were not visible instantly unless I ran

invoke InvalidateRect , [h_Edit_Window] , 0 , 0

which sometimes caused the letters written into the edit control to become visible right away.

Invoke InvalidateRect had this effect even though I had not written anything in the procedure WindowProc which would be used to detect a WM_PAINT message, it worked without that.

Even with that, the letters ABCD did not become visible when I wrote them beyond the active limit of where text filled the edit control.

I did some experiments. An edit control seems to start out with a really small area of memory, and you increase this area either gradually by typing into it, or by using invoke SetWindowTextA, which can load a lot of text into the edit control and increase its area immediately.

I was afraid that writing beyond the edit control's filled area with the direct address pointer, might crash the program. It sometimes did, but not always? Direct access beyond the edit control's filled area might be a bad idea. Obviously it's better to use invoke SetWindowTextA, instead because that properly expands the area.

However, I think with an address register only the writing which goes into the edit control's active area becomes visible on its window, and writing with an address register beyond that did not show up.

I tried a test of filling an allocated area of memory with lots of ascii blanks (number 20h), and a regular repeating pattern of carriage return and line feeds, and then using "invoke SetWindowTextA" to copy it all to the edit window. It worked, but some carriage return symbols with line feeds were essential.

I think if there was a carriage return symbol 0dh on its own, that crashed the program. The two symbols 0a0dh together in that order were Ok and they worked as a carriage return, to start the next line of text. (0a0dh is combined carriage return and line feed)

Before using the pointer, do a test to make sure it's not zero.

;----------------

About creating the edit control kind of window.

When you create a window with invoke CreateWindowEx, one of the parameters that you write in this invocation, the second parameter from left to right, should be the address of a short string of text which ends in a binary zero.

And this short string of text has to be the class name for creating the new window.

The so-called "class name". (In the second parameter of the function you use the label of this short string of text, without brackets, and the flat assembler converts the label, without brackets, into the address of where it is located in the data section of your program.)

The Windows operating system looks at this text when it creates the new window, and if it does not recognize the words then it creates an ordinary window. If it sees the word 'generic' it also creates an ordinary window.

But if it sees certain special words, it creates something else instead of creating a normal window. To see a list of those key words which create something else you can look up Microsoft's website with a Google search for "windows api CreateWindowEx".

If the operating system sees the word "edit", then it creates an edit control window, and typing can then be done in the window automatically.
 For example you might put in the data section of the program

class1 db "generic" , 0
edit_class db "edit" , 0

And you may then write without brackets the label edit_class as the second parameter of the invoke CreateWindowEx.
I have got the impression that Microsoft wants you to create the edit control as a secondary window. And you would have a normal window as well.
In an example program that came with the assembler, the edit control was made into a child window stuck onto the surface of an ordinary window. I hope that's not the only right way to do it.
I kept trying to make the edit control as much like a normal window as possible.

I wanted my edit control to have a working menu, and then managed to do that. I made two windows both edit controls, and I also made one normal window and one edit control. And I did an experiment to create an extra edit control when a certain key is pressed. That also worked.

When a window of the kind called edit control is created, it has at first lost the ability to receive messages. I mean that when the mouse is moved over it, or the focus is on it and you do any typing, or whenever the menu items are clicked on, the window should receive messages, which should go to WindowProc. But at first the window called an edit control has lost the ability to get those messages.

To explain how you give those messages back to it.
Next is an example of how you can create an edit control type of window. Before this runs you have to first register a window class, as a normal window.

That is when you create edit controls you register a normal window class before you create the edit window. I did not register an edit class, but just normal class. If you register as an edit class, nothing works at all.

;===============
 _class db 'normal window' , 0
  _edit db 'EDIT' , 0

```
;=========

    invoke  CreateWindowEx , 0 , _edit , _title , WS_VISIBLE or WS_OVERLAPPEDWINDOW , \
                   100 , 10 , 600 , 500 , 0 , [h_menu1] , [wc.hInstance] , NULL

     mov [h_Edit_Window] , eax
     invoke SetWindowLong , [h_Edit_Window] , GWL_WNDPROC ,  WindowProc
     mov [lpWindProc] , eax
;===============
```

Not shown in the above example ,  you firstly register a normal class (register a normal non-edit class). And then if you want a menu ,  run invoke CreateMenu at least once to obtain a menu handle saved into [h_menu1].

 You see the label _edit in the second parameter from left to right ,  the Fasmw assembler converts this label into an address ,  (because it is not in brackets) the address is pointing to the short text in your data section:   _edit db "EDIT" , 0

Just after creating the edit control window the important thing is the invoke SetWindowLong ,  which needs to have the flag   GWL_WNDPROC  and which is also given as its last parameter the address of WindowProc.

Invoke SetWindowLong returns with an important number in the eax register. You are supposed to save this number in a variable named [lpWindProc] ,  as you see. (It's supposed to be a long pointer to WindowProc.)

SetWindowLong is one of two invocations which are necessary to give the new edit control window the ability to receive messages and to work as a normal window.

Next inside the procedure WindowProc you need the function invoke CallWindowProc ,  something just like this:

  invoke CallWindowProc , [lpWindProc] , [hwnd] , [wmsg] , [wparam] , [lparam]
  ret

You need to place this in such a way that whenever a windows message arrives specifically for the edit control window ,  then this invoke CallWindowProc is going to run. I always put this at the end of WindowProc as its last operation before returning with ret. And I noticed invoke CallWindowProc puts something important into the eax register that should be in eax register when the computer reaches the "ret" operation.

But whenever the message was not specifically for the edit control window ,  then invoke CallWindowProc must not run.

Instead whenever a message is not specifically for the edit control, it has to be passed on to the invoke DefWindowProc which can be written just like this.

invoke DefWindowProc , [hwnd] , [wmsg] , [wparam] , [lparam]

Normally, whenever the procedure WindowProc runs, and there is any message which you yourself are not quite sure what to do with, then it is always important to pass that message to invoke DefWindowProc for processing.

DefWindowProc causes the Windows operating system to do default processing of the message, and is essential for different things including the creation of a new window, and mouse-drag to change size of a window.

So normally when you write the procedure WindowProc you have to make sure that invoke DefWindowProc is going to run whenever you are not quite sure what to do with a message.
This remains true when you create an edit control, except that messages which were specifically intended for the edit control window must not be passed to invoke DefWindowProc, they should be passed to invoke CallWindowProc instead.

And so you need to run a simple test to make the computer decide which of these two invocations to run. A simple test can determine whether a message was specifially for an edit control or not.

As an example of the simple test used to decide which invocation to run.
This following example is for 2 windows when one window is a Normal window and the second window is an edit control. [hwnd] addresses the handle field "hwnd" which you see in the top row of WindowProc. And [hCreatedWindow2] is the handle of the edit control window.

The start of the WindowProc procedure was this line:

proc WindowProc  hwnd , wmsg , wparam , lparam


                                    ;;Near the end of the WindowProc procedure ,
  .def:
      mov eax , [hwnd]
      cmp eax , [h_Edit_Window]
      jz .lps

      invoke  DefWindowProc , [hwnd] , [wmsg] , [wparam] , [lparam]

```
    ret

.lps:
   invoke CallWindowProc , [lpfnWndProc] , [hwnd] , [wmsg] , [wparam] , [lparam]

    ret                      ;;(Note at this "ret" the value in the eax register is important.)
```

This example just above here, was for a program experiment in which there was two windows, a Normal window, plus an edit control. Whenever WindowProc is called with a message which is specifically for a certain window , the handle of that window always is found in [hwnd]. You notice that in the test [hwnd] is loaded into eax to be compared to a window handle , or sometimes several windows handles. As the comparing operation

```
mov eax , [hwnd]
cmp eax , [h_Edit_Window]
jz
```

compares [hwnd] to the handle of the second window, which is an edit control , the test finds out whether the message was specifically for that window, and then jumps to run invoke CallWindowProc if it was for the edit control window.
Many messages were for the first window, which was not an edit control, and then it
must run invoke DefWindowProc.
The Windows operating system calls WindowProc several times while it is in the middle of the process of creating a new window, and when that is happening it must also run the invoke DefWindowProc, that's important.

( Assume hwnd is the window handle field in the top row of the start of WindowProc , and [hwnd] addresses it.)
In another experiment I made 2 windows which were both edit controls, and that worked with a slightly diffrent test and jump. Where both windows were edit controls, operating system calls to WindowProc during the actual process of creating a new window needed to be passed as usual to invoke DefWindowProc, and in that moment [hwnd] was not equal to either of the 2 edit window handles.

In another experiment I arranged so that pressing on the b key caused a third window to be created. It worked with similar testing of [hwnd], but testing for 3 windows handles. All three windows seemed to be working well, they all had a working system menu. And they could all be re-sized with a mouse drag at their edges.

So it seems I found the secret of making an edit control work like a normal window with messages and with a working menu.

;=============

This next example is if 2 windows are Both edit controls. It lets the computer run invoke DefWindowProc, at the moments when the operating system is in the middle of the process of creating a new window. That is sometimes necessary, but it turns out this is not always necessary. Put this somewhere at the end of WindowProc.

```
.defwndproc:                                  ;[hwnd] is in the 1st line of WindowProc.
    mov eax , [hwnd]
    cmp eax , [h_Editwindow1]                 ;This assumes 2 windows are both edit controls.
    jz .second
    cmp eax , [h_Editwindow2]
    jz .second
.def:
    invoke  DefWindowProc , [hwnd] , [wmsg] , [wparam] , [lparam]       ;Default processing

    ret
.second:

    invoke CallWindowProc , [lpWindProc] , [hwnd] , [wmsg] , [wparam] , [lparam]

    ret
```

;==================

The above example assumed that 2 windows are both edit controls. When one of the windows is not an edit control, you need to make sure that whenever [hwnd] is equal to that window's handle, then the computer will only go to invoke DefWindowProc.

In these tests I used a single WindowProc procedure which would be shared by several windows, but I read in some tutorials that you are really supposed to create a different WindowProc for each different window. The

```
invoke SetWindowLong , [hwindow] , GWL_WNDPROC ,  WindowProc
mov [lpWindProc] , eax
```

The SetWindowLong gives you a chance to make it work with a second procedure of the same type as WindowProc, but a procedure for the second window. Maybe you could make a copy of your procedure WindowProc, give that copy a slightly different name and give it different labels, and then pass its address to the invoke SetWindowLong in its 3rd parameter.

This example is to create a Normal window. If its class name is Not "edit", the operating system creates a normal window.
(The Windows operating system looks at, and sees the class name automatically.)
But not shown here, before creating the first window you need to register a normal class, (not an edit class) and you need to run invoke CreateMenu and save a menu handle to [hpopmenu1]
;========================

```
            invoke CreateWindowEx , 0 , \
                    _class , \
                  _title , \
                WS_OVERLAPPEDWINDOW or WS_VISIBLE , \
                20 , 20 , 500 , 500 , \
                0 , [hpopmenu1] , \
                [hInstance] , NULL            ;hInstance or 0 works
     mov   [hCreatedWindow] , eax


;============ Somewhere at the end of WindowProc.
  .defwndproc:
      mov eax , [hwnd]
      cmp eax , [hCreatedWindow]               ;The Normal window
      jz .def2
      cmp eax , [h_Edit_Window]                ;The edit control type of window
      jz .fin
    .def2:
      invoke  DefWindowProc , [hwnd] , [wmsg] , [wparam] , [lparam]
       ret
  .fin:
     invoke CallWindowProc , [lpfnWndProc] , [hwnd] , [wmsg] , [wparam] , [lparam]  ;

            ;;NOTE When it reaches ret , it has to have an untouched eax
      ret
```
;=============
This should create a second window as an edit control.
Preferably a program bit like this to create a second window should be called from near the beginning of the program. Or if it is going to run later on when something triggers the creation of a second window, call it from the end of the message loop, or somewhere unconnected to WindowProc.

The code for creating a second window should Not be placed inside WindowProc, since that can sometimes cause a recursive endless loop because the operating system calls WindowProc many times while it is in the middle of the process of creating a new window.

Assuming that it is used to create an edit control, CreateWindowEx should have these flags in its flags parameter

ES_MULTILINE or ES_AUTOHSCROLL or ES_AUTOVSCROLL which are all necessary for edit controls to work well in typing.

```
.second_window:
  cmp [h_Edit_Window] , 0
  jnz .rets

      invoke CreateWindowEx , 0 , \
              edit_class , \
               _title , \
              WS_OVERLAPPEDWINDOW or WS_VISIBLE or \
              ES_AUTOVSCROLL or ES_AUTOHSCROLL or \
              ES_MULTILINE , \
              400 , 20 , 500 , 500 , \
              0 , [hpopmenu1] , \
              [hInstance] , NULL        ;hInstance or 0 both work

      mov [h_Edit_Window] , eax
      invoke ShowWindow , [h_Edit_Window] , SW_SHOWNORMAL

      invoke SetWindowLong , [h_Edit_Window] , GWL_WNDPROC , WindowProc  ;essential
      mov [lpfnWndProc] , eax
  .rets:
      ret


edit_class db "edit" , 0           ;The word "edit" is seen by the operating system
_class db "generic" , 0
```

# Sound Waves and the Riff Header

I have done some experimenting with a method of creating and playing a sound track.
My first thought was that sound waves are called sine waves, and so if you make a number follow a sine wave, as the sine wave goes up and down, that value can be written into a sound track as a sound sample. The up and down of numbers following the sine wave should turn into a sound wave.

Most computers now have in them 2 or 3 different kinds of floating point coprocessors at the same time. I have programmed only the older type of floating point coprocessor.

Its instructions all start with the letter "f". It is easy to use it, except for a single fault in design, which I think is that when the register at the bottom of the floating point stack gets "lost" by a push, it should first be "empty". The register at the bottom of the floating point stack is always called st7. If it is lost while it's not empty, the unit malfunctions. But instructions which pop the stack, and also the instruction ffree st7, are able to mark st7 as "empty". Which prevents the problems.

The floating point unit finds the sines of angles, with a single instruction "fsin". And as well as loading floating point numbers, it can also load up integer numbers, converting them automatically into floating point numbers while it loads them.
Its outputs can easily be either integer numbers or floating point numbers, depending on whether the letter "i" is included in the instruction.

Whenever its output is an integer, everything below the decimal point is lost.
 So when you want to keep the information which is below the decimal point, it must first be multiplied by a large constant before being saved as an integer.
A multiplication raises the information to be above the decimal point, so it won't disappear.

When its outputs are in floating point form you have a choice of 3 different sizes for a floating number, 4 byte, 8 byte or 10 bytes sizes. Only the 4 byte size was used as sound samples. The 8 byte size was often used in calculations.

When you want to play sounds with the computer, I think using "invoke PlaySound" is the simplest way, it is so easy.
The whole process of writing a sound track and playing it is quite easy. But I did not make music, as that should be more difficult.

When you want to play a sound you always need to write a Riff header in the memory, and then write or copy all the sound data to the memory starting just beyond the end of the Riff header.
I am writing the specification of the Riff header lower down.

You have a Riff header with the sound data following it, and this can be played with invoke PlaySound.

But if you save this whole area of memory as a file, and give it a file a name extension of ".wav", it becomes a wav file and Windows media player can play it.

Since these sound files are not compressed, it doesn't play for very long. I timed that a 14 megabytes .wav file played for 1 minute with Windows media player.

## Sound using the floating point unit.

The program has filled the empty sound track with sine waves and played it as sounds.

Theoretically if you use a waveform that is not sine wave then it is a complex mixture of many sine waves. The displacement of any steadily vibrating object is called simple harmonic motion, and that is where the acceleration is always toward the center and is always directly proportional to the distance from the center. A sine and a cosine is like that.

A calculation of either sines or cosines with a steady increase of angle in each step can be used to fill a sound track. You have a number which you call an angle, and you steadily increase the angle in every step, and in every step calculate the sine of the angle with "fsin" and write that as a sound sample.

A proper sound track which has a RIFF header can be made from integer numbers or from floating point numbers. You have a choice.

Of course integers are the simple numbers that do not have a decimal point.

The floating point numbers all have decimal points and in this case they were of the 4 bytes form.

The Windows operating system can play either form of a sound track.

The integer form of the sound track was made from 2 bytes numbers as sound samples, a sample for the left ear, a sample for the right ear, again a sample for the left ear, and so on alternating. In this integer form the numbers were of 2 byte size, of values up to about 32000. Since 32767 is the maximum signed number which can fit in 2 bytes.

In the floating point form of a sound track, the numbers were all 4 bytes, but the numbers were all below a value of 1, with the important information all below the decimal point. Its range is usually plus 1 to minus 1, exactly like the range of plain sines and cosines. (Sometimes the range of up to +4 to -4 can also work).

So in the floating point form of sound track and sound samples, all the information is often below the decimal point. It can play like that, using the same invoke PlaySound.

When the sound track is played into headphones, each number called a sample, which the computer reads, should get converted instantly into a voltage of electricity in the headphones, or a speaker.

Each sound sample is just like the instant measurement of voltage which you would get if you were digitizing sound by measuring the voltage every twenty thousandth of a second or so and then writing it into a track.

A .WAV file begins with the RIFF header and it has a file name extension of .wav

Saving a playable sound track as a .wav file was quite easy , since you only need to save the whole area of memory as a file , beginning with the first byte of the RIFF header , which should be there anyway.

(I think Riff stands for Resource Interchange File Format.) The sound track data starting just beyond the end of this header.

So a Riff header has two purposes , it's either used to be able to play a sound that's in the memory , or it's necessary to create a .wav file , and in both cases the arrangement in memory is exactly the same.

My RIFF headers were in 2 different forms , depending on whether the data just beyond them is in integer form or in floating point form.

The method used to write the RIFF header , was to write down on paper the names of its fields , and the offsets of every field. The offset in the header is the address of the field relative to the start of the header (which is also the exact start of the .wav file).
And then to fill in the fields with the necessary numbers , and with 4 words in text which are necessary , in 4 fields for some reason.
If you don't understand all the fields you can try filling them in anyway.
I found the system works even if you don't understand the use of some fields.

Note the Windows operating system automatically checks for mistakes. And it makes silence if it detects any inconsistency.
A few of the fields involve calculations. They are not difficult. Just try to write a RIFF header , and it should work.

A riff header has a field in it for the sound sample rate in 'samples per second'.
In actual reality USB headsets are extremely sensitive to the exact rate of data which is sent to them , however , the Windows operating system separates you from the fact.
And when your program plays the sound track you notice that the samples per second field hardly affects quality , if it's roughly in the area of 20000 to 40000 , and hardly does anything except to affect the pitch you hear.

There are some meaningful fields in the riff header, and some of the fields can be fixed values which simplifies filling in the header. It's not difficult.

;===============

A bit more about using the floating point coprocessor to write in a sound track.
You increase an angle steadily and gradually, and with every increase in the angle you use the instruction fsin to find its sine. The sine is then suitable to be directly written into any floating point sound track, as a sound sample.

But the integer sound track is different. Most of the sine is of course in tiny fractions which are digits way below the decimal point. And since a number which is below the decimal point is all lost whenever it is converted from floating point form to integers form, then the numbers always have to be multiplied by a larger constant, an amplitude number, to bring it to be all above the decimal point. (I mean if you are writing an integer sound track). And after a multiplication it can be saved converted to integer for the sound data.

The sine of any angle has a maximum value of plus 1 to minus 1.
This is exactly the range which is used in a floating point sound track, but to create an integer sound track the sine of the angle has to be multiplied by an amplitude of sound, that may be a fixed number. You simply multiply the sines by an amplitude, and then write the result into the integer sound track.

Immediately the sine of an angle multiplied by an amplitude becomes an integer sound sample.
An address register writes the samples. When you are writing a 2 bytes number for each ear for stereo sound track, you write two samples and then just add +4 to the address register which is writing into the sound track, as each pair of sound samples is added.

The integer form of samples can be + and − numbers, which means that the maximum loudness or amplitude is approximately 32,000. Plus or minus. So 32,000 is an absolute maximum, and the sum of sounds should always add up to be a bit below it.

For example if you wanted to add 10 different sounds to the same sound track, then as you add the 10 sounds using "add", the maximum amount by which each "sine" can be multiplied, would then be only about 3,200. (Since 32,000 divided by 10 is 3,200.)

Assuming that 10 different sounds are to be added together on top of each other, the max amplitude of each, has to be a tenth the absolute maximum amplitude which is about 32,000.
As a 2 bytes number is added and by accident it goes above that 32,000 an overflow flag gets set.

It is sometimes important to test for overflow, with a conditional relative jump like "jno" for example which tests for overflow, ("jno label" means jump when no overflow. "Jo label" would mean jump if there is an overflow.)

And if overflow occurs one should not add anything more to the sound track.
Where there is some overflows, I hear a scratching noise. With a lot of overflow the scratching noise gets loud and it is really bad.

It's different if the RIFF header says the sound samples are going to be as floating point numbers.
In the floating point case you don't have to multiply the sine by a loudness value.
In the floating points, you actually have to divide the sines by some constant depending on how many sounds you are adding to the sound track on top of each other.
For instance I think that if you were adding together 10 different sounds you would need to divide all the sines by 10, just before adding them to the sound track.

I noticed that sometimes floating point sound samples can go in the range of +4 to -4, maximum, but sometimes the maximum range might be only +1 to -1. I don't know what affects that?

The floating point angles are all in Radians, which means that 180 degrees is the same thing as Pi Radians. A Radian is an angle where the arc traced out is the same length as the radius. The angle is steadily increased each time the operation fsin runs to make the sine of the angle, and it should then sound like a single pure frequency.

The lower the changes of angle between getting its sine and writing the sines as samples, the lower the frequency of the sound.
The amount of angle change in between the sound samples, is the main thing which affects the frequency of the sound.
Of course the greater the angle change in between your writing of sound samples, the higher the frequency.

The absolute maximum frequency you can make is 180 degrees per sample, which is really Pi Radians per every sample. 180 degrees is Pi radians. A Radian is the angle which traces an arc with an equal length to the radius.
Also, the absolute maximum frequency you can make is Half of the samples per second number, in the Riff header.
It seems that since at lower frequencies there is a much greater number of sound samples per 360 degrees, you might have a finer control of frequency when the frequencies are lower. I don't really understand that very clearly?

As any sound starts and then stops, the starting and stopping of its volume or loudness needs to be tapered gradually, at least to some extent.

And this is because of a theory that when loudness changes very suddenly it is an exact equivalent of a combination of many frequencies , rather than one frequency which you want.

And the theory must be right , since you do hear that as a click sound. And a tapering of loudness when the sound starts or stops avoids the click sound. The loudness at the start and at the end of a sound should be tapered rather than being very sudden , to avoid making a click sound.


;================================


One thing that was difficult was trying to make sounds seem musical. The best I could do was to use random numbers and keep trying different ways of using the random numbers until the sound was not unpleasant to hear. I did manage to make some sounds which sounded pleasant.

In some experiments there was a loud noise caused by an error. Any loud unpleasant noise must mean there's an error.

Mixing harmonics together did not on its own create an interesting sound , but it was sometimes interesting to use random numbers , then hear sounds with a complicated random pattern.

I tried the theory that notes contain harmonics , as a base frequency , with twice that , three times that , four times that , so on , combined together. When sounds which have those harmonics are turned on and off in a random pattern it can sometimes form a musical sound for a moment by chance.

Instead of always calculating the sine with fsin , one can create a sine wave table.

And then reading numbers from the table works instead of calculating them. This is a different technique which is faster. I actually tried that firstly.

In the case that I used a sine wave table , combinations of harmonic frequencies worked better or sounded a bit better than in the case when I used the floating point calculation fsin in every step. I have no idea why since it should have sounded the same.

Nearly random data from the memory somewhere can be used to decide on frequency , mixture of frequencies , length of sound , and speed of tapering loudness , and timing of when each sound starts.

Something which surprised me was that the rise and fall rate of the volume or loudness makes as big a difference to what one hears as the mixture of frequencies does.


Playing sound from the sound track can be done with a single function:

invoke PlaySound , [address] , 0 , 5

Turning off sound and making silence can be done with:

invoke PlaySound , 0 , 0 , 5

Its address field should point to the start of the riff header , (all the sound track data is just beyond the header.)

You notice the last 2 parameters were always zero and 5. The 5 is two flags.

The first step was for the program to ask the operating system to allocate a large enough area of memory. There has to be enough allocated memory for the sound track , and in one particular program I got the memory this way:

    invoke GlobalAlloc , 0 , 24000000        ;asks for 24 megabytes RAM

    mov [pointing2] , eax        ;save the address of the memory.

That was quite easy , and assuming that the address of the memory area is the number in [pointing2] , and that the sound track is already filled , I used this short program to write the riff header and then play the sound:

```
playing:
    call riff                              ;Call which writes the riff header
    invoke waveOutSetVolume , 0 , 0ffffffffh   ;set maximum volume
    mov ecx , [pointing2]
    invoke PlaySound , ecx , 0 , 5         ;Two flags SND_MEMORY OR SND_ASYNC = 5
        ret
```

Invoke PlaySound returns immediately and the operating system plays the sound for a length of time after that , which depends on the riff header. PlaySound has 3 parameters in it.
It returns immediately because it has the flag SND_ASYNC in the 3rd parameter.

It plays a sound that is in the memory , (rather than a sound that's in a file) because it also has the flag SND_MEMORY in its 3rd parameter. The two flags combined together are simply the number 5. Invoke PlaySound crashes the computer unless the allocated memory area is greater than the length specified in the riff header. You have to be sure that you have got enough memory allocated firstly. If the memory allocated is not long enough the computer will crash. In this example 24 megabytes was enough. The Windows operating system allows you to get much more memory than that.

```nasm
wav_file_header:    ;An example of a RIFF header for Integer sound that was working.


riff:
 mov esi , [pointing2]              ;address of memory area for both header and data.
 mov dword [esi] , "RIFF"           ;The words "RIFF" in capitals
;--------------------------
 mov eax , 015000000                ;Playsound crashes unless allocated area above this length
 sub eax , 8
 mov dword [esi+4] , eax            ;Write the file length minus 8 at offset +04.(8=chunk size)
;--------------------------
 mov dword [esi+8] , "WAVE"         ;The word "WAVE" in capitals
;--------------------------
 mov dword [esi+0Ch] , "fmt "       ;lower case word "fmt " with a blank space essential
;--------------------------
 mov dword [esi+10h] , 10h          ;format chunk size always 10h
 mov word [esi+14h] , 1             ;1=integers with no compression
 mov word [esi+16h] , 2             ;1= mono 2= stereo
;--------------------------
 mov ecx , 32000                    ;samples per second rate specified
 mov dword [esi+18h] , ecx          ;samples per second
 add ecx , ecx                      ;sample rate times 2 because 2 bytes per sample
 add ecx , ecx                      ;times 2 again because it is stereo
 mov dword [esi+1ch] , ecx          ;Bytes per second data rate = 4*32000
;--------------------------
 mov word [esi+20h] , 4      ;;;1= 8 bits mono , 2=16 bit mono or 8 bit stereo , 4=16 bit stereo

 mov word [esi+22h] , 16            ; binary bits per sample = 16
;--------------------------
 mov dword [esi+24h] , "data"       ;The word "data" in lower case
;--------------
 add eax , 8                        ;eax is file length again?
 sub eax , 44                       ;file length minus 44
 mov dword [esi+28h] , eax          ;Write file length minus 44 into offset +28h

;-------- at +2ch data starts.    (2Ch is 44 in decimal)
```

ret

The actual sound samples data can begin anywhere just beyond the RIFF header, as long as it is aligned by making the lowest 2 binary bits of starting addresses zero.

The arrangement of sound samples is actually really simple.
It was a 2 byte sample for the left ear which alternates with a 2 byte sample for the right ear, since the header specifies 16 bit stereo.

Samples per second has to be written at offset +18h (offset +24 in decimal) as a dword, and bytes per second has to be written at offset +1Ch (offset +28 in decimal) as a dword.
Samples per second will actually be pairs of samples, assuming that you have selected for "Stereo", by writing a number 2 at offset +16h (offset +22 in decimal).

You need to make sure that as it fills in the RIFF header, the computer does a simple calculation correctly to turn samples per second into bytes per second.
Samples per second was converted into bytes per second just by multiplying it by 4.

Bytes per pair of samples has to be written in offset +20h (+ 32 in decimal) as a 2 byte or word number, the number is 4 for 16 bit stereo.

Binary bits per single sample has to be written at offset +22h (+34 in decimal) as another 2 byte number.
The Windows operating system checks some things for errors, and when these numbers don't fit together you should hear only silence.
The actual sound data can start just beyond the riff header, the data has to be aligned so that the lowest 2 binary bits of the starting address is zero.

You see that there are 4 words of text in the riff header, these words were absolutely necessary since when any of the 4 words was slightly changed the Windows operating system just made complete silence.

These 4 words of text are also very case-sensitive. For example there is the word
 "fmt " which needs to be in lower case with one blank space after its letter t, and if this word does not have the necessary blank space you get silence.

The Windows operating system also seems to check that some of the fields you fill in are consistent with each other, and if any of the fields would not fit together or contradict, it just makes silence.

The sound samples in the playable sound track can be either all positive , or they can be made of both positive and negative numbers. I feel that the positive and negative combination sounds a bit better , when using integers.

```
;==============
```
Floating Point Sound.  WAVE_FORMAT_IEEE_FLOAT =3

Example of a RIFF header which worked with Floating Point sound samples.
The floating point samples were of maximum values Plus 1 to Minus 1 , (sometimes +4 to -4) and obviously they have decimal points , with most of the information naturally going below the decimal points.

```
riff:
  mov esi , [pointing2]                ;Address of an allocated area of memory
  mov ecx , 32000                      ;Samples per second in ecx now. 44100
  mov dword [esi] , "RIFF"             ;the word "RIFF"
;--------------------------
mov eax , 0e00000h
sub eax , 8
mov dword [esi+4] , eax                ;= file length minus 8 (chunk size)?
;--------------------------
mov dword [esi+8] , "WAVE"             ;word "WAVE"
;--------------------------
mov dword [esi+0Ch] , "fmt "           ;lower case word "fmt " with a blank space
;--------------------------
mov dword [esi+10h] , 10h              ;format chunk size always 10h
mov word [esi+14h] , 3                 ; 3= in floating point.  data 1.0 to -1.0 values
mov word [esi+16h] , 2                 ;1= mono 2= stereo
;--------------------------
mov dword [esi+18h] , ecx              ;write the sample rate in HZ at +18h
add ecx , ecx
add ecx , ecx                          ;x8 now if floating stereo 8 bytes per sample pair
add ecx , ecx
mov dword [esi+1ch] , ecx              ;bytes/sec = sample rate x channels x bytes/sample
;--------------------------
mov word [esi+20h] , 8                 ;Has to be 8 now , or else silent
mov word [esi+22h] , 32                ; 32 bits per sample
;--------------------------
```

```
mov dword [esi+24h] , "data"              ;"data" in lower case
;---------------
add eax , 8
sub eax , 44
mov dword [esi+28h] , eax
;--------                                  At +2ch the sound data starts
 ret
```

See that at the offset of +14h there is the code of 3. The number 3 specifies that the sound track is in floating point numbers. (A code of 1 meant integers numbers).
The constants are WAVE_FORMAT_PCM =1 , and WAVE_FORMAT_IEEE_FLOAT =3.

A few other changes go with the conversion of a RIFF header to floating point form.
The sample rate in Hz is now multiplied by 8 and then it goes in the bytes-per-second field at offset +1ch. The field at offset +20h is now 8. The bits per sample field at offset +22h is now 32. With all these changes it becomes a floating point header.
The address register which writes floating point sound samples , probably has to be aligned so that the lowest 3 binary bits of its address are zero , as it starts each pair of samples.

Import section

For the FASMW assembler it is necessary to have an "import section" usually at the bottom of your program. I don't actually understand what the import section does , but I notice it is something very important , as every single invoke function which the program uses always has to be declared there in the import section as a sort of double name. (Or you get an "undefined symbol" error message.)

 The example below is not a complete import section , it just shows the sound part of it. It has to be more complete than this , and examples of complete import sections come with the flat assembler , or Fasmw.
Invoke PlaySound has to be declared in your import section like this:
(with the others as well)(This below only shows a part of the import section.)
```
  ;==========================
```

section '.idata' import data readable writable

```
  library kernel , 'KERNEL32.DLL' , \
       user , 'USER32.DLL' , \
       gdi , 'GDI32.DLL' , \
```

```
comctl , 'COMCTL32.DLL' , \
winmm , 'WINMM.DLL' , \            ;Sound part is winmm , 'WINMM.DLL'
comdlg , 'COMDLG32.DLL'


import winmm , \                                   ;This sound part is necessary
        waveOutSetVolume , 'waveOutSetVolume' , \
        sndPlaySound , 'sndPlaySoundA' , \
        PlaySound , 'PlaySound'


;============================
```

Calculating a Frequency

I wanted to be able to specify the frequency. How do you get a specific frequency which you want? The frequency would be specified as an integer number in Hertz , or HZ which is the same as cycles a second. In one case I tried a way of doing it with a tuning fork at 440 Hz , and it seemed to be working exactly. But later on , the experiment was hard to hear , so I don't know.
To try to explain this idea for specifying the frequency in Hz.

A floating point number called an angle is increased by a small amount with every step , and its sine is calculated with "fsin" , and that sine can then be multiplied by some constant for loudness , and then written into the sound track as a sample.

So the small amount added to the angle with every step is what controls the frequency , the larger the amount the higher the frequency. Because the quicker the angle goes round and round in its circles the higher the frequency.
The absolute maximum frequency that can be created is 2 samples per 360 degrees , and therefore this is Half of the samples per second value in the Riff header.

The floating point unit uses angles in Radians , not in degrees. A 360 degree turn is 2 Pi radians. Obviously if the angle went around 2 Pi radians every 1 second , the frequency would be exactly 1 Hz , or 1 Cycle per second.
Assuming that you have in a register an integer which specifies the frequency you want in Hz.

Now the Riff header has in it a field called "samples per second" , at offset +18h beyond the start of the header.

You can make the samples per second field permanently, a value like 44100, or maybe 32000. And just leave this number the same all the time. I don't know what value makes the best sound? But it can be left the same all the time.

Your computer program needs to read this samples per second number to do a calculation with it, but that's only necessary if you want to specify a certain frequency.
The samples per second number stays the same whatever the frequency of the sounds you are creating in the sound track. You control the frequency with the amount that's added to the angle with every step.
A samples per second number that's much too low is obviously supposed to deteriorate sound quality, and it would make higher frequencies impossible.

If the amount that you increase the angle in each step would cause the angle to go through 360 degrees, or that is 2 Pi radians, every 1 second, then the frequency would be 1 Hz, or 1 cycle per second.
So supposing that in the Riff header, there is a samples per second value of 32000.
In that case, your angle would have to change by 2 Pi radians every 32000 steps, which means that in each step the angle needs to change by (2 Pi)/32000.

So it looks as if the increase of angle per step, in order to make a 1 Hz sound, is
(2 Pi)/32000 in that case, or in general, it is (integer)*(2 Pi)/(samples_per_second)

And of course increasing the change of angle per step, increases the frequency in proportion, so that to create a 100Hz sound, the increase of angle per step would be
 100*(2 Pi)/(samples_per_second).

So I think the way to do it, is to prepare in the memory a number equal to
(2 Pi)/(samples_per_second) and then to take the specified frequency in Hz as an integer number, and just multiply it by that in order to get the amount by which the angle should be increased in each step.

This is an example of programming which does that. Firstly preparing a number and saving it:
;========================
  frequency_proportion:  ;call once at the start to prepare the proportions number

```
    mov esi , [pointing2]           ;The address of the Riff header
    fild dword [esi+18h]            ;load samples per second number , from Riff
    fstp [samples_per_second]       ;converting it to floatig points
    fldpi                           ;load up pi
    fadd st0 , st0                  ;find 2* Pi
```

```
        fdiv [samples_per_second]           ;calculate the proportions number
        fstp [proportions_number]           ;save the important value in floating point
        ret


samples_per_second dd 0.0
proportions_number dd 0.0
calculated_frequency dd 0.0
;============================
```

Notice that when loading the samples per second number from Riff header, you need to specify its size using "dword".

Here is a program loop which could fill a sound track adding one frequency at a time,
and in asterisks a preparation which it makes. This is just a small part of a program.
Because it is using "add" to add sounds together, the sound track will need to be erased to zeros at the start.

```
add_sound1:
        cmp ebx , 0                         ;Called with the address of the sound track in ebx.
        jnz s3
        ret
  s3:
        and bl , 0fch                       ;align the address lowest 2 bits zero.
        push ebx
        push ecx
        ;=======
        fild [Hertz]                        ;* Load an integer frequency in Hz
        fmul [proportions_number]           ;* Multiply by the number found above
        fstp [calculated_frequency]         ;* Save Amount to add to angle in each step.
        ;======
        mov ecx , 80000h

    s2:                                     ;s2 is the sound track filling loop
       fld [angle]                          ;load the angle
       fadd [calculated_frequency]          ;Add the amount added every step
       fst [angle]                          ;replace the increased angle
       fsin                                 ;calculate the sine
       fmul [loudness]                      ;multipy by a loudness.
```

```
        fistp [output]                          ;converts it to an integer

        mov eax , [output]
        add [ebx] , ax                          ;write into sound track for the right ear
        jo s8
        add [ebx+2] , ax                        ;write into sound track for the left ear

        add ebx , 4
        cmp ebx , [upper_limit]
        jnb s8
        sub ecx , 1
        jnz s2
        mov [moves_up] , ebx
    s8:                                         ;jo should detect an overflow error?
        pop ecx
        pop ebx
        ret
        ;======================
```

The above example of a small part of a program should create a continuous tone. It is lacking in any way to change the loudness up and down and I needed to add that. I tried several different ways of making loudness go up and down. One method was for a byte in memory to containn a signal. A 0 for starting, a 1 for making loudness rise, a 2 for making volume steady, a 3 for making loudness fall. (not shown here).  It worked , but doesn't that seem complicated?

A different method which I also tried, was to make a second angle which would go round very much slower, as the amount added to this second angle in every step is much smaller or tiny. The sine or the cosine of the second angle, is then used as a second loudness value. For the frequency, the sine of the more quickly rotating angle is then multiplied by both loudness values, one immediately after the other. The rise and fall of loudness follows another sine wave,  but much more slowly.

Instead of just one multiply by loudness ,  there were two multiplications:

```
fmul [loudness]              ;fixed loudness
fmul [loudness2]             ;this one going up and down
```

;================================
The floating point coprocessor can handle an angle which keeps going up.

I said that the angle is increased a small amount with every step, and that implies that the angle goes up and up forever. In fact as it went round and round, the angle was going up and up forever, but the floating point coprocessor did not seem to mind.

I mean the floating point coprocessor is probably subtracting automatically a certain number of multiples of 2 Pi Radians, from every angle before calculating the sine or the cosine. The same as subtracting 360 degrees?

I tried testing every angle and then subtracting 360 degrees = 2 Pi radians from the angle whenver its value went above it.

The result was exactly the same sound. I wasn't sure whether I could hear any difference in the sound at all. Maybe it did improve a little?

This is the code used to try keeping the value of the angle below 360 degrees:

Check_angle can be called with an angle already in floating point st0.

```
    check_angle:              ;Probably all completely unnecessary
        fcom [twopi]          ;compares angle in st0 to two pi/
        call flags            ;Call to get flag bits into eflags
        jb check1             ;jump when carry flag set
        fsub [twopi]          ;subtract whenever was above 2Pi
    check1:
        ret

  flags:                      ;useful to let instruction fcom set carry and Z eflags.
      fstsw ax                ;floating point unit status word into ax
      mov al,ah               ;move carry bit and zero bit 1 byte lower for eflags
      and eax,0ffh            ;ah=0 prevented crash
      push eax
      popf                    ;pop carry flag and zero flag into main computer's eflags.
      Ret
```

I do not know whether keeping the angle in range improved anything?
I think it made no change of sound at all, but adding it slowed down the writing of the sound track quite badly. So it may be best not to use check_angle.

;==================

Whenever two frequencies are almost the same but just a tiny bit different , then as they are mixed together you hear a slow wavering, or it's called slow beats. The rate of the wavering as beats per second is equal to the difference between the two in Hz.

I would experiment with a tuning fork. When a frequency and a tuning fork are very sightly different, you should hear slow beats as loudness wavers caused by the constructive and destructive interference.


If you want an integer sound track , then should the conversion from floating point numbers to integer numbers be done as a very last step? Or should every sample be immediately converted into integers? I tried both ways of doing it. Listening I thought it sounded just a little bit better if it was done as the very last step.

If the sound track is at first in floating point , that did make a slight improvement of sound quality which I could hear when I tried both ways and it was mixing   frequencies. I had to get it to automatically decrease the loudness when any of the integers were overflowed. My program looked for overflow errors , and whenever there were several overflows counted , it decreased the loudness of the entire sound track , as a form of volume control. There wasn't too much difference between converting to integers immediately ,  or adding together floating point sounds and converting to integers as a last step. But converting as a last step does make a slight improvement in the sound.

This is a small part of a program. These program loops could write in a sound track a single pure frequency. The sound would not be very interesting.


```
add_sound1:
        and bl , 0fch                       ;align address register ebx , lowest 2 bits zero

        mov ecx , 50000h                    ;length of writing and sound playing
    s2: fld [angle]
        fadd [angle_incrementf]             ;Regularly increase the angle every time.
        fst [angle]
        fsin                                ;Calculate the sine , of st0 is assumed
        fimul [loudness]                    ;multiply by a loudness value integer

        fistp [output]                      ;st0 saved as an integer , and popped

        mov eax , [output]
```

```
        add [ebx] , ax              ;right ear    ;(Adding rather than loading)
        add [ebx+2] , ax            ;left ear

        add ebx , 4
        call do_taper               ;Try some way of tapering loudness?
        sub ecx , 1
        jnz s2                      ;another turn of this loop
        ret
        ;=====================
```

This small part of a program could add a sound when the riff header is written for floating point sound.

The sound track must be erased before using this.

The sound track would have to be erased to zeros before starting , if "fadd" is used.

```
        And bl , 0f8h               ;Align the address register ebx, lowest 3 bits zero
        mov ecx , 10000h            ;length of writing sound
s2:     fld [angle]                 ;load the angle and push it onto st0
        fadd [angle_increment]      ;angle increase per sample decides the frequency
        fst [angle]                 ;replace the angle
        fsin                        ;Calculates the Sin of the angle in st0. range +1.0 to -1.0

        fmul [loudness]             ;Multiply by a low floating value, maybe a value below +1
        fadd dword [ebx]            ;Add a floating point sample which is already recorded

        fst dword [ebx]             ;fst writes a floating point sample. Dword sized.
        fstp dword [ebx+4]          ;Right ear the same as left ear. Writes and pops.
        add ebx , 8                 ;move address register +8 forward

        call do_taper               ;some method of tapering the loudness?

        sub ecx , 1
        jnz s2
        ret
```

I think this is the format of a RIFF header.
RIFF stands for Resource Interchange File Format
;======================

| Offset | Size | | Name | Values |
|--------|------|---|------|--------|
| 0 | 0 | 4 | ChunkID | Contains the letters "RIFF" |
| +4 | +4 | 4 | Chunk size | File length in bytes minus 8 |
| +8 | +8 | 4 | Format | Contains the letters "WAVE" |
| +0Ch | 12 | 4 | Subchunk1ID | Contains the letters "fmt " (With one blank space) |
| +10h | 16 | 4 | Subchunk1Size | 16 for PCM |
| +14h | 20 | 2 | AudioFormat | PCM=1  (1=Integer)  (3=Floating Point form) |
| +16h | 22 | 2 | NumChannels | 1=mono,  2=stereo |
| +18h | 24 | 4 | Sample Rate | for example 8000 , 32000 , 44100 , |
| +1Ch | 28 | 4 | Bytes Rate | ==(NumChannels)*(Sample Rate)*(Bytes per sample) |
| +20h | 32 | 2 | BlockAlign | == (NumChannels)*(Bytes per sample) |
| +22h | 34 | 2 | BitsPerSample | 8 or 16  or 32  (I used 16 with integers or 32 for floating point) |
| +24h | 36 | 4 | Subchunk2ID | Contains the letters "data" |
| +28h | 40 | 4 | Subchunk2Size | == (NumChannels)*(NumSamples)*(Bytes per sample) |
| | | | | == The Length of Sound Data in Bytes |
| +2Ch | 44 | | Data | The actual start of sound data |

Data is signed integers -32768 to 32767.
At offset +40 the length of the data in bytes.

;======================

A table can be used instead of calculating sines. If a computer does not have a floating point unit.

At a time when my computer did not have a floating point unit , I thought the best way to create sine waves would be to create a sine wave table.
This would be a table of numbers that go up and down in the way that sine waves do.
And to use the table you would use two address registers. An address register that reads from it , and a second address register to write the value into a sound track. So one address register reads the table , and another one writes the sound track.

In order to get the address register to read any frequency at all from the sine wave table , you need to know exactly how many bytes distance,  the address distance, which corresponds to 360 degrees of turn. That single problem was the most difficult for me since at the time I did not have the floating point unit.
My program had generated the table but you need to know the distance corresponding to 360 degrees. When you find and know that number, an amount is added regularly to the address register

which does the reading from the table. And then, with every step, check whether the reading address overshoots 360 degrees. Whenever the reading-address overshoots beyond 360 degrees , the exact amount which corresponds to 360 degrees has to be subtracted from that address register.

This subtracting brings the address register back into the first circular turn of the table, and it will still be at the correct position. Because, of course, for example the sine of 15 degrees is always equal to the sine of 360+15 degrees. And the sine of 50 degrees is equal to the sine of 360+50 degrees. And so it is with absolutely any angle, if you subtract 360 degrees the sine will stay the same.

As an address register has amounts added to it, the larger the amount added each time, the higher the frequency. The writing address register meanwhile always has the same small amount added to it , just +2 or maybe +4. So that part is regular.

I generated my sine wave table using a program which only uses addition and subtraction , with also a positional dividing by a large power of 2.
A sine wave is defined as a wave with a negative acceleration that always points to the center , and this acceleration is always proportional to the distance from the center.

So to be able to generate a sine wave, use a number for distance from the center , another number for velocity. With each step subtract the velocity from the distance.
And simply dividing the distance from the center, by a really big, big enough value the divided distance can be used directly as the acceleration, which must then change the velocity in every step.
The program goes through many turns, or iterations (I mean many turns of the program, not of the sine) and whenever it has counted down a certain number of turns, it writes a single number into the sine wave table. Its writing address then +4 reguarly. 360 degrees corresponded to thousands of samples. It makes quite a long table, and it's quite accurately a sine wave.
I tested my sine wave table by using it to draw perfect circles or figure of eight so-called lissajous figures. Whenever my sine wave table was faulty in some way , the two ends of the circles didn't quite join up.
Of course you can now use the floating point coprocessor to create the table instead.
Reading from the table using an address register aught to be very much faster than calculating sines. Even the modern floating point unit , is unlikely to calculate that fast. And so , the method of creating a sine wave table and then just reading from it , should be a faster way. Is it? I did a rough timing test now , and found out that the operations using the floating point instruction "fsin" took about 80 nanoseconds. While the operations which read from a sine wave table , including testing the address for going beyond 360 degrees , took about 2.3 nanoseconds.This makes reading from a sine wave table about 34 times faster.
    ;=======================================

## A Random Sounds making program.

The following is a complete unfinished program, to create sounds on press any key, following random data which is read from the program code between two labels.

I tried a few ways of using the random data until the sound was sometimes pleasant.

The method of starting and stopping each sound was to make its volume follow a slower sine wave.

The program can save sound as a .wav file using its menu.

```
;Create random sounds.
            ;About 14 pages long when also saves sound file


 format PE            ;*
 entry start
  include 'win32a.inc'   ;or ax


 section '.data' data readable writeable

  hInstance dd 0
  _title db 'Sounds',0
  _class db 'Window',0

  pointing1 dd 0
 ;------
  h_menu1 dd 0
  h_menu2 dd 0
  h_menu3 dd 0

   hDC dd 0
   h_Window dd 0

 T1 db " Exit",0
 W1 db "End program",0                 ;500
  T2 db " Sounds   ",0                 ;501
  W2 db "(any key to make sounds)",0
  W3 db " Saving Sounds as a File  ",0 ;502

    msg MSG
    wc WNDCLASSEX 0;
```

```
    ofn   OPENFILENAME <>
    ;--------------------
    ;message box
    _words1 db "Saved the Sound",0
    _words2 db " message box",0
    _words3 db "an error",0

; file

    sound_file_length dd 0
    actual dd 0
    hcf dd 0
    ;-----------------
    szWav db ".Wav",0                    ;it needs full stop?
    szWavPath rb MAX_PATH                ;**This gets filled with path and file name.
    szWavFilter db "Wav Files",0,"*.wav",0,"All Files",0,"*.*",0,0

    soundsignal dd 0
; sound variables
    ratei dd 1                           ;rise and fall rates
    Hertz dd 0                           ;integer frequency
    divider dq 10000.0                   ;divider in rise and fall of volume
    loudness dq 05500.0        ;the sum of added sounds should never be above 32000.
    gradual dq 0
    pulse dq 0
    loudness2 dq 1.0
    texts db "ABCE       ",0
    pi dq 0
    thousand dq 1000.0
    twopi dq 0         ;regulating angle may be completely unnecessary and have no effect?
    ;----
    samples_per_second dd 0.01
    proportions_number dd 0.01
    calculated_frequency dd 0.01
    ;--------
    endsi dd 0                           ;this was to decrease end click, it worked
    iloudness2 dd 0
```

```
    hundred dq 100.0
;--
    upper_limit dd 0
    keyb db 0                          ;byte with keyboard input
    angle dq 2.0
    output dd 0
    moves_up dd 0


;-------------------------------------------------


section '.code' code readable executable    ; The word writable can trigger false positives

 playing:
        call riff
        invoke PlaySound,0,0,5      ;silence it?
        invoke waveOutSetVolume,0, 0ffffffffh

   mov edx,[pointing1]              ;*playsound crashes unless enough allocated memory
   invoke PlaySound,edx,0,5         ;SND_MEMORY or SND_ASYNC ;5
   ret

kbd:    cmp word [msg.message],WM_CHAR              ;when any key is pressed?
        jz kbd2
        ret
    kbd2:
        mov eax,[msg.wParam]
        sub al,60h
        mov [keyb],al

sound:
        mov ebx,[pointing1]
        cmp ebx,0
        jnz s1
        ret
    s1:
        call riff
        call frequency_proportion
```

```
    invoke TextOut,[hDC],10,20,texts,10      ;ABCE only to see whether this is running
        Fninit                               ;Fninit not necessary
        ffree st5
        ffree st6
        ffree st7
        mov ebx,[pointing1]
        add ebx,30h                          ;skip over riff sound header

        fldpi
        fst [pi]
        fadd st0,st0
        fistp [twopi]

        ;==============
        mov esi,[pointing1]                  ;to riff header
        mov eax,esi
        add eax,[esi+4]                      ;read the file length adding it to file start address
        mov [upper_limit],eax

        call erase
        mov [moves_up],ebx                   ;**load into moves up necessary.
        mov ecx,60                           ;how much random sound gets added
      s10:
        call randoms                         ;Set variables with random numbers.
        call add_sound1                      ;Add more and more sound with this call.
        dec ecx
        jnz s10

        call playing                         ;Call to play the sounds
        ret

;----------------------------------------
    randoms:
        push ecx                             ;must save ecx
        invoke GetTickCount                  ;? * Only to make it slightly different every time
        pop ecx
```

```
        cmp edi,sound                  ;Compare to the address of the label.
        jnb y1
        mov edi,sound                  ;keep the address between two labels

    y1: cmp edi,erase
        jb y2
        mov edi,sound                  ;load the address of the label
    y2: and eax,03fh                   ; from tick count?
        add edi,eax                    ;add so that its slightly different each time
        ;---
        mov eax,0
        mov al,[edi]                   ;[edi] reads random numbers for random sound.
        and al,01fh
        add al,1
        inc edi
        mov [ratei],eax                ;rate of volume rise and fall
        mov ax,[edi]
        and eax,3ffh
        add eax,60
        mov [Hertz],eax                ;an integer frequency specified in HZ
        add edi,1
        test cl,7
        jz y4
        test al,6
        jnz y3
    y4:
        mov ebx,[moves_up]
    y3: ret



erase:  push ebx
        mov ecx,1000000h
        mov eax,0
    ers1:
        mov [ebx],eax
        add ebx,4
```

```
        cmp ebx, [upper_limit]
        jnb ers2
        sub ecx,1
        jnz ers1
    ers2:
        pop ebx
        ret

    flags:                      ;useful to let instruction fcom cause set eflags
        fstsw ax                ;floating point unit status word into ax
        mov al,ah               ;move carry bit and zero bit 1 byte lower for eflags
        and eax,0ffh            ;ah=0 prevented crash
        push eax
        popf                    ;pop into main computer's eflags.
        ret

    checkangle:                 ;Probably unnecessary
            fcom [twopi]        ;compares angle in st0 to two pi/
            call flags
            jb check1
            fsub [twopi]
    check1:
            ret

add_sound1:
        cmp ebx, 0
        jnz s3
        ret
    s3: and bl, 0fch                        ;align address
        mov [endsi], 0
        push ebx
        push ecx
        fldz
        fstp [pulse]
        ;=======
        fild [ratei]
        fdiv [divider]                      ;for rise and fall of volume
```

```
    fstp [gradual]
;=======
    fild [Hertz]
    fmul [proportions_number]
    fstp [calculated_frequency]
;======
    mov ecx, 20000h

s2:
    fld [pulse]
    fadd [gradual]
 ;;    call checkangle            ;probably completely unnecessary
    fst [pulse]
    fsin
    fstp [loudness2]
    fld [angle]
    fadd [calculated_frequency]
 ;;    call checkangle            ;probably completely unnecessary
    fst [angle]
    fsin
    fmul [loudness]
    fmul [loudness2]
    fistp [output]

    mov eax, [output]
    add [ebx], ax                 ;add for sound in left ear ?
    jo s5
    add [ebx+2], ax               ;right ear
    jmp s7
s5: sub [ebx], ax      ;undo. avoid writing if an overflow error (too loud volume)
s7:                    ;better not to jump to exit
    add ebx, 4
    cmp ebx, [upper_limit] ;
    jnb s8
;--------                         the next part is just to decrease ending end clicks,
    cmp [endsi], 1     ;decrease end click by making end wait until lower volume
    jnz s12
```

```
        fld [loudness2]
        fmul [hundred]
        fabs
        fistp [iloudness2]
        mov eax, [iloudness2]
        cmp eax, 10
        jb s14
        jmp s2
    s12:
        sub ecx, 1
        jnz s2
        mov [endsi], 1
        jmp s2
    s14:
        mov [moves_up], ebx
    s8:
        pop ecx
        pop ebx
        ret
        ;=====================
;; samples_per_second dd 0.01    ;moved to data section
;; proportions_number dd 0.01
;; calculated_frequency dd 0.01
    ;--------
    ;===========
frequency_proportion:              ;calculation for proportions so a hertz fequency
    mov esi, [pointing1]
    fild dword [esi+18h]           ;" dword" load samples per second number
    fstp dword [samples_per_second]    ;converting it to floating points
    fldpi                          ;load up pi
    fadd st0,st0                   ;find 2* Pi
    fdiv [samples_per_second]      ;calculate the proportions number
    fstp [proportions_number]      ;save the important value in flosting point form
    ret

riff:
  mov esi, [pointing1]
```

```
    mov ecx, 32000                  ;other values can be instead.  44100
    mov dword [esi], "RIFF"         ;"RIFF"
;-------------------------
    mov eax, 01200000h              ;Playsound crashes the program unless enough allocated
    sub eax, 8                      ;1200000h maybe 65 seconds of sound.
    mov dword [esi+4], eax          ;= file length minus 8 (chunk size)?
;-------------------------
    mov dword [esi+8], "WAVE"       ;"WAVE"
;-------------------------
    mov dword [esi+12], "fmt "      ;fmt with one blank space
;-------------------------
    mov dword [esi+10h], 10h        ;format chunk size always 10h
    mov word [esi+14h], 1           ;1=integers and no compression
    mov word [esi+16h], 2           ;1= mono 2= stereo
;-------------------------
    mov dword [esi+18h], ecx        ;sample rate in hZ
    add ecx, ecx
    add ecx, ecx
    mov dword [esi+1ch], ecx        ;bytes/sec = sample rate x channels x bytes/sample
;-------------------------
    mov word [esi+20h], 4           ; 2=16 bit mono or 8 bit stereo, 4=16 bit stereo

    mov word [esi+22h], 16          ; bits per sample
;-------------------------
    mov dword [esi+24h], "data"
;---------------

    add eax, 8                      ;add 8 not at all necessary?
    sub eax, 2ch
    mov dword [esi+28h], eax        ;? really file size minus 2ch

;-------- at +2ch data starts
    ret
    ;===============

start:
```

```
    invoke  GetModuleHandle, 0
    mov [hInstance], eax
    ;=========================
    mov dword [wc.cbSize], 30h
    mov    [wc.hInstance], eax
    invoke  LoadCursor, 0, IDC_ARROW
    mov    [wc.hCursor], eax
    mov [wc.lpfnWndProc], WindowProc
    mov [wc.hbrBackground], COLOR_WINDOW+1   ;background +3=black +1=white
    mov [wc.lpszMenuName], _class
    mov [wc.lpszClassName], _class
    ;------------
    invoke  RegisterClassEx, wc
;----------------------------------------
    invoke CreateMenu
    mov [h_menu1], eax

    invoke CreateMenu
    mov [h_menu2], eax
    invoke CreateMenu
    mov [h_menu3], eax
;------------------------------------------------

    invoke AppendMenuA, [h_menu1], MF_POPUP, [h_menu2], T1        ;exit
    invoke AppendMenuA, [h_menu2], 0, 500, W1                     ;End program
;--------
    invoke AppendMenuA, [h_menu1], MF_POPUP, [h_menu3], T2      ;sound
    invoke AppendMenuA, [h_menu3], 0, 501, W2              ; play sounds when 501
    invoke AppendMenuA, [h_menu3], 0, 502, W3         ;save sound as a file  when 502
    ;------------------------------------------------

    invoke  CreateWindowEx, 0 , _class, \
    _title, WS_OVERLAPPEDWINDOW, \ ;
    1, 1, 400, 500, 0, [h_menu1], 0, 0

    mov [h_Window], eax
    invoke GetDC, [h_Window]
```

```
    mov [hDC], eax

    invoke ShowWindow, [h_Window], SW_SHOWNORMAL
    ;========================

    invoke GlobalAlloc, 0, 1800000h
    mov [pointing1], eax

    invoke FreeConsole
;========================

msg_loop:
    invoke  GetMessage, msg, 0, 0, 0
    cmp     eax, 1
    jb      ending
    jne     msg_loop

    invoke  TranslateMessage, msg

    invoke  DispatchMessage, msg
    cmp [soundsignal], 1
    mov [soundsignal], 0        ;turn off so it only runs once, important
    jnz no
    call sound                  ;sound if the menu is clicked
  no:
    call kbd                    ;sound if any key is pressed
    jmp   msg_loop

  ;==========================

proc WindowProc hwnd, wmsg, wparam, lparam

    cmp     [wmsg], WM_COMMAND
    jne     .notcommand
    cmp dword [wparam], 500
    jz .wmdestroy
    cmp dword [wparam], 501
```

```
        jz .make_sound
        cmp dword [wparam], 502
        jz .saving_sounds
    .notcommand:
     ;---------------------------
        cmp     [wmsg], WM_CHAR
        je      .character
        cmp     [wmsg], WM_DESTROY
        je      .wmdestroy
.def:
        invoke  DefWindowProc, [hwnd], [wmsg], [wparam], [lparam]
        ret

    .make_sound: mov [soundsignal], 1          ;must only run once
          ret
    .character:
            mov eax, [wparam]
            cmp eax, 27                        ;27=1bh was the escape character
            jz .wmdestroy
            jmp .def

.saving_sounds:
        mov [wparam], 0                        ;erase to prevent rerunning
        call saving_sounds
        ret

    .wmdestroy:

        invoke  PostQuitMessage, 0
        xor     eax,eax
        ret
endp



; =================

    saving_sounds:
```

```
        mov eax,400000h                          ;length to save in bytes
        mov [sound_file_length],eax

    mov ebx, [pointing1]   ;now to write the sound file length into the RIff heading
    sub eax, 44                                  ;this subtract might be unnecessary
    mov [ebx+28h], eax                           ;Write into Riff.
        add eax, 44
        sub eax, 8
        mov [ebx+4], eax

;-----------------
    call get_save_file_name

    invoke CreateFile, szWavPath, GENERIC_READ or \              ;\ continued
    GENERIC_WRITE, FILE_SHARE_WRITE, 0, 2, 20h, 0

    mov [hcf], eax
    cmp eax,-1
    jz error

    invoke WriteFile, [hcf], [pointing1], [sound_file_length], actual, 0
    invoke CloseHandle, [hcf]
    mov ebx, [actual]
    cmp ebx, [sound_file_length]
    jnz error
saved:
    invoke MessageBoxA, [h_Window], _words1, _words2, 0
      ret

   error:
      invoke MessageBoxA,[h_Window],_words3,_words2,0
      ret
    ;=================

get_save_file_name:
```

```
        invoke RtlZeroMemory, ofn, sizeof.OPENFILENAME
        invoke RtlZeroMemory, szWavPath, MAX_PATH

        mov [ofn.lStructSize], sizeof.OPENFILENAME
        mov eax,[h_Window]
        mov [ofn.hwndOwner], eax
        mov [ofn.lpstrFilter], szWavFilter
        mov [ofn.lpstrFile], szWavPath
        mov [ofn.nMaxFile], MAX_PATH
        mov eax, OFN_EXPLORER OR OFN_PATHMUSTEXIST \
        OR OFN_HIDEREADONLY OR OFN_OVERWRITEPROMPT

        mov [ofn.Flags], eax
        mov [ofn.lpstrDefExt], szWav

        invoke GetSaveFileName, ofn

        ret
;=================================

ending:
            invoke GlobalFree, [pointing1] ;
            invoke ReleaseDC, [h_Window], [hDC]
            invoke FreeConsole
            invoke DestroyWindow, [h_Window]
            invoke ExitProcess, 0
;=================================
section '.idata' import data readable writeable

 library kernel32,'KERNEL32.DLL',\
        user32,'USER32.DLL',\
        gdi32,'GDI32.DLL',\
        comctl32,'COMCTL32.DLL',\
        winmm,'WINMM.DLL',\
        comdlg32,'COMDLG32.DLL'

   include 'INCLUDE\API\ADVAPI32.INC'
```

```
    include 'INCLUDE\API\COMCTL32.INC'
    include 'INCLUDE\API\COMDLG32.INC'
    include 'INCLUDE\API\GDI32.INC'
    include 'INCLUDE\API\KERNEL32.INC'
    include 'INCLUDE\API\SHELL32.INC'
    include 'INCLUDE\API\USER32.INC'
    include 'INCLUDE\API\WSOCK32.INC'

 import winmm,\                              ;this necessary one was not in the INCLUDE\API\
     waveOutSetVolume,'waveOutSetVolume',\
     sndPlaySound,'sndPlaySoundA',\
     PlaySound,'PlaySound'

; above ends ABCE  15 pages random sounds
;==================================================
```

## Something about using the floating point unit.

I think most computers contain 2 to 3 different kinds of floating point coprocessors all at the same time, and they each have different registers, and different programming methods are used for each of them.  I only learnt to program the oldest kind.

The oldest floating point unit is ready to run, and so to use it you only need to write some floating point instructions, and you can do that anywhere in your programs.

The floating point instructions are not case sensitive, so they can be written either in capitals or in lower case.  They all begin with the letter F which can be in capital or lower case.
At first my main interest was converting integer numbers into floating point, and the reverse, since this conversion is done simply and easily with the floating point instructions fild [label] (load integer & push) and fistp (store integer & pop).
Of course integers are the simple numbers which do not have decimal points.

At first when I tried programming the floating point unit, the mathematics results were often completely and totally wrong, and it frequently crashed the program.
Or else it caused the computer to slow down, and slowing down could show that exceptions were being triggered.

What was going wrong?? I think the problem was only that the bottom of the floating point stack was being "lost" while it was "not empty".
Whether it was empty to begin with or not as your computer program starts, could depend on what the operating system did with the fpu before your program starts.
To explain it lower down, the problem and its solution is easy.

In general Floating point instructions can be written in the same area as normal program instructions, and so you have in the same area of program a mixture of both normal and floating point instructions.

Floating point numbers (of the oldest form) can be of 3 different sizes.
They can be 4 bytes numbers. They can be 8 bytes numbers, and they can be 10 bytes numbers. The more bytes, the greater its accuracy.
 I was always using the 8 bytes floating form and the 4 bytes integers in the memory.

 Whenever you load a number into the FPU, the floating point unit pushes it onto a stack which consists of 8 special 80 bits  long registers. (80 bits is 10 bytes).
 Whatever the number's size was when in the memory, I think it is converted instantly into a 10 bytes precision form, and it is pushed into st0.

St0 is the top of these 8 special registers. These 8 registers are named ST0 to ST7.

St0 to St7 are eight registers which are of 10 bytes size each, and they are called a stack. Since they are made to work like a stack, numbers loaded to or from the memory are always "pushed onto st0" or "popped from st0."

All the 8 numbers in the stack move to the next register, up or down when there is a push or a pop. That stack is totally separate from the computer's normal stack. It does not use a stack pointer. It is never used for return addresses, as it only holds the up to 8 floating point numbers.

Whenever you load a number from the computer's memory into the floating point unit,
it is **always pushed** onto the stack's first register which is called st0. The number which was previously in st0 is now moved to st1, and the number that was in st1 is now in st2. And the number that was in st2 is now in st3.
And so on. This is called pushing onto the stack. Now the number which was in st7, is lost, because I think it has nowhere to go.

So I think pushing involves losing a number from st7, and that happens whenever any number is loaded from memory into the floating point unit, if and only if there was something in st7, since these registers can be marked as being Empty.

Now the 8 special registers of 80 bits each, called st0 to st7, can each be marked internally as being empty. There is a special binary bit which marks st0 to st7 as either empty or full.
I think whenever a number is "popped" from st0, it probably marks st7 as being empty, as an empty state rises up from the bottom of the stack. So at the lowest bottom of the stack, the st7 should automatically be marked as empty when there is a pop. And during any pop all the whole stack rises up, the top of stack called st0 is lost but it is simultanously copied to the memory. The pops never cause any problems, and on the contrary can prevent a problem.

At the bottom of the stack, when there is a push, you should make sure that st7 is to start with empty. Whenever st7 was not empty, so that a push causes a filled st7 to be "lost", it seems to trigger a serious malfunction and the whole of the floating point unit malfunctions.

 Therefore st7 should be "empty" or at least marked as empty, whenever there is going to be a push. And any load from memory to the fpu is a push.

As far as I can tell, the floating point unit has a fault in its design, so that when st7 is "not empty" when there is a push, all maths calculations go wrong, and as well, there may be a triggering of an exception which crashes the program or slows it down.

Whether or not the floating point registers are empty at the time when your computer program starts running, could depend on what the Windows operating system has done with the fpu some time before your program starts running.

With one of my laptops, I discovered I could start the floating point program with a maximum of 2 pushes, and a third push would trigger the trouble and the whole floating point unit malfunctions. This implies clearly that when my program starts on the laptop, st6 and st7 must already be "empty", but, unfortunately, st5 must have been "full".

So in a second push, the starting st5 becomes st7. When there is a third push, the number which Windows operating system had left in st5, becomes "Lost" from st7 at the bottom of the stack.
So when I did 3 pushes, the third push triggered a malfunction in the whole floating point unit, as st5 became st6 then became st7 and was then lost.

To be able to use more than 2 pushes, I had a habit of starting my program with a series of several instructions which were "pops". (Floating point instructions which end with the letter "p" are pops). These are instructions which were not intended to do anything but just pop the floating point stack. For example I would start out a program section with these three:

fistp [label]        ;Store as an integer and pop, (the instruction ends with the letter "p")
fistp [label]
fistp [label]

This method worked well for me, it got the floating point unit working well.
Every "pop" probably marks st7 as "empty", and if you start with 3 pops, then that should make sure that at least three registers, st5, st6 and st7 are all "empty" and therefore they will cause no problems if you write up to 3 pushes next.

There is another completely different way to solve the same problem! There is the instruction ffree st7, and this instruction simply marks st7 as being empty.
When you write
 ffree st7
before every single instruction that is a "push" then the malfunction is never triggered.
As an alternative you could also start out your program with a series of ffree's like

          ;Just mark the registers as empty so that pushes can be written next.
ffree st4
ffree st5
ffree st6
ffree st7

Which would mark st4 to st7 as "empty" and so make sure that you can do up to 4 pushes in a row without any risk of problems.

Anyway you need to keep track of whether st7 is going to be empty or full, as it must be "empty" before there is any push.
Anyway the floating point unit is very good, as long as you avoid this particular problem.

Since the floating point stack is never used to save the return addresses of calls, the floating point unit should never have been designed to malfunction when there is merely a small mistake in st7. To make it easy to count pushes and pops, a floating point program can be divided into short sections with some separating line or a space. I used to use a semicolon then a line of dashes.

As you program the floating point unit, you find it easy to program, and it works well, all except for this one problem of malfunction and errors being triggered when st7 was not empty while there was a push.


Inside the floating point unit the floating point numbers are stored in a kind of code which follows a specification which is rather complicated, and so the numbers are not readable to my eyes.

Loading your decimal numbers into the floating point unit can be easy because you can just write simple decimal numbers in the program, and the assembler then automatically converts them into the specification used by the floating point unit, and it is converted before a program starts running. They have to have a simple decimal point, and it is the decimal point that tells the assembler to convert them.

To get the assembler to do it, you just put a full stop in the middle of the number as a decimal point. For example:

number1  dq 10.003

The assembler knows that this is a floating point number because of its full stop,
which is its decimal point. Number1 is therefore a decimal number with a decimal point to the assembler and it will convert it into the special floating point specification. You must write "dq" in between the label and the number. The dq stands for Double Quad which simply means the 8 Bytes precision size of numbers.
The simple floating point instruction:

fld [number1]

Will load the decimal number 10.003 by pushing it onto the top of the floating point stack. It becomes immediately register St0.

In order to get the assembler to do that automatically its creator must have studied the special format of floating point numbers, which is rather complicated.
Though the assembler will convert any number which has a decimal point into the floating point form, I do not know of any very simple way of converting a floating point number into decimal text, so I created a subroutine which does it using the powers of ten method.

The 2 letters "dd" can be used to declare 4 bytes floating point form, while the 2 letters "dq" should be used to declare 8 bytes form, and the 2 letters "dt" should be used to declare a number in 10 bytes floating point form.
Note in "dt" the "t" stands for ten.

For example, the simple decimal number 100.21 (One hundred and 2 tenths and 1 hundredth) can be declared in this way for 8 bytes floating point form:

label dq 100.21

And as it assembles your program the Flat Assembler converts this into the real
floating point form which is ready for loading into the FPU with instruction fld [label].
The same number can be in the much less accurate 4 bytes form like this:

label dd 100.21

Or in the greatest accuracy 10 bytes form, as

label dt 100.21

But the 10 byte form did not always work so I used the 8 byte form.
Simple decimal numbers like 0.001 and 100.05 can be declared in 8 bytes form by:

label1 dq 0.001
label2 dq 100.05

A series of several separate floating point numbers can go on one line and they should be separated by commas.
 Label dq 0.01,100.3,200.0

This is 3 simple decimal numbers separated by commas.

It is possible to load up the second of these numbers, remembering that they are each 8 bytes long, so the second number will be at offset +8

fld [label+8]
It loads the second floating point number and pushes it onto ST0. (In this example it would load decimal number 100.3)

I am not sure about a zero, but that was not important. The flat assembler seems to think that
label dq 0.0
should be an integer, but maybe it is not a mistake.
 One could think of either loading zero as an integer, or instead to load a floating point zero there happens to be one special instruction:
fldz
which simply pushes a constant zero onto ST0. (Its "z" stands for constant zero).

As an example of some calculation, these 4 instructions:

```
fld   [Number1]         ;load (and push) a floating point angle or number onto St0
fsin                    ;Find the sine of the angle in st0. (angles are in Radians).
fmul [Number2]          ;Multiply by another floating point number, result in St0
fst   [Number3]         ;Store the result as a floating point number ("st" for store)
fistp [Number4]         ;Store as an integer, and Pop. ("i" for integer, "st", "p" for pop)
```

 To get a result in a simpler form, you need to store it as an integer, and the floating point instructions with the letter "i" in it simply changes the result into an integer as it saves it to the memory.
It is rounded off and all the detail which was below the decimal point disappears.
 If the decimal numbers were:

Number1 dq 10.0
Number2 dq 200.4
Number3 dq 0.0
Number4 dd 0              ;with dd and no full stop the last one is an integer

The result should be the Sin of 10 Radians multiplied by 200.4

There is a problem which is converting a floating point result into decimal text numbers, and I have not found a simple way of doing it, which is why I prefer results as integers.
There is just one instruction which converts a floating point in st0 into packed BCD, and then, I needed a complicated program loop to convert the packed BCD into decimal ascii text form.

At first I was mainly interested in the instructions which contain the letter "i" as they convert integers into floating point, or floating point into integers in memory, very simply.

Though they are simple and very easy to use, these instructions round off numbers and remove completely all the detail which was below the decimal point.

Obviously the main information of a number might well be below the decimal point, and all of it disappears.

Of course the assembler only does its decimal to floating point converting once, before the program starts running, and converting in the opposite direction doesn't happen.

The system makes it very easy to calculate multiplications, divisions, squares, sines, cosines. The sines or the cosines can be used to create sound waves in a sound track, since sound waves are sine waves. And as well, floating points can be used to create drawings, and circles and ellipses. Using the floating point sines and cosines, drawings can bend or rotate, and you don't need graphics software.

Loading out from the floating point unit, to the memory, as a floating point number, is simple with

fst [label]                 ;Store but does not pop

and with

fstp [label]                ;Store and also pop.

And the variable can be declared with

label dq 0.0

Floating point numbers inside the fpu are so simply converted into integers by the instructions "fist" or "fistp". But of course converting into integers loses all information that was below the decimal point.

I wrote a subroutine for converting 8 byte floating point into decimal text, so you can print a result of calculations on the screen.

The instructions which convert the form of the numbers in both directions, integer to floating point, are the simple loads to and from memory, but you add to the name of the instruction the letter "i" as the second letter in their names, which "i" stands for integer.

For example
fild [label]                ( "f" "i" "ld" For Float, Integer, Load)

This is an instruction which loads an integer from memory and immediately converts it into a
floating point form, it also pushes it onto the floating point unit's own special stack.
That is it is pushed onto register ST0 which is the name of the top of the stack.
The name "fild" must stand for Floating, Integer, Load.

Fist [label]                              ( "f" "i" "st"  For Float, Integer, Store)
is an instruction which simply copies ST0 to the memory while converting it from the
floating point form into an integer form.
The name "fist" must stand for Floating, Integer, Store.

 Integers are of course the simple numbers which have no decimal points, and they can be called
binary or hexadecimal which is the same thing depending on how you look at them.
In conversion to integer form anything below decimal point disappears except
for the fact that it is rounded off, which would cause the number 5.6 to become a 6.

Fistp [label]              ( "f" "i" "st" "p"  For Float, Integer, Store, Pop)
does the same thing as fist, but it also pops the top of the floating point stack, you can tell that
because its name ends in the letter  "p" . Since it pops the number, the number is lost from the top
of stack, st0. (and probably st7 gets marked as empty, which is a useful thing.)

As the fpu stack's ST0 is "popped", ST1 becomes named ST0, and ST2 becomes ST1, and so on, up to
ST7 becomes ST6. And new st7 becomes empty.
In general any operation which loads from memory to floating point unit, is always automatically a
"push"  operation.

And in general any instruction which loads from the fpu to the memory, can be either a  "pop"  or
not a  "pop",
depending on whether the letter  "p"  is the last letter of its name.

**You need to remember** that all the instructions which load from memory into the floating point
unit, are always at the same time "pushes".

And you need to remember, that all the instructions which load from the floating point unit to the
memory, can be "pops" but only if you write the letter "P" at the end of their names. You often have
to write the letter "p" at the end of the instruction's name, because you often have to balance pushes
with pops.
;=================================

The instruction fninit can be used at the start of your program, to initialize the fpu.

A list of the floating point instructions. A computer usually contains 2 or 3 different kinds of floating point units, and this list is only for the older kind of floating point unit.

| | |
|---|---|
| F2XM1 | Compute 2x–1 |
| FABS | Absolute Value |
| FADD | Add |
| FADDP | Add and Pop |
| FBLD | Load Binary Coded Decimal |
| FBSTP | Store BCD Integer and Pop |
| FCHS | Change Sign |
| FCLEX | Clear Exceptions |
| FCMOVcc | Floating-Point Conditional Move |
| FCOM | Compare Floating Point Values |
| FCOMI | Compare Floating Point Values and Set EFLAGS |
| FCOMIP | Compare Floating Point Values and Set EFLAGS |
| FCOMP | Compare Floating Point Values |
| FCOMPP | Compare Floating Point Values |
| FCOS | Cosine |
| FDECSTP | Decrement Stack-Top Pointer |
| FDIV | Divide |
| FDIVP | Divide |
| FDIVR | Reverse Divide |
| FDIVRP | Reverse Divide |
| FFREE | Free Floating-Point Register (Marks a specific register as "empty") |
| FIADD | Add Integer |
| FICOM | Compare Integer |
| FICOMP | Compare Integer |
| FIDIV | Divide Integer |
| FIDIVR | Reverse Divide Integer |
| FILD | Load Integer (A number from memory pushed onto St0) |
| FIMUL | Multiply Integer |
| FINCSTP | Increment Stack-Top Pointer |
| FINIT | Initialize Floating-Point Unit |
| FIST | Store Integer |
| FISTP | Store Integer and the Pop |
| FISTTP | Store Integer with Truncation |
| FISUB | Subtract Integer |
| FISUBR | Reverse Subtract Integer |
| FLD | Load Floating Point Value (from memory pushed onto St0) |
| FLD1 | Load Constant number 1 (1 is pushed onto St0) |
| FLDCW | Load x87 FPU Control Word |

| | |
|---|---|
| FLDENV | Load x87 FPU Environment |
| FLDL2E | Load Constant |
| FLDL2T | Load Constant |
| FLDLG2 | Load Constant |
| FLDLN2 | Load Constant |
| FLDPI | Load Constant number Pi |
| FLDZ | Load Constant number zero |
| FMUL | Multiply |
| FMULP | Multiply |
| FNCLEX | Clear Exceptions |
| FNINIT | Initialize Floating-Point Unit |
| FNOP | No Operation |
| FNSAVE | Store x87 FPU State |
| FNSTCW | Store x87 FPU Control Word |
| FNSTENV | Store x87 FPU Environment |
| FNSTSW | Store x87 FPU Status Word |
| FPATAN | Partial Arctangent |
| FPREM | Partial Remainder |
| FPREM1 | Partial Remainder |
| FPTAN | Partial Tangent |
| FRNDINT | Round to Integer |
| FRSTOR | Restore x87 FPU State |
| FSAVE | Store x87 FPU State |
| FSCALE | Scale |
| FSIN | Sine     (Finds sine of number in St0 result in St0) |
| FSINCOS | Sine and Cosine |
| FSQRT | Square Root |
| FST | Store Floating Point Value     (Store St0 to memory) |
| FSTCW | Store x87 FPU Control Word |
| FSTENV | Store x87 FPU Environment |
| FSTP | Store Floating Point Value,    (Store St0 to memory, and then Pop) |
| FSTSW | Store x87 FPU Status Word    (Can use it to read C and Z flags) |
| FSUB | Subtract |
| FSUBP | Subtract and Pop |
| FSUBR | Reverse Subtract |
| FSUBRP | Reverse Subtract and then Pop |
| FTST | TEST |
| FUCOM | Unordered Compare Floating Point Values |
| FUCOMI | Compare Floating Point Values and Set EFLAGS |
| FUCOMIP | Compare Floating Point Values and Set EFLAGS and then Pop |
| FUCOMP | Unordered Compare Floating Point Values and Pop |

| | |
|---|---|
| FUCOMPP | Unordered Compare Floating Point Values |
| FWAIT | Wait |
| FXAM | Examine Floating-Point |
| FXCH | Exchange Register Contents |
| FXRSTOR | Restore x87 FPU, MMX, XMM, and MXCSR State |
| FXSAVE | Save x87 FPU, MMX Technology, and SSE State |
| FXTRACT | Extract Exponent and Significand |
| FYL2X | Compute y * log2x |
| FYL2XP1 | Compute y * log2(x +1) |

Floating Point Compares

Some of the comparing instructions do not set the ordinary flags register (which is called Eflags) in the CPU, and so they can't easily be used with conditional jumps. These set a different flag register which unfortunately cannot be used with conditional jumps.

Obviously it is very important to be able to use a compare instruction and then a conditional relative jump.

The comparing instructions which do set the conditional flags are fcomi and fucomi.

I noticed that if you load floating point numbers with different sizes, fcomi compares between them did not always work correctly.

I mean the numbers can be of sizes dd for 4 bytes, dq for 8 bytes, or dt for 10 bytes, when you load them. Default size seems to be 8 bytes. I am not sure, maybe it it necessary for them to start with the same size if you are going to compare them, and to get correct results of the comparison?

The following short subroutine or program can load the fpu Carry sign and Zero sign bits into the usual computer's Eflags register. And so it can let you use those other compare instructions with conditional relative jumps:

```
transfer_flags:
    push eax
    fstsw ax                ;spelled  f s t s w   ax (floating store status word into ax)
    mov al,ah
    and eax,0ffh            ;You must zero higher part.
    push eax
    popf                    ;popf eflags register with value that was in eax
    pop eax
    ret
;=======================================
```

## An error of recursion.

I did an experiment with a short program, and there was a problem which I think is called recursiveness. It was something so strange and unexpected.

I wanted a click on a menu item to cause a call to "invoke CreateWindowEx" so that a secondary window would be created, after creating the first window.

So I copied the "invoke CreateWindowEx" which created the first window, and arranged for a click on my menu item to cause a call to the copy of it. Something went wrong, and then after a while I found out what was wrong.

Now I think whenever you want to create a second window or a third window, some time after creating the first, that can work easily, but the "call" to do it should preferably not be inside WindowProc.

It was a mistake to do that from within WindowProc.
To explain what happened is quite simple. Whenever you run 'invoke CreateWindowEx' the computer automatically calls the special procedure WindowProc a number of times while the computer is actually still right in the middle of 'invoke CreateWindowEx.'

It created the secondary window. And I had made the size and coordinates of the secondary window different from the first, but something was wrong as it did not want to be minimized with the click on its corner minimize button.

I suspected perhaps there were several identical secondary windows directly on top of each other, and so I arranged for the X coordinate of the second window to be changed every time the invoke CreateWindowEx was called.

Now sure enough I could see a whole long series of many secondary windows was being created, their positions being shifted a bit like a stack of cards.
Obviously new windows kept on being created at a rate of at least 30 new windows a second! There were hundreds of new windows and more of them created constantly.

So to try to get the creation of a secondary window to run only a single time, I added just above the start of the copy of

invoke CreateWindowEx

a test for the handle being zero. That did not work. (When CreateWindowEx returns, it gives you a handle in the eax register, and you have to save that handle. I was saving the handle in a variable as [hWindow2]. If this still contained a zero , then invoke CreateWindowEx has not finished , or the computer had not returned from working in it.)

But when I tried it , I was very surprised that the CreateWindowEx was creating a whole long series of many new windows again , as before.
The test for the window handle still being zero , had no effect at all on anything.
And it never stopped more and more windows from being continually created.

In reality , when "invoke CreateWindowEx" is in the middle of running , the Windows operating system calls the procedure "WindowProc" many times.
And you see the amazing thing is , that it calls WindowProc before the invoke CreateWindowEx has finished running. I mean long before the computer has come out from running that function.

So what was happening , it was that while the computer was right in the middle of invoke CreateWindowEx , and certainly hadn't finished it , it was calling WindowProc. As it called WindowProc it started running "invoke CreateWindowEx" again.

And again and again it ran invoke CreateWindowEx , without ever having finished running even the first copy of it.
And the experiment proved that over and over again , while the computer was inside CreateWindowEx , and had definitely not emerged from it , it was continually repeating calling WindowProc and restarting CreateWindowEx.

I think this is called recursive behavior , and the simple solution to stop it , was to add just a little bit of programming just in front of invoke CreateWindowEx.
It was this:

create_second_window:

```
    cmp [entry1] , "Busy"
    jz avoid_entry                      ;this did it.
    mov [entry1] , "Busy"               ;Setting the word BUSY to prevent reentry.

  invoke  CreateWindowEx , 0 , _class , \
      _title , WS_OVERLAPPEDWINDOW or WS_VISIBLE , \ ;
      [Ex] , 1 , 310 , 400 , NULL , [hmenu1] , 0 , NULL ;
```

Any particular number would do , where I happened to use the word "Busy".

You see that if the word "Busy" is there in the variable [entry1], the conditional jump skipped over to avoid_entry, it avoided reentering the invoke CreateWindowEx.

To prevent the recursive error, that signal needed to be written before not after CreateWindowEx starts, since the computer has not emerged from running it at the moment when the operating system will call WindowProc again and again. And so nothing placed below it would work.

(The Windows operating system always knows the address of the procedure traditionally called "WindowProc" because whenever a Windows program starts, it has to do register the class of the first window, and that gives the Windows operating system the address of "WindowProc" during the registration process.)

I found with a counting-up test that the Windows operating system was actually calling WindowProc between 40 times and 59 times when just one of the CreateWindowEx was right in the middle of running. That is the computer was actually inside CreateWindowEx in the operating system while it also called WindowProc so many times! WindowProc was being called again and again, at least 30 times every second, before it had even finished working on the first of the calls. I think this is an example of something being recursive.

```
;----------------
  error:
        invoke  MessageBox , [hCreatedWindow] , D1 , D2 , MB_OK
        ret
D1 db "Eax was zero" , 0
D2 db "box" , 0
entry1 dd 0
Ex dd 100
hWindow2 dd 0

create_second_window:

  cmp [hWindow2] , 0                    ;No good. This compare to 0 did not help
  jnz avoid_entry                       ;Did not help.

  cmp [entry1] , "Busy"
  jz avoid_entry                        ;this did it.
```

```
    mov [entry1] , "Busy"                ;Setting the word Busy to prevent reentry.
    add [Ex] , 10                        ;An add to X so every run X coordinate increased.

    invoke  CreateWindowEx , 0 , _class , \
       _title , WS_OVERLAPPEDWINDOW or WS_VISIBLE , \
       [Ex] , 1 , 310 , 400 , 0 , [hmenu1] , 0 , 0

    mov [entry1] , "EXIT"
    cmp eax , 0
    jz     error
    mov [hWindow2] , eax         ;Save the handle.There was 38h runs of WindowProc while BUSY
  ;-------------
       invoke  ShowWindow , [hWindow2] , SW_SHOWNORMAL      ;This invoke did not call WindowProc
    invoke UpdateWindow , [hWindow2]        ;This UpdateWindow caused one run WindowProc
       ret
   avoid_entry:
   ret
;===============
 ; The problem was avoided completely by calling create_second_window from the message loop

     invoke  TranslateMessage , msg

     invoke  DispatchMessage , msg
     cmp [msg.message] , WM_COMMAND
     jnz no1
     cmp [msg.wParam] , 501             ;501 was a system menu Id.
     jnz no1
     call create_second_window           ;// There was no problem when it was here.
   no1:
```

The automatic many-times calling of WindowProc during the creation of a window is apparently a normal thing ,  and to avoid these errors ,  it's probably better if a call which creates new windows is not inside WindowProc.

To be absolutely sure that I could know whether or not the automatic calls to WindowProc were caused by DispatchMessage, msg I tested for that possibility in the message loop. And it wasn't anything to do with DispatchMessage.

```
    cmp [entry1] , "Busy"
    jz no2
    invoke  DispatchMessage , msg      ; There still were 56 calls to WindowProc.
  No2:
;=======================================
```

# Converting a floating point number into text. And creating a new DLL.

I do not know any instruction which can show a floating point number as the equivalent text on the screen, so I created a subroutine which does that. You save a floating point number, and then call this subroutine to convert it into the decimal text which includes a decimal point in text.

The subroutine uses the common powers of ten method, in which all the powers of ten are subtracted from the test number. Starting with the highest power, which was decimal 1 followed by 16 zeros, and going down to lower and lower powers of ten.
   To use the subroutine, is simple, the esi register has to be pre-loaded with the address of the floating point test number, which has to be in qword size. (8 bytes size).

And the ebx register has to be the address of a small blank area of text memory, into which the
   decimal text string is going to be written.
 As the subroutine is called with esi and ebx preloaded, it correctly converts a floating point number at address [esi] into a decimal text number, at address [ebx].
   The result includes a decimal point, and may include a – sign.
   The result was accurate to almost 16 decimal places, but nothing improved the accuracy above that.
   The ebx register was loaded using the instruction
   mov ebx, space_for_text

Once you call the subroutine and have the decimal text as a result ,
   invoke TextOut , [hDC] , 10 , 20 , space_for_text , 200

was used to show this result as text numbers on the screen.
And [hDC] was the device context of the window, obtained by invoke GetDC.

Firstly it was not necessary at all for the subroutine to be made into a procedure ,
but though that's not necessary I made it into a procedure as an experiment.

   Secondly it was not necessary for the procedure to be made into a DLL , but as an experiment I made it into a DLL , following the example of a simple DLL which comes with the flat assembler. That also worked.
  So here you have a triple experiment, converting floating point numbers into text ,
    the maybe unnecessary converting of the subroutine into a procedure.
And then an interesting converting of the procedure into a DLL.

Once converted into a DLL, the following invoke was able to run it:

  invoke float , esi , ebx                                 ; I had called the new DLL "float".
  ;ret
  After that you needed the TextOut to show it.
  Converting the subroutine into a procedure, was a question of adding to it a top
  line starting with the word "proc" and then the two parameters for esi and ebx.
  For ending the procedure, use the word "endp", something called a macroinstruction.

After that, making it into a DLL was done by adding the word "DLL" to the top line
 of the program, and creating an export section as shown below here, and a line
 with the words "fixups" had to be there for some reason I do not understand.

To give the program the ability to call the new DLL, with "invoke float , esi , ebx"
 the program needed some extra lines in its "import section" which normally goes at
 the bottom of the program. The following was added in its import section:

    library kernel32 , 'KERNEL32.DLL' , \
     user32 , 'USER32.DLL' , \
     gdi32 , 'GDI32.DLL' , \
     comctl32 , 'COMCTL32.DLL' , \
     winmm , 'WINMM.DLL' , \
     comdlg32 , 'COMDLG32.DLL' , \
     sides , '2Gr floating.dll'          ;The lowest line was now added (with name of the Dll)

  import sides , \        ;in making the dll, a reloc line doing nothing at very bottom was necessary?
    float , 'float'

; You see the added lines were    " sides , '2Gr floating.dll'" and then the import line for "float , 'float'

;The program below created a DLL which was working.


  format PE DLL
;; format PE GUI 4.0 DLL


  include 'win32a.inc'

```
section '.code' code readable writable executable ;


   proc float , one , two            ;Proc "float" with two parameters.
       mov esi , [one]                ;DLL used with invoke float , esi , ebx
       mov ebx , [two]

       fistp [blank]                  ;Now try quadrillions having 16 zeros
       fistp [blank]                  ;any blank pop2 to make sure st7-st6 is empty
       mov cx , 40                    ;cx =40 now as a maximum number of places
       mov dx , 17        ;dx counts down 16 result digits since above 16 wasn't accurate
       mov ah , 0                     ;ah inhibit left side zeros

       fld qword [esi]                ;Qword. load one test number at a time , qword was enough


       ;========
       fadd [adjusts]                 ;??? adjust to prevent 0.01 becoming 0.0099999999
       ;========
       fcom [zero]                    ;detect when a number is negative by cmp to zero.
       call flags                     ;a carry when number was less than zero
       jnb n9
       mov word [ebx] , "--"          ;write a minus sign if it was negative , then "fabs".
       add ebx , 2
       fabs                           ;** Make it + with fabs
   n9:
       ;----------
       fld [quadrillions]             ;start off powers of ten with greatest power.
       fstp [power_of_ten]            ;Start off with 10 to the 16 power.
    n3:
       mov al , "0"                   ;al = the character "0"
    n2:
       cmp al , "9"                   ;a test for "9" better here to prevent an error
       jz n1
       fcom [power_of_ten]            ;power of ten is compared.
       call flags                     ;Get the flags so that a conditional jump can be used
       jb n1
```

```
        fsub [power_of_ten]                ;power of ten is subtracted.
        add al , 1                         ;increase the character in al ,  going up to "9".
        jmp n2
n1:
        fld [power_of_ten]
        fdiv [ten]                         ;divide a power of ten by ten to get next test power
        fcom [hundreth]                    ;test it to find a decimal point
        call flags
        jnz n4
        mov byte [ebx] , "."               ;writing the decimal point
        mov ah , 1                         ;ah=1 allowing zeros after a decimal point
        inc ebx

n4:
        fstp [power_of_ten]                ;** replace the power of ten ,  now divided by ten
        cmp ah , 0
        jnz n5                             ;avoids many zeros on the left hand side
        cmp al , "0"
        jz n6
        mov ah , 1                         ;ah=1 to unblock writing of text zeros
n5:
        mov [ebx] , al                     ;write a decimal digit 0-9 from al
        inc ebx
n6:
        cmp ah , 1                         ;skip dec dx when ah=0
        jnz n7
        dec dx                             ;dx to limit number of digits to 16 which were accurate
        jz n8
n7:
        dec cx                             ;cx counts down cycles of the loop
        jnz n3
n8:

        mov dword [ebx] , 0a0d0a0dh        ;double line space
        fistp [blank]
        add ebx , 10
        ret                                ;ret to leave the procedure.
```

```
flags:
    push eax                    ;useful to let instruction fcom cause set eflags.
    fstsw ax                    ;floating point unit status word into ax
    mov al , ah                 ;move carry bit and zero bit 1 byte lower for eflags
    and eax , 0ffh              ;ah=0 prevented crash
    push eax
    popf                        ;pop into main computer's eflags.
    pop eax
    ret 0                       ;"ret 0" to end subroutine inside a procedure
;=====================
; ## Note These variables could all be moved to the data section.

    blank dd 0                  ;Note:  fsub/ fadd only did dq.
    zero dq 0.0
    hundreth dq 0.01            ;ten to 16th power starts 'quadrillions'
    ten dq 10.0                 ;the powers of ten get divided by ten each time.

    quadrillions dt 10000000000000000.0     ;16 zeros above the decimal point. ok
    power_of_ten dq 0.0                     ;quadrillions becomes the starting power of ten
    adjusts dq 0.0000000000000000139        ;???  16 zeros then 13
    ;--------------------

    endp                        ;end the procedure

;=======

    section '.idata' import data readable writeable

library kernel32 , 'KERNEL32.DLL' , \
        user32 , 'USER32.DLL' , \
        gdi32 , 'GDI32.DLL' , \
        comctl32 , 'COMCTL32.DLL' , \
        winmm , 'WINMM.DLL' , \
        comdlg32 , 'COMDLG32.DLL'
```

```
include 'C:\0 computer\INCLUDE\API\ADVAPI32.INC'
include 'C:\0 computer\INCLUDE\API\COMCTL32.INC'      ; need to change pathways
include 'C:\0 computer\INCLUDE\API\COMDLG32.INC'
include 'C:\0 computer\INCLUDE\API\GDI32.INC'
include 'C:\0 computer\INCLUDE\API\KERNEL32.INC'
include 'C:\0 computer\INCLUDE\API\SHELL32.INC'
include 'C:\0 computer\INCLUDE\API\USER32.INC'
include 'C:\0 computer\INCLUDE\API\WSOCK32.INC'

;========= This DLL also has to have this export section.

section '.edata' export data readable ; writable

    export 'C:\0 computer\2Gr floating.DLL' , \        ; The name of this DLL
            float , 'float'                            ;The double name of the procedure

                ;reloc line was Essential but don't know why?

section '.reloc' fixups data readable discardable      ;this must be necessary?
                                                       ;even though nothing below it

;-===============================
```

## About 64 bit programs

What I have read in Wikipedia about the Microsoft x64 calling convention.

The first 4 parameters of invoke functions should use particular registers, and they are
 rcx, rdx, r8, r9
in that order. Additional arguments are pushed right to left.
Callers responsibility is to allocate 32 bytes of 'shadow space' on the stack right before calling the function, regardless of how many parameters, and to pop the stack after the call. (Is the shadow space all done automatically by the Fasm assembler?)

There is a stack alignment of 16 bytes.
The registers rax, rcx, rdx, r8, r9, r10, r11          are all volatile (caller-saved)
The registers rbx, rbp, rdi. rsi, rsp, r12, r13, r14, r15       are all non-volatile (callee-saved)

Values in any of the volatile registers might be changed by the invocation and so you have to save them if you want to save the numbers they contain.
When the called function is entered the stack will be composed of in ascending order,
Return address, 32 bytes shadow space, 5$^{th}$ Parameter. The shadow space is used to spill rcx,rdx,r8,r9. (what does spill mean?)
These 4 registers can only be used for parameters 1 through 4.

This was my note about the Wikipedia page. I have noticed with the Fasmw assembler with 64 bit programs, that you should use these 4 registers, rcx,rdx,r8,r9 in that order for the first 4 parameters of the invocation.

I have noticed that when you do not use those 4 registers in the right order, then some invocations may work anyway, but others completely crash or malfunction.

So in 64 bit programs it is obviously important to use those 4 registers in that order for the first 4 parameters. (Nothing like that was necessary for 32 bit programs, in 32 bit programs you can use any register, except maybe not eax or ebp).
It is usually not necessary for all the first 4 parameters to be in registers.
It is confusing to me that the rule that one must use those 4 registers rcx,rdx,r8,r9 in that specific order, is important for some functions invocations, but might not matter so much with some others. In the case of invoke MessageBox, it was important, as the program might crash badly. (While in 32 bit mode MessageBox was the simplest function to use, it actually seemed difficult in 64 bit mode because I kept forgetting to use those 4 registers in the right order.)
When the invocation has more than 4 parameters, I think that on the right hand side of those which go in the 4 specific registers, you can use any of the non-volatile registers?

The stack pointer in 64 bit mode.

There is a strange rule in 64 bit mode which does not exist in 32 bit programs, and it can sometimes be difficult. I have found a solution to the problem, but maybe there is a much better one I don't know about?

In 64 bit mode, the stack pointer, rsp, has to be cleared to 0 in its lowest 4 binary bits.

The first 4 binary bits are called bits b0 to b3, and their value alone is 1,2,4,8.

If any of these 4 binary bits in the stack pointer is not 0, then the invocation might not work and the whole program might crash.

So this is important, but how does one make sure those 4 binary bits are always 0 when an invocation starts?

When a 64 bit program starts running, I assume that these 4 binary bits are already 0.

But I have seen in some example programs, that the stack pointer was adjusted right at the beginning of the whole program, and I don't know why it was necessary. For example, at a program's start.

```
sub rsp,6*8           ;This was only there once at the start. A sub is safe, do not add.
and sp,0fff0h         ;Logical And with 0fff0h clears the lowest 4 binary bits to zero.
```

Whenever a normal "call" is made to a subroutine in another part of your program, this of course sets binary bit 3 of rsp, because in 64 bit mode an 8 bytes long Instruction Pointer is pushed onto the stack. And the stack pointer rsp is therefore decremented by 8.

Whenever the stack pointer rsp is decremented by 8, this inverts its binary bit 3, which is worth 8.

Of course this is about normal calls, such as "calls" to a subroutine, not the functions or invocations.
 So assuming that to begin with the 64 bit stack pointer is correctly 0 in its lowest 4 binary bits, as soon as you make a call to another area of your program, the binary bit 3 is going to become set to 1, of value 8.

Therefore if you try to run any function invocation in the other area of your program which you have called, it might crash badly and the whole program is likely to crash.

64 bit programs can crash because of that one binary bit in the 64 bit stack pointer.

Now this rule seems strange to me, I don't know why there is this rule?

One way of dealing with this problem is to start and end any such subroutine with a push of an 8 bytes register. Like "push rcx" and then "pop rcx" for example. Because a push of any 8 bytes register will always invert the binary bit 3 of the stack pointer, and if it was a 1, turn it back into the good zero.

You can even more easily put a "push rcx" just in front of the "call" operation, and put the "pop rcx" just beyond the "call" operation, and that worked just as well, but is maybe more easy to work with. Like this,

push rcx
call label
pop rcx

So you know that in 64 bit mode the operation "call" will surely be inverting binary bit 3 of the stack pointer, and that this can cause serious trouble.

But placing one "push rcx" just in front of the operation "call", with a pop just after the call, should make it right. It will invert binary bit 3 again replacing a 0 in it to make it 0 as it was before.
The number of pushes (and pops) has to be an odd number. That is 1 or 3 or 5 or 7
pushes, then at the other side of the call the same odd number of pops.
So the problem is solved, but it's a bit difficult to have to think about it.

You do have to think about this. Obviously an odd number of pushes inverts binary bit 3, in any series of pushes of 8 bytes registers, while an even number of pushes does not change it.

==============================
Using for example an 8 byte register push/pop, this should fix crashing problem.
In 64 bit mode any CALL creates an 8 byte push of extended instruction pointer EIP, and any RET is an 8 byte Pop of EIP.
This is supposed to be a drawing of nested calls.

```
Start:                      ;Assume bits 0 to 3 of stack pointer are =0 to start with.
  (safe)
  push rcx                  ;the push inverts and therefore sets to 1, bit 3 of stack pointer
  call program1             ;The call inverts and therefore clears to 0, bit 3 of stack pointer
  Pop rcx                   ;the pop balances
  (safe)
  jmp loop                  ;Ends. (All 64 bit mode Calls cause an 8 byte pushing of the IP.)


  program1:                 ;Now stack pointer b3=0  (So invoke functions are safe)

      (functions are safe)  ;Now stack pointer b3=0
  push rcx                  ;the push inverts and therefore sets to 1, bit 3 of stack pointer
```

```
        call program2              ;The call inverts and therefore clears to 0, bit 3
        pop rcx                    ;(Ret has set b3.) The pop clears b3 of stack pointer to 0
              (functions are safe)         ;b3=0
        ret                        ;after RET b3=1


    program2:                      ;Now b3=0 again  (So invoke functions are safe)

              (functions are safe)       ; b3=0 again
        ret                        ;after RET b3=1

;==========
```

A different way of making the lowest 4 bits of the extended stack pointer zero, was: First save the stack pointer into a variable. Then subtract any large enough number
from the stack pointer, and then use AND sp,0fff0h to clear to zero the lower 4 binary bits of the stack pointer. And then as soon as the invoke functions have run, replace the original value of the stack pointer. (Note that the AND was to the lower 16 bit part of the stack pointer).

```
    Call program1
    jmp loop

    program1:
       mov [save_rsp],rsp
          sub rsp,28h
          and sp,0fff0h                  ;using AND to 16 bit part of the 64 bit stack pointer.
          (Invoke function can run here)         ;Binary bits b3-b0 =0
          mov rsp,[save_rsp]             ;recover the stack pointer immediately
          Ret
```

This worked as well, but obviously it is simpler to use a simple push/pop of a 64 bit register.

About the rules for the registers RCX/RDX/R8/R9
The rule that the first 4 parameters of functions in 64 bit mode should be in registers rcx,rdx,r8,r9 in that order, was important to many functions including this one.

invoke CallWindowProc, [window_address], [hwnd], [wmsg], [wparam], [lparam]

It works when all 5 of its parameters are labels in rectangular brackets, as above.

# Mouse Inputs

This was about reading the mouse messages in a way that worked with two laptops, which have Windows 7, and Windows 10.
Mouse coordinates were relative to the top left corner, which is approximately 0,0.
 Y increased as you go Downward, as X increases to the Right.

The mouse and the laptop touch pad do the same as one another. So a touch pad is like a mouse. The theory is: Whenever the mouse or the touch-pad moves and the mouse cursor is over the surface of your window, the operating system creates mouse messages, and it puts the messages in a queue.
The messages are at first in an internal queue, and always the function GetMessage, must run, often like this

invoke GetMessage, msg, 0, 0, 0

to take the messages out of the message queue and to put them into the small data structure named MSG, which always must be declared somewhere in the data section of the program with the two words

msg MSG

(A description of MSG is in the next and last chapter, about "Keyboard Inputs")
Whenever the mouse cursor is moved over the window which your program has created, it makes the message WM_MOUSEMOVE. The message goes into the queue. And GetMessage takes it out of the queue and puts it into MSG. And the this can easily be tested for, from anywhere in the program, for example with:

cmp [msg.message], WM_MOUSEMOVE           ;An equals is flag z, and so jz would jump.
jz mouse_did_move

At the same time as this message in [msg.message], the message structure also contains mouse coordinates of 2 different kinds.
There are mouse coordinates relative to the top left corner of the window which you have created, and they appear in the message field [msg.lParam].

The upper 2 bytes of [msg.lParam] are the Y, which increases as you go vertically downwards. And the lower 2 bytes of this field are for X. Which increases as you go to the right.

Then there are also the 2 coordinates of the mouse relative to the whole screen, or maybe it is called the desktop.
They appear in the message parameters [msg.pt.x] for horizontal and in [msg.pt.y] for vertical.
As these are relative to the top left corner of the whole screen, not the window.

But the mouse has to be over the window even to get coordinates which are about the whole screen, since when the mouse was not over the window it did not get any mouse messages.

So in order to read this other sort of mouse coordinate, you can write this from anywhere in the program, for example:

mov eax, [msg.pt.x]                    ;get X into register  eax
mov ecx, [msg.pt.y]                    ;get Y into register  ecx

When the assembler sees [msg.pt.x] written, what does the assembler do with it?  The "msg" is the label which you give to the message structure MSG when you declare it somewhere in the data section of your program with the two words

msg MSG

 and the actual names of those two fields inside it are "pt.x" and "pt.y".  The assembler knows automatically the addresses of these fields partly because it has found information about the MSG structure in the include file named

\EQUATES\USER32.INC.
And the assembler will automatically convert the instruction

mov eax, [msg.pt.x]
into a load which has the correct address to read that part of the message data. If you wanted to, you could write a load that has the right address offset yourself, but that's not necessary since the assembler does it automatically.

The coordinates of the mouse arrow relative to the window you create, coordinates found in [msg.lParam], must be the main useful ones. They would be used more often than the other coordinates which are relative to the whole computer screen.
You can read [msg.lParam] from almost anywhere in the program, except maybe not from inside certain possible procedures?

If the computer is running inside WindowProc, then you can assume that the field [lparam] should contain the identical number as the field [msg.lParam].

To read either X or Y you firstly test [msg.message] for equal to WM_MOUSEMOVE.

WM_MOUSEMOVE    is a constant, which temporarily has the meaning that the mouse has moved. And then you should read the X and the Y coordinates of the mouse relative to the top left of your window, from [msg.lParam].

Now about reading the two coordinates,
The X is in the lower 2 bytes of the [msg.lParam] field, and the Y is in the upper 2 bytes of it.
So you have to separate the upper 2 bytes from the lower 2 bytes, and there must be several common ways of doing that:
mov eax,[msg.lParam]                    ;This reads an X coordinates from lParam into ax.
and eax, 0ffffh                         ;X is in lower 2 bytes. Remove the upper 2 bytes.

When you want to read the mouse Y coordinate from [msg.lParam], it is in the upper half of [msg.lParam].
 And so you can read Y with:

mov eax, [msg.lParam+2]                 ; Notice the added offset of +2    for Y coordinate
and eax, 0ffffh                         ; Y is now in the lower 2 bytes of eax

For some reason when I try the 2 byte load "mov ax, [msg.lParam+2]"    that caused an error message of "operand sizes do not match". Therefore used a 4 bytes load into eax.

The other common way of reading exactly the same upper part of [msg.lParam] into AX, is
mov eax , [msg.lParam]
shr eax , 16                            ; 16 shifts right move the upper part down into AX.

I think many people read it with these 16 shifts.

Since the Y coordinate increases downwards, and you can sometimes prefer the coordinate to increase upwards, you might find the height of the window in pixels or in scan lines, and subtract the Y coordinate from that number.
 The subtraction should make a better Y coordinate which is zero at the bottom left side of the window, and which increases upwards. After a subtraction you can have a coordinate which is 0,0 at the bottom left corner, instead of the top left corner.

I have read that at the moment when the mouse cursor leaves the area of the window, there should be a WM_MOUSELEAVE message. (value =2a3h). But it Never worked at all when I looked for it.

I find with my laptop that when the mouse cursor leaves the main area of the window but stays over one of the window's thick or narrow borders, then the messages WM_MOUSEMOVE stop coming, and instead there comes a different message which is WM_NCMOUSEMOVE.
This different message continues when the mouse is over the borders area.

And at the same time, the X,Y coordinates in the field [msg.lParam] changes to become Equal to the POINT structure coordinates, that is it changes to the coordinates for the whole screen.
When the mouse cursor gets back to the main area of the window, things change back.
But unfortunately as soon as the mouse cursor goes entirely outside of a window, the messages all stop.

Obviously the writing [msg.pt.y] must mean to the assembler, "the Y part of the pt part of the MSG structure."
I think the idea behind this way of writing it must be that people have preferred to read names, rather than to read numbers.

There is an interesting listing of mouse messages in the file named:
INCLUDE\EQUATES\USER32.INC
You have to be careful never to damage this file since the assembler uses it automatically to work. The assembler should stop working if you damaged this file.
This file called USER32.INC also defines many data structures, including MSG. Please see my Keyboards inputs chapter about that.

For another example you can read a mouse X coordinate into AX and a Y coordinate into DX with this programming, relative to top left corner of a window:

```
 cmp [msg.message], WM_MOUSEMOVE
jnz no_mouse
mov eax, [msg.lParam]
mov edx, [msg.lParam]
shr edx, 16                              ;Now X is in AX and Y is in DX.
```

To read the coordinates relative to the whole screen's Top left, instead of a window,
```
cmp [msg.message], WM_MOUSEMOVE
jnz no_mouse
mov eax, [msg.pt.x]
mov edx, [msg.pt.y]
```

And while the mouse cursor is over one of the window's borders, the test has to be for WM_NCMOUSEMOVE instead. (it has the extra 2 letters NC)

About the handles when you create several windows together:
Your program might create several windows. When you make several windows, you need to store the handles to each window when you create it.

I have made the handles visible on a hexadecimal view, and looking at it, you find that when a message is created by the Windows operating system, the handles of windows go automatically into the field
[msg.hwnd]

The [msg.hwnd] field in the message structure immediately changes when the mouse cursor moves from one window to another window, as there are both windows on the screen.

Therefore to find out which window the mouse cursor is over, you can compare the field [msg.hwnd] to the saved handles of the windows.

The assembler looks through the INCLUDE files such as USER32.INC to automatically convert names into numbers. When the names of constants are written in block capitals, the assembler converts them to the exactly equivalent numbers. If you yourself write the numbers instead of writing the names, it has exactly the same result, the assembled program comes out the same. Here are several names and equal numbers, which you can see in the INCLUDE file I mentioned.
WM_MOUSEMOVE = 200h
WM_NCMOUSEMOVE = 0A0h
WM_LBUTTONDOWN = 201h    ;Left mouse button down        All in [msg.message] field.
WM_RBUTTONDOWN = 204h    ;Right mouse button down
WM_LBUTTONDBLCLK = 203h    ;detect a **double** click

Windows do not detect mouse double clicks **unless** you used the flag CS_DBLCLKS.
When you are filling in **the field [wc.style] just before** you create the window.
;The Registered Window structure "wc" should include this constant or flag before the window is created, to allow a window to later detect the mouse double-clicks:

mov [wc.style], CS_DBLCLKS    ;when filling in the [wc.style] field for WNDCLASSEX
I checked whether this is really necessary for double click detecting, it was.
;-------------------------------


There was another way to read mouse coordinates relative to whole screen, but it also stopped as soon as the mouse was outside of the window area. It was not very useful.
I tried

invoke GetCursorPos, point2

Firstly it is necessary to declare in the data section of the program, the existence of a POINT stucture. These two words can declare it:

point2 POINT

Your program can call regularly the "invoke GetCursorPos, point2" but it is not necessary to use it since reading MSG is just as good.
The mouse coordinates should appear in your separate POINT structure. (This works separately from the message system). You can then read the second point structure for mouse coordinates like this,

    invoke GetCursorPos, point2    ;
mov eax, [point2.x]
mov [X], eax
mov eax, [point2.y]
mov [Y], eax

call draw_pixel_xy                ;This call was just a draw dots test.
Ret

# Keyboard inputs & messages

The best way of reading inputs from the keyboard, is to test the message field called [msg.message] for the constant WM_CHAR, and then when the constant is there, to read the alphabetical character from the message field called [msg.wParam].

 The theory of it is that whenever you press on the keyboard or move the mouse, the Windows operating system posts messages about it, and it puts these messages into an internal queue.
A queue builds up containing more and more messages, and your program should read the messages and remove them from the queue.
Both reading and removing from the queue, is done together with the one function

invoke GetMessage, msg, 0, 0, 0

This function removes a message from the queue and places the message inside the small data structure called MSG.
In all Windows programs it is normal to declare the existence of a MSG data structure somewhere in the data section of the program, usually with the two words:

msg MSG

This is important. If your program did not remove messages from the operating system's message queue,
the queue would overfill, and you might get a crash or a warning with the words "not responding".
When the function "GetMessage" has put a message into the MSG data structure, other parts of your program can easily read the message information. (Which includes keyboard inputs)

The MSG structure has approx 7 fields, and these fields are given these names, which have to be written this way for the flat assembler:

| | |
|---|---|
| [msg.hwnd] | The window handle field |
| [msg.message] | The type of message field |
| [msg.wParam] | The message information |
| [msg.lParam] | Extra message information |
| [msg.time] | The time field |
| [msg.pt.x] | The Point X |
| [msg.pt.y] | The Point Y |

These 7 parts of the message structure are so often used that you need to learn them, or at least how to write their names in brackets as shown here, and the names are case-sensitive. It may be useful to memorize most of them. You see they are all in lower case except for the letter "P" of wParam and of lParam, the only capitals.

You write the label "msg" and then a full stop, and then the name of the field.

The [msg.message] field contains a constant number which identifies what basic type of message. With the flat assembler you commonly need to write compare instructions which compare this field with a constant number which is normally written as a word in block capitals, starting with letters "WM" for Windows Message,
such as WM_CHAR or such as WM_KEYDOWN.

The flat assembler automatically searches for the block capitals constants in an include file, and converts them into the corresponding number which they are equal to.
 For example the assembler will find this in an include file:
WM_KEYDOWN = 100h

And as the program is assembled, it converts the word into the number 100h which means something to the Windows operating system. You can write the number if you want to, and that will work equally as well, but usually let the assembler do it for you.

You should look in the include file USER32.INC if you would like to see the complete list.

The next field, [msg.wParam]  contains important message information. What it contains depends on the basic type of message.

The field [msg.lParam]  contains more message information.

And when [msg.message] = WM_MOUSEMOVE, then the mouse coordinates relative to the top left corner of your window, are usually in the field called [msg.wParam].

The lower 2 bytes half of that is for X and the upper 2 bytes half of it is for Y.

And mouse coordinates relative to the whole screen are in the message fields [msg.pt.x] and [msg.pt.y]

## A bit about message loops.

In all Windows programs you have to have a Message Loop, which has in it these three functions: I think all examples which you download together with flat assembler, have a message loop which looks like this:

```
msg_loop:
   invoke  GetMessage, msg,0,0,0        ; Remove messages from the queue and put into MSG.
      cmp    eax,1                      ;
      jb     ending                     ;end the program when eax=0
      jne    msg_loop                   ;This jump doesn't ever run at all!


      invoke  TranslateMessage, msg              ; always necessary
      invoke  DispatchMessage, msg               ; always necessary
   call parts_of_the_program
      jmp msg_loop
```

I have no idea why they always write the message loop this way, since one of those jumps doesn't ever run. And a message loop can at least sometimes work equally well, written like this instead:

```
 msg_loop:
      invoke  GetMessage, msg, 0, 0, 0     ;the most important function
      cmp    eax, 0
      jz ending                            ;end the program when eax=0
                                           ;At this point eax is always=1 ?

      invoke  TranslateMessage, msg        ;always necessary
      invoke  DispatchMessage, msg         ;always necessary
   call parts_of_the_program
      jmp msg_loop
;============================
```

Below the DispatchMessage, you can write calls which call various other parts of your programs. You can aso place there tests for the keyboard inputs, though the tests can be anywhere.
To make a loop there is the unconditional jump to the top of the message loop:
Jmp msg_loop

 And the computer often goes round and round in this loop, and the GetMessage will remove messages from the queue and put them into the MSG data structure.

The TranslateMessage makes an adjustment to the data. The DispatchMessage, causes the special procedure named WindowProc to be called, and the message structure data copied to it, actually copied to the stack for it.

 Incidentally the operating system knows the address because you give it the address of WindowProc whenever you fill in the WNDCLASSEX data structure at the very beginning of a program, and register the class of a new window as a program begins.

WindowProc is the only procedure which is always essential, and it's essential because the Windows operating system is also going to call it about 20 times as the program starts, before and especially during the creation of a window, and before the computer ever gets to your message loop.

There is a special very important function which the operating system really needs inside WindowProc, because the operating system can only create a window when this function is there, and it is also used to do some kind of essential default processing in WindowProc:

   invoke  DefWindowProc, [hwnd], [wmsg], [wparam], [lparam]        ;( Essential and important.)

But though it is essential, WindowProc can be kept short if you want it to be short. You don't need to make it long or put much in it, and you can decide to do your keyboard inputs completely outside of it, and the keyboard inputs can easily be either in message loop, or called from the message loop.

While GetMessage is essential, it has a disadvantage which is that it often blocks the running of the program until a message is written into the queue. This means that the computer program could stop running if you do not touch the keyboard or move the mouse, and just wait. It all stops and just waits. To prevent this blocking, you can use the function

invoke PeekMessage, msg, 0 , 0, 0, 0          ; 4 Zeros, while GetMessage had 3 Zeros.


It copies the message at the front of the queue into MSG, but it does not actually remove the message from the queue.

In the message loop, unlike GetMessage, the PeekMessage never blocks the flow of the program. And when there are no messages, the PeekMessage function returns immediately with a zero in the eax register.

You can test for the zero in the eax register after PeekMessage, and then skip over the message loop at any time when there are no messages in the queue, and that can be done to prevent the program from freezing and waiting for a message. But you still need GetMessage to remove the messages from the queue.

As soon as a message is moved from the queue to the MSG structure, other areas of your computer program can have access to it. (You can read the message in MSG from almost anywhere in the program).

When you declare the MSG data structure in the data section of your program with the two words

msg MSG
The small msg on the left is your label, which theoretically could be changed.

The keyboard inputs should be read from the MSG structure, as that is probably the best way of doing it.
(If someone is typing, all the alphabetical characters in all the text writing, are in ascii code.
And "ascii" stands for American Standard Code for Information Interchange. Many books contain a complete list of the ascii table.
 I find that sometimes but not always you need to look at the ascii table.)

In order to read an alphabetical character from the keyboard, you can use these instructions:

```
cmp [msg.message], WM_CHAR        ; WM_CHAR means a character key was pressed
jnz not_character                 ; jump away on condition nz for not equal
mov eax, [msg.wParam]             ; The AL register now contains the character in ascii code.
```

WM_CHAR stands for character, and it is simply a constant. That is when your program is assembled the assembler will automatically look up this word in a list of constants, and replace the word with the number which is equivalent.

You see that you should firstly test the field called [msg.message] for WM_CHAR and then, if it's there you know that an alphabet key on the keyboard has been pressed.
Then, you can always read the alphabet code from the field called [msg.wParam].
The field [msg.wParam] is 4 bytes long, and the alphabetical character is always in its lowest byte AL. So if it has been loaded into eax, the alphabetical character is always in the register AL. Since register AL is the lowest byte of EAX.

The Windows operating system has taken care of the effects of the shift key automatically, as the character code in AL is already affected by the shift key in the way it should be, and is either lower case or a capital letter.

If you want to create a typing routine which will type your words onto an area of memory (without using an edit control), then I think it is enough to decide when to actually type characters by doing that one test with:
 cmp [msg.message], WM_CHAR
 jz do_typing

And if the compare finds WM_CHAR then you can assume that it is the right time for typing the character which you find in the lowest byte of [msg.wParam].

And when you are doing typing, you don't need to use a test to detect either WM_KEYDOWN or WM_KEYUP. Because of the way the Windows operating system is made, WM_CHAR should be enough for detecting when to type an alphabetical letter.

As you press on the alphabetical keys of the keyboard, the Windows operating system creates 3 messages one after the other, all in the field [msg.message].
The first 2 messages come quickly one after the other, they are WM_KEYDOWN and then WM_CHAR. And a bit later on when the key is released, the message is WM_KEYUP.
(All in the field [msg.message])

Non alphabetical keys are different.
As you press on a non-alphabetical key, the Windows system creates only 2 messages.
They are WM_KEYDOWN immediately, and then when the key is released WM_KEYUP.

There is no WM_CHAR when the key was non-alphabetical.

Microsoft calls the non-alphabetical keys "Virtual keys".
These 3 messages, and the 2 fields called [msg.message] and [msg.wParam], are what you have to remember when you want to use the keyboard.

The escape key has a character code of 27 even though it looks non-alphabetical.
To detect the escape key, which can be used as a way of ending the program, you can also test for WM_CHAR in [msg.message] but then you test for the escape code which is 27, in [msg.wParam].

The message structure has these different fields. I noticed something about how the flat assembler actually works. The flat assembler looks for the definition of the message structure in an include file, USER32.INC, and this gives the assembler the ability to automatically recognize whether you have spelled the field names correctly. The fields have case-sensitive names, and if you misspell the names you get an error message.

..........


If you want to find out when a virtual key (a non alphabet key) is released, you can certainly use the WM_KEYUP message. But at the time of writing I still don't know if there is an accurate way to detect when an alphabet key is released. The problem could only exist at times when several keys were held down together.

I have found that you can easily do typing using just detection of the WM_CHAR. The character to be typed is then in the lowest byte of [msg.wParam].

About the non-alphabet keys, to read a virtual key input,

```
cmp [msg.message], WM_KEYDOWN
jnz not_down
mov eax, [msg.wParam]        ;this may read a virtual key code into the eax register.
```

This should get virtual key codes into the lower part of register eax, which is the register AL. (For example a left shift key is virtual key code 10h, and a control key is virtual key code 11h.

To see when a virtual key is released, you can use a test

```
cmp [msg.message], WM_KEYUP
```

And when there is a WM_KEYUP message, you can look at [msg.wParam] to see which of the virtual keys is being released, as its code should be in AL from the least significant byte of [msg.wParam].

Assemblers like the flat assembler seem to automatically understand the data structure called MSG. I think the assembler obtains this information from a certain include file, INCLUDE/EQUATES/USER32.INC.  And an experiment with the include file could confirm this. I think the MSG structure contains 7 fields. You need to be very careful not to damage the include file, since the assembler really needs it. If the include file were damaged the assembler would stop working.

The assembler reads include files, usually starting from the same folder that the assembler itself is in. The assembler automatically reads about the MSG data structure from the include file:

\INCLUDE\EQUATES\USER32.INC

 If you look in this include file, you will find this:(Without the extraX)

```
struct MSG                          ;This is in USER32.INC and it tells the assembler about MSG data.
  hwnd    dd ?                      ;The flat assembler learns the names of the fields from here.
  message dd ?
  wParam  dd ?
  lParam  dd ?
  time    dd ?
  pt      POINT
ends
```

Also in the same Include file there was the definition of the POINT structure:

struct POINT
  x dd ?
  y dd ?
Ends

You see that normally the MSG data structure has 7 fields in it, and each field is 4 bytes. The letters "dd" mean 32 bit numbers, I think dd stands for Data Double-word.

And **simply as an experiment** I added one extra line, "extraX dd ?" to the INCLUDE file, and tested assembly of my program. Because of this one extra line, the flat assembler allowed the instruction:

mov eax, [msg.extraX]    ;Not a real field

Previously it would have called this instruction an Error. It was case sensitive, so lower case and upper case letters are quite different.

struct MSG                      ;A temporary experiment only.
  hwnd   dd ?
  message dd ?
  wParam  dd ?
  lParam  dd ?
  time    dd ?
  pt      POINT
  extraX  dd ?         ;extraX is not normally in it. *****
ends

With the experiment over, I **removed** the "extraX dd?" And re-saved the INCLUDE file USER32.INC exactly as it was to begin with.
It's important to keep the INCLUDE files intact and not to change them, as the assembler really needs them to work. If the include file was damaged, the assembler would of course stop working. So the include file tells the assembler about all the data structures, and the assembler then reports an error message if you write something wrong.
The assembler seems to automatically recognize many hundreds of constants which you notice are written in block capitals, such as the constants WM_CHAR or WM_KEYDOWN for example.
The reason behind it must be that people prefer to see words rather than to see numbers. Someone thought that you would prefer to see a word. My opinion is that when the word is a complete word,

they are right, but when the word is a strange complicated abbreviation it might be as hard to remember as the number.

When a program is assembled, each constant as a word in capitals is converted into a simple number.

If you yourself write that number instead of the word, it will have exactly the same effect, and that works as well. Since the assembler always turns the name of the constant into the corresponding number anyway while it creates an .exe file.
\INCLUDE\EQUATES\USER32.INC

For example
WM_KEYDOWN = 100h
WM_KEYUP   = 101h
WM_CHAR    = 102h

The assembler automatically looks through the include file whenever it gets to a word written in block capitals, and it finds the word, if it is there, in these lists of equates. If you write

cmp [msg.message], 102h

This will test for WM_CHAR and it is exactly the same result to write either the number or the word.

I see in the include file USER64.INC that If the computer program is written for 64 bit mode, the POINT structure can be the same, but the message or MSG structure becomes longer with 64 bit fields like this:

```
struct MSG                  ;64 bit form. "dd" =32 bits and "dq" = 64 bits.
  hwnd   dq ?               ;"dq" means Double Quad word.
  message dd ?,?
  wParam  dq ?
  lParam  dq ?
  time    dd ?
  pt      POINT
          dd ?
Ends
;--------------------------------
```

Just as an example. To create a variable in memory which will show whether the control key is down:

control_key dd 0
;-----------

```
        cmp [msg.message], WM_KEYDOWN
        jnz not_down
        mov eax, [msg.wParam]
        cmp eax, VK_CONTROL              ;VK_CONTROL=11h
        jnz not_control
        mov [control_key], eax           ;Record that it has been pressed
        jmp end

not_down:
        cmp [msg.message], WM_KEYUP
        jnz not_up
        cmp [msg.wParam], VK_CONTROL
        jnz not_conrol2
        mov [control_key], 0             ;erase it with zero when it has been released ?
;-------------------------
```

This is another example of a message loop:

```
  msg_loop:
 invoke PeekMessage, msg, 0, 0, 0, 0         ;Optional  PeekMessage  (Not always used.)
         cmp eax, 0
             jz skips                         ;When no message, skip over GetMessage.

         invoke  GetMessage, msg, 0, 0, 0
         cmp     eax, 1
         jb      ending                       ; When eax=0 the program should end
         jne     msg_loop                     ; This one jump "jne" never ever runs. So it's unnecessary!

         invoke  TranslateMessage, msg
         invoke  DispatchMessage, msg
skips:
         call typing
             call other_parts_of_program                ; Lots of calls can be here
         jmp msg_loop
```

The following is some example which is Not important, of detecting several different virtual keys, which are any of the
non-alphabetical keys. The variables you use have to be declared in a data section.
This chapter is mainy over,

```
    cmp word [msg.message], WM_KEYDOWN
    jnz no1
    mov eax, [msg.wParam]
    mov [save_wParam], eax

    cmp eax, VK_SHIFT
    jnz no0
    mov [shift1], eax              ;show shift
    jmp no10
  no0:
    cmp eax, VK_CONTROL
    jnz no12
    mov [ctrl1], eax               ;show control
    jmp no10
  no12:
    cmp eax, VK_F12+1
    jnb no10
    cmp eax, VK_F1
    jb no10
    mov [function], eax            ;show function
    jmp no10
;===================================== Character
  no1:
    cmp word [msg.message], WM_CHAR
    jnz no2
    mov eax, [msg.wParam]

    mov [last_alphabet], eax       ;show character
    mov [alphabet], eax            ;show character (until released)
    jmp no10
;============================== Key Up
  no2:
    cmp word [msg.message], WM_KEYUP
    jnz no3
```

```
        mov eax, [msg.wParam]

        cmp eax, VK_SHIFT
        jnz no4
        mov dword [shift1], 0            ;erase a record of the shift
        jmp no10
    no4:
        cmp eax, VK_CONTROL
        jnz no5
        mov dword [ctrl1], 0             ;erase control
        jmp no10
    no5:
        cmp eax, VK_F12+1                ;Detect a range of function keys.
        jnb no7
        cmp eax, VK_F1
        jb no7
        mov [function] ,0                ;erase function
        jmp no10
;=================== Aphabet lifted
    no7:                                 ;when eax= [msg.wParam]
        cmp eax, 20h
        jb no10
        cmp eax, 80h                     ;for certain keys like <>?@~
        jnb no6
        cmp eax, 60h
        jnb no10
    no6:
        mov dword [alphabet], 0          ; ;erase character when released?
                                         ;Only Partly working but pgup/down erases.
        jmp no10
    no3:
        jmp no10
;==============================
 no10:

        jmp   msg_loop

;==============================
```

The 4 Arrow keys.
```
;VK_LEFT = 25h          VK_UP = 26h
;VK_RIGHT = 27h         VK_DOWN = 28h
;VK_PAGEUP = 21h        VK_PAGEDOWN = 22h
```

```
;=============================================
```

There is the alternative method of keyboard inputs called invoke GetAsyncKeyState.

You give it the name of the specific virtual key you are interested in, such as VK_SHIFT as its one parameter. After it runs, the most significant binary bit of eax is set when a key is being held down, and the least significant binary bit of eax is set when the key was pressed at some time after the last call to invoke GetAsyncKeyState. But Microsoft says it is not reliable because more than one program could be running at a time.
The message loop must be running as usual.

```
 ;Note** I looked up Getasynckeystate
 ;Ls bit called Bit 0 =1 if key was pressed since the last call to GetAsyncKeyState
 ;because another program might have called it, its considered not reliable
 ;The most significant bit =1 if held down now.
; When most significant bit =1 a test should show that the number is Negative.
  keystate:  ;Note ** It shows when key pressed and released, it did not show caps lock states.
      invoke GetAsyncKeyState,VK_LMENU   ;*Result the left alt toggles 12h/00 on off
                                         ; LMENU and RMENU the Alts??
      mov [menukey],0
      and eax,eax
      jns nomenu
      mov [menukey],VK_MENU  ;**=12h
  nomenu:
      invoke GetAsyncKeyState,VK_CAPITAL   ;*It shows whether caps lock is down
                                           ;but it does not show the state.
      mov [caps1],0
   ;  and eax,eax
   ;  js caps
      test al,1          ;also does not show whether toggled
      jnz caps
      ret
   caps: mov [caps1],VK_CAPITAL
      ret
```

```
;=========================================================
These show a few of the Virtual key codes, a complete list is inside
 the file INCLUDE\EQUATES/USER32.INC


    VK_LBUTTON   = 001h        VK_RBUTTON   = 002h        VK_CANCEL    = 003h
    VK_MBUTTON   = 004h        VK_BACK      = 008h        VK_TAB       = 009h
    VK_CLEAR     = 00Ch        VK_RETURN    = 00Dh        VK_SHIFT     = 010h
    VK_CONTROL   = 011h        VK_MENU      = 012h        VK_PAUSE     = 013h
    VK_CAPITAL   = 014h        VK_ESCAPE    = 01Bh        VK_SPACE     = 020h
    VK_PRIOR     = 021h        VK_PGUP      = 021h        VK_PGDN      = 022h
    VK_NEXT      = 022h        VK_END       = 023h        VK_HOME      = 024h
    VK_LEFT      = 025h        VK_UP        = 026h        VK_RIGHT     = 027h
    VK_DOWN      = 028h
```

## index

| | | | |
|---|---|---|---|
| 64 bit considerations | 129, 250 | Resource section | 94 |
| 64 bit open file name | 131 | Ret | 56 |
| Allocating memory | 104 | Riff Header | 200, 202, 211 |
| Authentication | 137 | Sendgrid co | 140 |
| Base 64 code encoding | 162 | Send email | 141, 145 |
| Bitmap address | 42, 47 | Servers | 139, 156 |
| BitBlt | 34 | Sending to server | 157 |
| Camera window | 17 | SMTP | 135, 138, 145 |
| Create Dibsection | 47 | Sound | 193 |
| Create edit control | 187, 192 | Timers | 167 |
| Create file | 115, 125, 128 | Typing | 71- 77 |
| Create font example | 149 | Virtual allocate | 110 |
| Creation Disposition | 134 | | |
| Clipboard | 172 | | |
| Create window example | 12, 27 | | |
| DLL | 63 | | |
| Download a page only | 100 | | |
| Edit controls | 181 | | |
| Electronic SMTP conversation | 143 | | |
| File Flags | 133, 134 | | |
| Filter string used | 11, 123 | | |
| Floating Point | 228 | | |
| Floating point instructions | 236 | | |
| Floating point conditional jumps | 238 | | |
| Floating point output to Text | 244 | | |
| Frequencies | 204 | | |
| Get Open File name | 122 | | |
| Get window text | 183 | | |
| Global alloc | 104 | | |
| Header for Bitmaps & bmp | 48, 178, 179 | | |
| Hex view of memory | 30 | | |
| Internal file pointer | 120, 121 | | |
| **Keyboard Inputs** | 260 | | |
| Message | 34, 165 | | |
| Menus | 83 | | |
| Mouse Inputs | 254 | | |
| PeekMessage | 166 | | |

Program code lists      11-16, 17-24, 25-33, 35-49, 145-164, 213-227

Printed in Great Britain
by Amazon